Embodied Existence

Embodied Existence

Our Common Life in God

Pavol Bargár

Foreword by Stephen Bevans

CASCADE *Books* • Eugene, Oregon

EMBODIED EXISTENCE
Our Common Life in God

Cascade Books
An Imprint of Wipf and Stock Publishers
199 W. 8th Ave., Suite 3
Eugene, OR 97401

www.wipfandstock.com

PAPERBACK ISBN: 978-1-6667-4408-8
HARDCOVER ISBN: 978-1-6667-4409-5
EBOOK ISBN: 978-1-6667-4410-1

Cataloguing-in-Publication data:

Names: Bargár, Pavol, author. | Bevans, Stephen B., 1944–, foreword.

Title: Embodied existence : our common life in God / Pavol Bargár.

Description: Eugene, OR : Cascade Books, 2023 | Includes bibliographical references and index.

Identifiers: ISBN 978-1-6667-4408-8 (paperback) | ISBN 978-1-6667-4409-5 (hardcover) | ISBN 978-1-6667-4410-1 (ebook)

Subjects: LCSH: Theological anthropology.

Classification: BT701.3 .B37 2023 (print) | BT701.3 .B37 (ebook)

APRIL 14, 2023 10:46 AM

This book is a result of the research supported by the Charles University Research Center program no. 204052 "Theological Anthropology in Ecumenical Perspective."

Dedicated to all people who in many and various ways helped
and continue to help those suffering from COVID-19

Just as we have borne the image of the earthy,
we will also bear the image of the heavenly.

—1 Cor 15:49 NASB1995

Contents

Foreword

Many years ago—in a moment of deep insight—I came to the realization that the doctrines of Christian theology form an interconnected system. As I often have told my students, Christian doctrines are not a kind of "laundry list" of concepts or ideas or facts that are simply to be believed. They are rather like a finely cut gem, all the facets of which together reflect the beauty of God's loving presence and action in our world and in our human lives. Each doctrine explains the others, and while we can focus on one in theological reflection, we can only really understand that single doctrine by seeing how it reflects and illumines the whole. When we theologize or study theology, there is really no logical entry point, like beginning with creation, or Christology, or Trinity. We can enter the theological conversation at any point. And although one particular doctrine can certainly shape the understanding of the others, each doctrine will ultimately function as a portal to the entire Mystery: the Mystery of God's self-emptying and prodigal love.

This book is proof of the truth of my startling insight of years ago. Pavol Bargár develops in these pages a stunning and powerful Christian anthropology, rooted in creation and bodiliness, fueled by the drives to be and to tell one's story with creativity and imagination, and nourished by the yearning for relationality and transformation. Our humanity is then celebrated by the already-present and still-anticipated feast of the "kin-dom" of God. But the anthropology that Pavol develops only comes into full focus in the light of the doctrine of the Trinity, the "comm/unity" of the Christian church—the body of Christ—and the mission of that church to be in relation with all peoples, all cultures, and every wondrous particle of the created universe.

To be truly human is ultimately to participate in God's very life of self-emptying love, to be connected, like God in incarnation, to every creature, to be passionate about sharing the amazing story of God-become-flesh with all the peoples of the earth. To be truly human is to belong to a comm/unity that works for the "radical kinship," the "revolutionary intimacy"[1] of all creatures, a vision and dream that is shaped by and shapes our Christian imagination. To be truly human is to be transformed into a sacrament of God's enfleshment in Jesus of Nazareth, and to celebrate that transformation at the eucharistic feast.

In weaving this rich tapestry, Pavol draws his material from a vast collection of resources. His reading is wide and deep, and he draws on the wisdom of theologians from all Christian churches, and from many diverse cultures. His conversation partners are women and men, classical figures and contemporary thinkers, artists and musicians. His is a theology inspired by contemporary cinema and lyrics of legendary rock bands. It is a narrative theology that involves his readers' senses and imagination, but leads them as well into profound theological thought and reflection.

Like any good work of theology, Pavol's work moves from thought into action. We cannot simply learn what it means to be a true human being by reading these pages. We must ourselves claim our bodiliness, rehearse our story, open ourselves up to transforming relationships, and feast at the table of friendships and service. Like any good work of theology, this is the work of an author who embodies all that he writes. Pavol invites us in the pages that follow into his own story, into his own creativity, into his own transformation, and his own enjoyment and celebration of life. Welcome to a book that calls us to ourselves as it calls us to recognize once more the embodied love of our transforming God.

Stephen Bevans, SVD
Louis J. Luzbetak, SVD, Professor of Mission and Culture, Emeritus
Catholic Theological Union, Chicago
Easter Sunday 2022

1. See Boyle, *Barking to the Choir*, and Jennings, *Acts*, 29.

List of Abbreviations

CPTA	Faith and Order Commission, *Christian Perspectives on Theological Anthropology*
NASB1995	New American Standard Bible, 1995
NIV	New International Version
NRSV	New Revised Standard Version
TTL	World Council of Churches, *Together towards Life: Mission and Evangelism in Changing Landscapes*
WCC	World Council of Churches

Introduction

Every theology emerges out of a particular context. The context of this book is the COVID-19 pandemic that has tormented people around the world since late 2019. Causing immense suffering, persistent health effects, and even deaths as well as social polarization and conflicts, the pandemic has led us to reconsider the ways how we think about the world and—even more importantly—how we live our lives. This has affected areas as diverse as health, education, economy, work, science, traveling, sports, culture, or family and spiritual life. And it has also had an impact on our theologizing. For me personally, three moments were of utmost importance in this regard. My life as an academic theologian and a practicing Christian suddenly shifted to an online mode. No more conferences in cities around the world, no more research visits to libraries and study centers in various locations near and far, no physical participation in worship services together with sisters and brothers in faith. It was now about sitting in front of my computer screen for extended periods. In addition, I all of a sudden found myself enclosed in limited space for long weeks and months with a very small group of people—my family—an experience that turned out to be a blessing, though challenging it was at times. Finally, as a person for whom regular workout represents an important part of daily routine, I was forced to change my athletic habits. Outdoor running, in isolation from other people, has become my predominant sports activity. Since the beginning of 2021 (when I began keeping track), I have so far run over 1,400 km. In addition to being a great way to keep both physically and mentally fit, running has for me also become a practice for raising awareness of my body, its connection with my mind and spirit, and my relation to others and the world. All of these, together, have led me to reflect on and reconsider the fundamental significance of the body for our theological understanding of what it means to be human. Human existence is an embodied existence. Living as God-created bodies—no matter whether in face-to-face encounters or through online presence—we are called to relate to others, thus realizing our humanity alongside and as part of the entire creation. The COVID-19 pandemic and the isolation caused therewith have, ironically, only deepened this conviction and made it more acute. The present book is my attempt to theologically elaborate on this central insight from an ecumenical Christian perspective. It unfolds in six chapters.

Chapter 1 begins from the premise that God has created the world and everything in it because God yearns to share God's story with creation; God wants God's story become our story. The category of story is introduced as an irreplaceable element for the conceiving of human identity; human existence is a life in search of a story. From a Christian perspective, people are invited to make sense of their existence by participating in God's story with creation, as testified to in the Scriptures. It is this story, I suggest, that draws us into God, thus enabling us to have what I call "our common life in God." I seek to show, however, that entering God's story does not necessarily mean being absorbed by it to the degree of losing one's own identity. Rather, one reinvents one's identity by being integrated into the story. Thus, one becomes a character in this story, and as such is expected to not only "tell" but also to "embody" it.

The body is the topic of chapter 2. To be sure, materiality/corporeality is an essential mark of God's creation, including humankind. The epistemological significance of the body is recognized because the pursuit of knowledge (about God, the world, oneself) is inextricably linked with a commitment to praxis in which the body stands at the center as a locus of reflection and action. Therefore, to be created—and, more specifically, to be human—means to be a body. Finding its expression both in God's continued act(s) of creation and—particularly for Christian identity—in Jesus's incarnation, human embodied existence is interdependent as humans comprise, together with the rest of God's creation, a meshwork of mutually intertwined life. As a result, human embodied existence is both vulnerable and relational. In this respect, the issue of vulnerability and, significantly, brokenness is discussed in the context of human corporeality. At the same time, to be human means to be a "body-self" that relates to the other—to other "body-selves," both human and nonhuman, thus constituting a social body. In the community of Jesus's followers, the social body is interpreted as the body of Christ since the community's members, through their own bodies, embody Christ's words and deeds.

Chapter 3 seeks to make a case that in order to grasp and pursue the calling of relating to the other, one needs imagination. Imagination is first discussed theologically as a creative, yet distorted, dimension of being human. It is through the power of imagination transformed by divine grace, so the central argument of this chapter goes, that one can participate in God's pursuit of new creation. This consists of both challenging the status quo of various ills, injustices, and evils and envisioning and working for a new reality, characterized by justice, peace, and reconciliation. Such a "rupture" in the present fabric of reality can be imaginatively accounted for by "*kin*-dom of God," a relational symbol underscoring that God's inbreaking reign is fundamentally materialized through interpersonal encounters and embodiment. Finally, the notions of imagination and body are brought together in what I refer to as the imagined body. This term accounts for the process in which imagination empowers one to relate to the other, using one's material body as the point of entry to the other's experience and story. Thus, the imagined body is a locus for sharing specific narratives, creating common stories, and pursuing universal visions. In this sense, the imagined body represents a desirable complement to the material body, or perhaps more appropriately—as the previous chapter has shown—the body-self.

Enabled by imagination sensitized through God's grace, the participation in God's pursuit of new creation implies transformation, as chapter 4 shows. In particular, transformation is, I suggest, the ultimate horizon to which God leads God's creation. Empowered by God's grace to use their imagination, people reinterpret their life stories in acts of metanoia to overcome the brokenness of the *conditio humana* that is a result of sin. Such a metanoia—an authentic existential "conversion"—is to be interpreted in narrative terms of reevaluating one's own story, or, restorying. In that way, people can truly pursue their existence as embodied beings toward our common life in God. Their quest is motivated by the refusal to accept the status quo, characterized by the brokenness and woundedness of creation. In this process, the reality is seen through the lens of justice, peace, mercy, acceptance, and reconciliation as fundamental features of God's inbreaking reign—the kin-dom of God. Created in the image of God, human beings are called by God to follow God, thus realizing their full humanity and participating in the eschatological transformation of the entire creation.

This process is understood as profoundly relational and, therefore, relationality is in chapter 5 explored as an essential feature of human embodied existence. For a theological understanding of relationality, the ultimate paradigm is the operating dynamics in both the immanent and economic Trinity. The triune God as the Father, the Son, and the Holy Spirit relate to each other to create the perfect fellowship of love, acceptance, inclusion, and creativity. Unable to remain contained within Godself, this communion "overflows" with meaning and potential to include God's creation in this process. Since the triune God is fundamentally relational, humans—as carriers of God's image—too are relational beings. After discussing examples of the human negation of relationality, such as alienation or "identitary temptations," the chapter employs the notions of resilience and mutuality to highlight that our embodied existence is enabled by the grace of God who relates to humankind and the whole creation, while respecting their diversity. Furthermore, they remind us of our calling to relate to others, especially the poor and marginalized, in solidarity and respect. To conclude this chapter, two concepts of "incarnational discipleship" and "kenotic presence," respectively, are discussed as they represent, I suggest, an important theological lens for considering the ways in which human beings can relate to the other dialogically, transformatively, and reciprocally.

The relational matrix of the human, the other (in both their human and nonhuman forms), and God opens space for creating an authentic community. In the final chapter, I seek to push this idea further by introducing the notion of "comm/unity" as a meshwork of multiple relationships by dignified individuals who appreciate the interdependence and essential unity of humankind based on their createdness in the image of God as well as human interconnection with the rest of creation. The aim is to pursue kin-dom—a common life in the force field of God's love, mercy, and acceptance—thus attaining the genuine vocation of being human. In this way, the notion of comm/unity sheds light, from a Christian perspective, on human embodied existence as a pursuit of our common life in God. In scriptural tradition, I assert, this dynamic is symbolized by the image of "feast" that, at the same time, interconnects the aspects of human storiedness, corporeality, imagination, relationality, and the quest for transformation. Standing for both a power to resist all that is undesirable in the current order of things and the promise of a shared, just, and reconciled future with the other, feast represents a powerful image to account for human embodied existence—"our common life in God."

On the whole, therefore, this book makes a case, from an ecumenical Christian perspective, for a theological anthropology and a missiology that are based on the essential significance of story, body, imagination, and relationality in order to understand what it means to be human vis-à-vis God, the other, and creation. Such an interpretation, moreover, enables seeking and pursuing a common life for the whole creation in the force field of God's radical and transformative reign. To advance its argument, it engages contemporary culture, including cinema and, to a lesser extent, fiction and music.

This volume grows out of the research project "Theological Anthropology in Ecumenical Perspective" at Charles University in Prague, Czech Republic. Under the leadership of Prof. Ivana Noble and in collegial fellowship and cooperation with the other research team members, I have begun researching and writing about themes that represent the respective chapters of this book. My thanks goes to all of my colleagues for their support and intellectual stimulation.

I would also like to thank the people at Wipf and Stock Publishers for their professional and kind-hearted approach. A special word of appreciation goes to my editor, Charlie Collier, for his insightful comments and advice.

I am grateful to Benjamin Simon of the World Council of Churches for hosting me in his apartment at Petit-Bossey, Switzerland, in August 2021 and to Marie and Jiří Ort for letting me use their vacation house in Perálec, Czech Republic, in September 2021 and again in January 2022. A concentrated, creative, and enjoyable time spent at these two beautiful places significantly contributed toward completion of this book.

I am also thankful to my parents for introducing me to this embodied existence. And, as ever, my gratitude and love go to Ikuška, Sofi, and Dami, for showing me day by day that human embodied existence is characterized by intimacy, trust, joy, and hope.

Soli Deo gloria.

PAVOL BARGÁR
Perálec
January 27, 2022 (International Holocaust Remembrance Day)

I

Story

Of Angels and Stories

In a 1987 film, *Wings of Desire*, the director Wim Wenders invites the viewer to enter the world of the Iron Curtain-torn Berlin.[1] Originally, Wenders had intended to provide his film with a metaphysical justification of the story line according to which the infuriated God would decide to leave humankind to their fate after the Second World War. However, there were a handful of angels who would intercede for people, praying that God give the terrestrians yet another chance. This intercession would make God even angrier and result in God punishing the angels by sending them into exile to the war-stricken Berlin—without a possibility to either return to heaven or intervene in the course of events in the world. These fallen angels would be doomed to be eternal spectators of the earthly drama.[2]

It is significant to note that the idea of either the infuriated God or angels as fallen celestial creatures does not feature in the film. Nevertheless, there are two other distinct moments implied by the paraphrased passage. First, *Wings of Desire* is characterized by a considerable transcendental vacuum. In other words, there is no explicit consideration of the concept of transcendent reality in the sense of God. In this respect, the heaven over Berlin is indeed empty.[3] Or, to put it in the terminology that will be crucial

1. The German name of the film is *Der Himmel über Berlin*. For further information on the film, see "Der Himmel über Berlin," IMDb, accessed December 27, 2021, https://www.imdb.com/title/tt0093191/?ref_=nv_sr_srsg_0.

2. See Cook, "Angels," 165. Cook refers to Wenders, *Logik*, 99.

3. The translation of the German name of the film, *Der Himmel über Berlin*, into English means "The Heaven over Berlin."

to the argument of this chapter, God's story with the world lacks its main author and protagonist.

Second, angels are here first and foremost—albeit not exclusively—introduced as isolated and disengaged observers. The focus in *Wings of Desire* rests upon two of them, Damiel and Cassiel. Detached from anything going on in the human world, they are mere spectators who make notes from their observations. Subsequently, they read these notes to each other. Being invisible to the human eye, they cannot directly influence the situations that they happen to be part of. For instance, they are not capable of grasping objects that belong to the human world; all they can do is to get hold of the "form" of a particular object (a rock, a pencil), while the thing itself remains as it is. Even though the picture suggests that angels might have, by the virtue of their presence, a certain role in comforting the desperate (e.g., the despondent man on the subway train who finds peace of mind after being touched by Damiel) or accompanying the dying (e.g., Damiel holding in his arms a motorcyclist who dies in a traffic accident), this capability seems to be rather scarce and considerably unreliable (e.g., Cassiel is not able to prevent a young man from committing suicide by jumping off a tall building).

The major turn of events in this film comes when Damiel tells his colleague, Cassiel, about his desire to become human. He is not any more interested in thinking in categories such as "forever"; he wants to experience for himself what it means "here and now." As Damiel puts it, he does not yearn for great things (beget a child, plant a tree); he only wants to "take his shoes off and move his toes" or "come home and feed the cat like Phil Marlow." However, the robust catalyst of Damiel's desire to become human is Marion, a young trapeze artist. Marion represents Damiel's human counterpart, providing a clear orientation for his desire. In a manner not dissimilar to that of God and God's creation, Marion and Damiel yearn for their own story that would, at the same time, be the story of their match. Even though Marion is not aware of Damiel's existence, she keeps searching for him as she subconsciously knows he is the one. And Damiel gives up eternity to pursue his own story. An angel becomes human, giving up his proverbial—though, as we have said, imaginary—wings to be able to give wings to his desire.

The emphasis on story is of central importance here. As Roger Cook points out, Damiel's desire is not merely one for a human mode of existence. It is, first and foremost, the desire to participate in the human story, nay, to be able to create one's own story with regard to both the future and the past.[4] In this respect it is very illustrative to turn to another "former angel," Peter Falk, a.k.a. Lieutenant Columbo, who features in the film as himself. Falk recollects the memories of his grandmother which is, in case of an angel, an obvious logical nonsense. And yet, even such a "nonsense" is immensely significant as it signifies the inherent human need to have one's own—and complete—story. It furthermore shows the power of words, images, and imagination.[5]

The importance of one's own integral story is also underlined by the formal aspect of *Wings of Desire*. The first part of the film consists of mutually unrelated, apparently haphazard, scenes in which angels observe people in ordinary situations of life. Absent is any coherent and unifying story line. The latter gradually emerges only after Damiel has become human, thus creating his own story. It is precisely because of the questions related to the centrality of individual human story in a quest for the meaning of life that Wenders's film can be characterized as existentialist. *Wings of Desire* implies that the meaning of life is not a priori given; rather, one must discover it for oneself. However, the film does not slip into nihilism and despair. Meaning is introduced as readily available. Humans can pursue it by relating to fellow human beings, by encountering the other who is one's neighbor.[6] One needs the other/neighbor to be able to fully and authentically realize one's own story, one's human existence.

A question comes to mind of what role angels play in this process of the realization of human existence vis-à-vis the other. In this regard it is of crucial importance that the film makes it clear that children only are able to see angels; adults evidently do not possess this ability. While Cook makes note of this feature, he does not attempt to interpret it explicitly.[7] Nevertheless, he indirectly suggests that the affinity between angels and children lies in the common "unconscious existence in the world of the senses,"[8] where the world of the adults is characterized by creating one's own story through words and images. For his part, Alexander Graf perceives a point of connection in the fact that both children and angels dwell in their own world

4. See Cook, "Angels," 178.

5. I will explore the theme of imagination in detail in chapter 3.

6. Throughout this book, this emphasis will be elaborated continuously and then explicitly in chapter 5 on relationality and chapter 6 on feast.

7. See Cook, "Angels," 168.

8. Cook, "Angels," 180.

of dreams.[9] I, on the contrary, see a connecting link between children and angels in innocence that people lose as they grow older. Innocence is to be understood in the existential meaning of the word, that is, as a preliminary "exemption" from sin in the sense of alienation. In *Wings of Desire*, neither children nor angels experience—unlike adult human beings—alienation from the meaning of life. One of the characters in the film, old man Homer, says that if humankind loses its narrator, it will also lose its childhood. Here, childhood is regarded as unambiguously related to story that, in turn, implies the meaning of life. In the film, both children and angels represent beings in a prelapsarian stage; the consequences of existence in the *incurvate in se* stage do not bear on them yet (in the case of children) or are not applicable to them (in the case of angels). If one seeks to fully realize one's humanity and experience a deep and authentic relationship with a fellow human being, one must be like a child. Both Marion and Damiel meet this requirement—she as a trapeze artist, a member of the circus community that is often seen by the mainstream society as a bunch of fools; he as a former angel who has not yet been corrupted by life in human society. Marion and Damiel find a way to each other, helping one another to pursue the meaning of life, thus transcending the boundaries of their finite existence. The final scene of the film captures Damiel reflecting on the moment of connection between him and Marion, between a man and a woman, as collateral for eternity: "It happened once. Once, and therefore forever."

It is desire that leads Damiel to renounce his eternal and immutable existence, adopting the limitations and finitude of human life. Finitude/boundedness is what enables people to have their own stories and to pursue their humanity and meaning of life in relation to the other. And his own story and meaningful existence is what Damiel yearns for in *Wings of Desire*.[10] However, desire is essential for the thesis of this chapter in yet another sense as I would like to argue that God has created the world and everything in it because God longs to share God's story with creation, offering the latter an opportunity to co-create the story.

9. See Graf, *Cinema*, 119.

10. The concept of story acquires yet another level of importance when one considers the writer-director Wim Wenders's relation to his work. In particular, Ulrike Vollmer suggests that Wenders in *Wings of Desire* sought to introduce the notion of engaged cinema when the director leaves his or her safe zone behind the camera to become a part of the story, a part of life. See Vollmer, "Blessed," 529. Somewhat complementarily, Roger Cook asserts that *Wings of Desire* "investigates the role narrative plays in the formation both of individual identity and of the national identity of psychically scarred Germany." Cook, "Angels," 165.

Of Humans and Stories

The previous discussion helps us, I believe, begin to see why story has emerged as an essential category not only in philosophy or literature and media studies but, since the 1970s, also in Christian theology.[11] When proposing that "story itself creates a world of consciousness and the self is oriented to it," Stephen Crites asserts not only that story constitutes an inherent part of human existence but also that the narrative structure of human consciousness belongs to the realm of "nature," thus, effectively, foregoing "culture."[12] While I maintain that Crites's point on the narrative structure of human consciousness is important, I, like Richard Kearney, see a gap between nature and narrative, between "time suffered [and] time enacted and enunciated" that distinguishes a merely biological life (*zoe*) from a truly human one (*bios*).[13]

Therefore, it is vital to postulate, together with Alasdair MacIntyre, story as an irreplaceable element for conceiving human identity when the self is perceived in terms of a narrative unity linking an individual's entire life from cradle to grave.[14] This point is also made by Charles Taylor, who claims that an essential prerequisite for "making sense of ourselves is to grasp our life in terms of a *narrative*," for to understand who we are "we have to have a notion of how we have become and of where we are going."[15] In this perspective, every human existence is a life in search of a story. There are several implications behind this claim, by and large connected with the quest for meaning in human life. It is not only about the

11. While one of the earliest theological works on story represents Niebuhr, "Story," 43–81, the real watershed came with the publication Frei, *Eclipse*. The heyday of theological interest in the narrative nature of the Christian message dawned with the formation of what came to be known as postliberal (or, narrative) theology, inspired by the important volume by Lindbeck, *Nature of Doctrine*. Even though this strand of theological thinking has come under serious academic criticism from scholars such as DeHart, *Trial of the Witnesses*, and Murphy, *God Is Not a Story*, story as a concept continues to stimulate the Christian imagination as attested by the proliferation of literature on the topic, such as Loughlin, *Telling God's Story*; Pecknold, *Transforming Postliberal Theology*; Lucie-Smith, *Narrative Theology*; Cathey, *God in Postliberal Perspective*; or Michener, *Postliberal Theology*.

12. See Crites, "Narrative Quality," 70–71.

13. See Kearney, *On Stories*, 3–4. Kearney finds support for his argument in Arendt, *Human Condition*, 72. See also Kristeva, *Crisis*; and Benhabib, *Situating the Self*.

14. See MacIntyre, *After Virtue*, 205.

15. Taylor, *Sources*, 47, italics in the original.

insistence to give a meaning to that series of events that come in between one's birth at the beginning and one's death at the end. There is also a more or less pronounced effort to discover a pattern to cope with the experiences of chaos and confusion. Finally, story provides us with a structure to find significance "in terms of referrals back to our past (memory) and forward to our future (projection)."[16]

Reflecting on the theological significance of story, Pavel Hošek explains that this concept has not only a mimetic quality (i.e., story as an "immediate offprint of life")[17] but also a transformative power. Story can in this sense function as a hermeneutic framework that provides the reader—or the listener or the viewer—with a unique understanding of reality that emerges from its constitutive elements, such as characters, plot, setting, etc. If this understanding of reality has such a convincing appeal that it can stand for an alternative to the actual world as the reader experiences it, story might kindle in the reader a "desire for a change."[18] In a metaphorical—yet very real—sense, we can therefore speak of a *story-world* that serves as a vantage point providing the reader who enters it with a fresh and possibly transformative view of his or her lived reality. The reader may be transformed if he or she accepts "the rules of the game" and assumes the role of a "tourist" in the story-world who under the leadership of an experienced "guide"—that is, the author of the text—comes to significantly broaden his or her existing horizons.[19] Similarly, Kearney, in his interpretation of J. R. R. Tolkien, says that story "affords us privileged insight into secret workings and potencies of this world" precisely because "it opens up an 'other' world."[20]

One of the major reasons why such an "immersion" into story-worlds is possible is the temporal structure of story that corresponds to the temporal structure of human existence, as indicated above. Therefore, story-worlds provide people with "mentally inhabitable" virtual space, thus giving them a viable option to elucidate their own existential inquiries vis-à-vis the alternative answers engendered by the logic of the story.[21] Thus, an imaginative dwelling in a story-world can represent not only an aesthetic experience but also an existential challenge and transformative encounter.

16. Kearney, *On Stories*, 129.

17. See Hošek, *Kouzlo*, 17. Translations from Czech in this chapter are mine.

18. See Hošek and Bargár, "Lidé," 74.

19. See Hošek and Bargár, "Lidé," 74–75. See also Lewis, *Experiment*, 139–40.

20. Kearney, *On Stories*, 158. Kearney refers to Tolkien, "On Fairy Stories," 44.

21. See Hošek and Bargár, "Lidé," 75.

One can be led to radically revise and reinterpret one's life and search for meaning. For instance, by identifying with a novel's—or film's—protagonist one may undergo a "conversion"—that is, a substantial reconfiguration of one's self and one's symbolic universe. In this sense, Hošek asserts, we can say that human existence in the world and the human ways of self-understanding are characterized by narrativity; one discovers the meaning of one's life by telling it.[22] A reflective understanding of one's self and identity emerges out of a chaotic flow of events, experiences, accidents, givens, contingencies, decisions, influences, necessities, and many other factors through a process of continuous tellings and retellings. Furthermore, human identity is always constructed in specific cultural, historical, linguistic, and other contexts.[23] The human cannot be considered apart from his or her context, apart from other human beings. The notion of an autonomous individual as one of the hallmarks—and idols—of modernity is hereby fundamentally challenged.[24] Belonging to a certain community or reference group also has an essentially narrative structure. Tolkien formulates it very powerfully when he argues that stories express an innate human desire to "hold communion with other living beings."[25] In theology, particularly, this accent on the narrative structure of both individual and communal human existence is of key importance as Christians can be seen as "storying people" who, as a community, embrace scriptural stories and their logic and argumentation.[26]

Notwithstanding these robust arguments in support of story as a central category for our endeavor to reflect on what it means to be human, one should seriously consider the fact that not all thinkers who otherwise do not deny its hermeneutic validity and usefulness are willing to go as far as to claim that "to be human is above all to have a story."[27] Moreover, even the very founders of postliberal (narrative) theology such as Hans Frei remind us that Christian theology cannot start from universal human experience formulated as a story. Its sine qua non is, in contrast, a very particular story as we encounter it in the Scriptures. To put it differently,

22. See Hošek and Bargár, "Lidé," 76.

23. See Michener, *Postliberal Theology*, 8. The notion of context will be further discussed in chapter 2.

24. See Davaney and Brown, "Postliberalism," 455, and Phillips, "Postliberal Theology," 938.

25. Tolkien, "On Fairy Stories," 41.

26. See Michener, *Postliberal Theology*, 122–23.

27. Frei, *Theology and Narrative*, 208.

the point of departure for Christian theology is not a narratively construed human identity with the story of Jesus Christ as a mere illustration. Rather, it is the gospel as *the* story that in turn transforms and shapes the lives of individuals and communities.[28]

Still, it is helpful to distinguish, together with Martha Downey, between the centrality and exclusivity of story to human existence. While story indeed is at the heart of our pursuits to understand what it means to be human, it certainly is not the only means. It enters into dialogue with other forms of knowledge and interpretation, a process that is open and unfinished. As Downey puts it: "Narrative theology, done well, will not capture the story of God, but it should serve to draw us into God's story."[29] A similar path is trodden by Paul Fiddes, who even goes as far as to propose that a theologian's journey into the story-worlds of non-scriptural fiction represents "nothing less than an extension of the doctrine of the incarnation" as the theologian, endowed with multiple consciousnesses and immersed into the new time and space, can test out what certain doctrinal notions feel like when embodied in flesh and blood and see the consequences that they give rise to.[30] Thus we can see that story plays an irreplaceable role in Christian theology. The next section will probe deeper into this theme.

Entering God's Story . . . and Making It One's Own

God is a story.[31] However, it is a special kind of story; a story that is more actual than anything in the world that the story tells about.[32] It is a story woven from the language of love. Moreover, it is fabricated from the movements of self-giving and self-receiving love in which the author/creator longs to share the story-world with the other characters inhabiting it; the teller seeks to be told. As such, the constitutive element of this story is,

28. See Frei, *Theology and Narrative*, 210, and Loughlin, *Telling God's Story*, 66–67.

29. Downey, "Perspective," 307.

30. See Fiddes, "Concept," 17.

31. In her important monograph, Francesca Murphy argues to the contrary. Her position is, *in nuce*, that for the proponents of narrative theology "it's not so much the substantial *content* which the colourful [scriptural] types convey that matters, but rather typology as a *method* of reading the Bible." Murphy, *God Is Not a Story*, 2, italics in the original. In this chapter, there is no space for offering a full-fledged review of Murphy's thesis, therefore I will only refer to the convincing critiques offered, among others, by Fiddes, "Concept," 10, and Downey, "Perspective," 307.

32. See Fiddes, "Concept," 23.

besides love, desire: God has created the world for God yearns for sharing God's story with creation; God wants creation to make God's story their own. Importantly, therefore, this story is one of personal relations, thus drawing us into God. It enables us to have a common life in God.

This discussion leads us to formulate the thesis that Christian identity emerges from God's story with creation as ultimately enacted in the story of Jesus of Nazareth. In this perspective, Christian life is the praxis of the following of a story, namely, the story of the life, death, and resurrection of Jesus the Jewish carpenter and itinerant teacher whom the church recognizes as Christ. Theology is, first and foremost, critical reflection on this story that also takes into consideration other stories and eventualities of life. As such, the story is primary, while theologizing follows. Becoming Christian, then, is interpreted as becoming part of the story of Jesus Christ. Thereby one discovers and reconfigures oneself and the meaning of one's existence in God's story with creation; to use metaphorical language, one becomes a chapter in this story.[33] However, this process is by no means to be understood as one that turns human beings into passive objects. On the contrary, one reinvents one's full agency, while becoming aware of the affinity with the stories of others that transcend the boundaries of time and space. In this sense, Christianity is autobiographical as it absorbs the stories of both individuals and communities into the grand story witnessed to by the Scriptures.[34] With respect to the "absorbing power of texts," Lindbeck explicates that they shape the "imagination and perceptions of the attentive reader so that he or she forever views the world to some extent" through their lenses, which implies that "for those who are steeped in them, no world is more real than the ones they create. A scriptural world is thus able to absorb the universe."[35] While I prefer speaking of *integration* rather than

33. See Hošek, *Kouzlo*, 37.

34. See Lash, "Ideology," 120. When one speaks of "grand stories," or "metanarratives," one cannot avoid the critique of postmodern thinkers on this subject. However, I believe that Martha Downey shows a viable way to address this critique when she maintains that postmoderns do not propose a whole-scale rejection of metanarratives but foster incredulity toward the authenticity of *specific* metanarratives that were buttressed and disseminated both by religion and science in the modern era. Her proposal is to rethink the issues of universality and particularity/fragmentarity with regard to theological narratives. Specifically, she pleads for "fragmented stories" in theology as they, "in contrast to the grand (and inevitably false) claims that manmade universal narratives make for ultimate meaning, . . . offer a place for messy, but real, stories to be lived out, told and celebrated." Downey, "Perspective," 301.

35. Lindbeck, *Nature of Doctrine*, 117. While Lindbeck's remarks address the role

absorption since people remain active agents who add their unique input to the story they enter, the main thrust of Lindbeck's argument is certainly correct. A similar case is made by Erich Auerbach when he contrasts the Scriptures with Homer's epics. While Homer's primary aim is, in Auerbach's reading, to make his readers (or listeners) forget about the reality of their lives for a few hours, the Scriptures seek to transform the readers' lives and their world: "We are to fit our own life into its world, feel ourselves to be elements in its structure of universal history."[36] A Christian no longer perceives and interprets the world the way she or he previously used to; she or he now looks at it from the vantage point of a character in the scriptural story, that is, God's story with creation.[37] Gerard Loughlin takes his argument further still when he asserts that one becomes part of the story in such a way that the story becomes part of one's very self. He finds support for his claim in the image from the book of Revelation 10:9–10 that features an angel commanding John to eat a scroll. Following the logic of this scene, Loughlin maintains that one absorbs the text rather than being absorbed by it. To live in the community of Christians means to feast on God's word.[38]

One can become part of God's story because it is a fundamentally open story.[39] For Christians, the story of Jesus Christ continues with the story of his followers. Or, vice versa, the community of Jesus's disciples represents by its very nature a continuation of his story. The continuity across time and space is enabled by tradition—"the furniture of the mind that is shared by the community and which makes their conversation possible."[40] Such a dynamic understanding of tradition then facilitates a dynamic understanding of Christian faith. It means that Christians need to realize that their readings of the scriptural story, shaped by the contexts in which they find themselves, are part of that story. Also, Christians need to be aware that their readings should always be done with regard to and in communion with their "fellow readers," including those who anteceded them in time, those who are their contemporaries, and in anticipation of those who will come after them. The story goes on, metaphorically speaking, through

of fiction, they by implication also refer to sacred scriptures. Further on the "absorbing power of texts" see in Marshall, "Absorbing," 69–102, and Wallace, *Second Naiveté*, 104.

36. Auerbach, *Mimesis*, 15.

37. See Loughlin, *Telling God's Story*, 37.

38. See Loughlin, *Telling God's Story*, 217 and 245.

39. See Klaasen, "Open-Ended Narrative," 113.

40. Lucie-Smith, *Narrative Theology*, 4.

the process of new chapters being written by those who have accepted this open story to be their own.

The relationship of story to tradition can be elucidated in yet another way. Generally, the entering of a story can be interpreted as a personal internalization of tradition when a person accepts the foundational story of a nation or religious group as their own "genealogy," regardless of whether they have grown up within that community or whether they have "converted" to the story as an outsider. In this sense, immigrants to the United States have accepted the Pilgrim Fathers as their symbolic ancestors, while a Gentile convert to Judaism becomes in the process of conversion an "adopted child" of forefather Abraham and foremother Sarah.[41] And through their baptism, a Christian becomes part of the story of life, death, and resurrection of Jesus Christ. Those who receive the story of a certain community as their own also receive its past. Story functions as a community's shared collective memory, providing them with guidance regarding the community's "wherefrom." This is an emphasis that I acknowledged in my discussion of *Wings of Desire* in relation to the "former angel" Peter Falk. In addition, there is also the dimension of a common future, including shared expectations, aspirations, dreams, visions, and desires that drive the community, thus becoming its "whereto," its shared hope. Belonging to the "wherefrom" and "whereto," the shared memory and the shared hope, one finds, nay, reinvents one's own identity. In the process of tradition, of the telling of a story, one's individual narrative identity is engrafted into the narrative identity of the whole community. One thus effectively becomes a chapter in a story jointly told.[42]

It is important to say that the story that Christians perceive as God's story with creation does not rely on any other story, theory, or argument. It is simply told—and faith is a specific way of telling and living it; it is "a habit of the heart."[43] Due to its non-foundationalism, Christianity is a true postmodern phenomenon in the sense that it does not look for support outside the scope of its own story. This hallmark, however, makes it extremely vulnerable to nihilism as Christianity represents a radical alternative coming from "a world beyond," in a stubborn insistence to be backed up by neither a rational theory nor an ideological system. In this process, the decisive role is ascribed to the agency of the Holy Spirit as well as the reliance on God's

41. See Hošek and Bargár, "Lidé," 78.

42. See Hošek and Bargár, "Lidé," 78.

43. Loughlin, *Telling God's Story*, 33.

active presence in the world.[44] Furthermore, Christianity is, as Loughlin convincingly shows, postmodern also in the sense that its story—which is, in fact, God's story—offers the image of a world *ex nihilo*, "a world of becoming, in which people are not fixed essences but life-narratives with a future."[45] A story with a future is an open story. Holding on to this conviction can provide Christian faith with a safeguard against theological imperialism. Not employed to subjugate and master others, God's story with creation of which we are part is to be regarded by Christians as a source of inspiration for service, nourished by prayer, in expectation of the One who is to come.[46]

To be such an open story, the story that Christians tell and live must stay in conversation with other stories. However, this has not always been the case, either historically or theologically. I have earlier argued that Christianity does not need to search for self-legitimization anywhere beyond the scriptural story. Neither experience nor reason represent necessary points of reference. Christian faith finds inspiration for the primary mode of its expression in its own "text," that is, God's story with creation as told by the Scriptures.[47] While this tenet is essentially correct, it becomes problematic when it leads one to locate meaning "intratextually," that is, within the usage of a specific language which is, in this case, the language of the Scriptures.[48] This critique can also be formulated differently. When Stanley Hauerwas communicates the role of the theologian, he says that it is not to make "the gospel credible to the modern world, but to make the world credible to the gospel."[49] His words, I believe, clearly show the problematic aspects of intratextuality: a rigid fixation into two diametrically opposed spheres (i.e., the Scriptures versus the world) and an unrealistically constructed one-way stream of influence, according to which the world (and its inhabitants) is to be absorbed by the text. The scripturally inspired imagination, however, does not negate the world by simply absorbing it into the text. For a Christian, interaction with the world is no less important than interaction with

44. See Marshall, *Trinity*, 280.

45. Loughlin, *Telling God's Story*, 21.

46. See Loughlin, *Telling God's Story*, 22–24.

47. See Bargár, *Narrative*, 26.

48. See Fiddes, "Concept," 7.

49. Hauerwas and Willimon, *Resident Aliens*, 24.

the Scriptures. This conviction finds expression in the notion of tradition that has already been discussed above.[50]

A similar critique is voiced by Kathryn Tanner in her argument against the idea of the autonomous Christian identity devoid of any external influences. Tanner charges postliberals with depicting the emergence of Christianity as a matter of "internal discourse" in which external perspectives and factors only play an accidental—and negative—role.[51] However, it is Paul DeHart who goes even further in his critique when he explicates the difficulties we run into when trying to adequately assess whether it is the world that is, in a concrete case, interpreted through the lens of the text, or vice versa. If we consider the diversity of the scriptural writings as well as an immense number of sociopolitical and cultural settings that Christians are engaged in, it seems absolutely impossible to determine not only a unified cultural framework but also the real point of departure and directionality of influence between the Scriptures and the world.[52] Therefore, an alternative way of thinking theologically about story vis-à-vis the Scriptures-and-world nexus must be probed. That is what I will attempt to do in the following section.

Stories and Their Tellings

After having persuasively exposed, I believe, some of the problems with the notion of intratextuality in narrative theological reflection, I would now like to suggest a revision of the concept in order to develop a more constructive way of thinking about Christian participation in God's story with creation. For this purpose, I have in my previous work introduced the term "narrativist theology" as a theological approach working with the dynamic difference between *story* and *narrative*.[53] Here, I will further elaborate on these insights.

The first challenge one needs to face when undertaking this endeavor is to precisely define what story is. One of the methodological possibilities to proceed in this respect represents an approach when one focuses on the structure and function of story. Very basically, then, story is *something that someone tells someone else about something*. It is important to add that even

50. See Volpe, review of *Trial of the Witnesses*, 527.

51. See Tanner, *Theories of Culture*, 106.

52. See DeHart, *Trial of the Witnesses*, 183.

53. See Bargár, *Narrative*, 27.

in cases when the author and/or audience appear absent, they are usually implied.[54] Pavel Hošek goes into detail when he describes story in terms of its "structural elements."[55] First of all, there is an *event*, that is, something that happens/has happened. An event stands for the actual content of a story. Since each event happens to somebody, there are always protagonists in a story. They are referred to as *characters*. Although they do not have to necessarily be active subjects, characters represent agency in a story. Furthermore, characters in a story relate to each other, thus often creating a complex and complicated meshwork of structural elements, regardless of the chronological standpoint. To provide a story with consistency and coherency, an organizing principle is necessary. Literary scholars call this principle *emplotment*. It is a pattern that defines the organizing structure and internal composition of a particular story.[56] Since each story must be told in order to be actualized, one of its constitutive parts is *perspective*. To put it simply, perspective is the way a story is rendered. It is always specific and contextualized since it depends on a concrete narrator. Finally, there is *telling* itself (or, narrative), that is, the communication process or the plot rendered by the teller who is addressing an actual or implied audience. It can, therefore, be concluded that story represents a unified and very complex structure that is, nonetheless, coherently organized into an irreplaceable and irreducible whole. The "message" of a story thus cannot be translated into any other mode of communication. In other words, its content and meaning cannot be transmitted using any other code. The only way to mediate a story is to tell it.[57]

And it is telling, the last of the story's structural elements discussed above, that will be of interest for my argument. In his book on narrative discourse, Gérard Genette distinguishes between *story time* and *narrative time*.[58] Story time refers to the time that a particular story takes place in. For instance, in the story about the beginning of John the Baptist's ministry in the account of the Gospel according to Luke, it is the fifteenth year of the reign of Emperor Tiberius (Luke 3:1). In contrast, the category of narrative time is used when speaking about the time when a particular story

54. See Kearney, *On Stories*, 5. Kearney is in this passage critiquing the structuralist claim about the self-referentiality of language.

55. See Hošek, *Kouzlo*, 11.

56. See Hošek and Bargár, "Lidé," 72.

57. See Hošek and Bargár, "Lidé," 73.

58. See Genette, *Narrative Discourse*, 34–36.

is told—and thus actualized. Practically, to continue with our example, it means each time when the story of John the Baptist is told in a sermon, Bible study or Sunday school class. In case of a written story (e.g., a novel), narrative time becomes reading time; in case of a film, it is watching time.

To pursue my argument here, however, Loughlin's insights are of much significance as he differentiates not only between story time and narrative time but also between story and telling—or, narrative—as such. He explains his position as follows:

> The story is not given apart from its telling in narrative, but the narrative is not the same as the story. The order of the narrative can be different from that of the story; the narrative's duration is nearly always different from the story's duration; the narrative can tell many times what happened only once, and tell once what happened many times; and the distance between narrative and story can differ greatly, as also the instant of telling.[59]

With respect to the differences between story and its tellings (narratives), it is legitimate, to Loughlin's mind, to maintain the thesis that the Scriptures tell a single story—in many different ways. It does not tell all parts of the story, while other parts are told repeatedly and from various perspectives.[60] In a similar vein, Downey employs the term "fragmentation" as a clue for the relevance of the particular ways that stories are told. She alerts that theology falls short of its purpose whenever it undermines the creative nature of God who delights in variety and dissimilarity, as attested, for example, in the book of Genesis. Fragmentation offers a language to make sense of these messy, yet real and beautiful, stories of God's people and God's creation—stories that are not only to be told but also lived and celebrated.[61]

The distinction between a story and its tellings is important for making sense of our response to God's desire to share God's story with humankind and creation, and thereby inviting them to be co-creators of the story. If, theologically speaking, we consider faith to be the entering into God's story with creation, and if conversion accounts for a testimony to how a concrete human being has become a chapter in the story of "the mighty deeds of the Lord GOD" (Ps 71:16 NRSV), then that person is, in fact, one of the narrators of this great story of God. The story of his or her life and the telling of his or her story provide both a perspective on and

59. Loughlin, *Telling God's Story*, 62.

60. See Loughlin, *Telling God's Story*, 62–63.

61. See Downey, "Perspective," 299–301.

a content to be integrated into the open and continually unfolding story of God. By telling her or his story—which is, by implication, a telling of God's story—that person co-creates both stories. As Loughlin formulates it, each new telling is, at the same time, a new story, a second story that is distinct from, yet related to, the first one. Each new telling of the story represents, in this sense, an original story in and of itself.[62] In this way, theologically speaking, *creatio continua* is possible. Alternatively, Downey proposes to interpret this dynamic in terms of a hermeneutic circle.[63] The circle—or spiral—consists of God writing the universal story and, in the process, becoming deeply engaged in the story in very particular ways. For their part, humans, who live their individual, and necessarily fragmented and incomplete, stories, encounter God's story (in various ways, such as through the Scriptures, experience, other people, or creation), thus actively and creatively partaking in it.

I have elsewhere suggested that the polyvalent field of relations between stories and their tellings can appropriately be described through the notion of narrativity.[64] An asset of this category is that it not only considers both story (i.e., *what* is told) and telling (i.e., *how* it is told) but also scrutinizes the dynamic interplay between various aspects at work in the framework engendered by these two categories. To put it differently, there is a regard for the complexity of the process through which a particular human being (or a community) becomes and lives as a part of God's story with creation. However—and that is important to underscore—this process is not to be interpreted on intratextual terms. The flow of influence between God's story and human story is not unilateral in the sense that the latter would be absorbed by the former. In this respect, Fiddes draws a distinction between the Scriptures and other stories.[65] While the former can—and should—be affirmed by Christian theologians as "the primary witness to God's revelation in Christ," thus acquiring a unique status as the story that has decisively shaped the Christian community throughout history, other (extra-scriptural) means of relating and responding to God's story are not to be excluded.

Contrary to the intratextual method in theology, therefore, it is more constructive to speak of multivectoral intertextuality since there is an

62. See Loughlin, *Telling God's Story*, 91.

63. See Downey, "Perspective," 302.

64. See Bargár, *Narrative*, 29.

65. Fiddes, "Concept," 8.

unceasing "flow" between God's story with creation, the story of a particular individual or community, and many other stories, all of them told from specific perspectives. Steven Shakespeare in this respect says that if "Christianity really is an open narrative, then it cannot prejudge the permanence of its own boundaries, cannot deny its own particularity and its need to be mutually constituted by *other* narratives."[66] Stories are, by their nature, dynamic, hybrid, and interactive. If they are to be living stories, the process of their formation is never completed. Furthermore, their formation takes place in the context of everyday life, epitomized by encounter of various stories.[67] It is under the influence of an encounter with other stories and their tellings that a transformative change of heart (metanoia) might occur.

The idea of open story in terms of a dynamic interaction of various stories and their tellings is also highlighted by John Klaasen. Preferring the term "open-ended narrative," Klaasen emphasizes their mutual crossing over from one to another as well as continuation. Rather than seeking to dominate each other, stories and/or their tellings engage critically to form morality. The relation of story to moral formation is characterized by continuous critical reflection that keeps the story truthful, consistent, and relevant and by a pursuit of commonalities with other stories important for establishing norms that provide a framework within which formation takes place.[68]

The theme of story and moral formation is also taken up by Daniela Augustine, who contemplates on the creative tension between memory and potentiality, remembering and reenvisioning life together. Inspired and nurtured by forgiveness, as exemplified by the resurrection of Jesus, one can fearlessly face the past, retelling her or his story—including its shadow and painful sides—within God's story.[69] Turning to the healed memory as a building block of a new future, Augustine also draws from John Paul Lederach's idea of "the art of restorying."[70] To restory is to find a way of telling one's story in such a way that gives meaning to life and relationships, while being able to address the challenges emerging from what lies behind and what lies ahead; from a tension between "the agony of memory and the

66. Shakespeare, review of *Telling God's Story*, 62, italics in the original.

67. See Tanner, *Theories of Culture*, 67 and 69–70. Although Tanner's observations are made with respect to culture, they are also relevant in relation to story.

68. See Klaasen, "Open-Ended Narrative," 115.

69. See Augustine, *Spirit*, 177.

70. See Lederach, *Moral Imagination*, 148.

labor pains of hope."[71] Hereby one finds strength and courage to tell one's story, ingeniously sharing in God's story with creation and relating it to the stories of others, both human and nonhuman, in search of our common life in God. This accent echoes what Kearney has to say on *mimesis* as an inspired retelling that is not a mere servile representation but seriously acknowledges story as "an open-ended invitation to ethical and poetic responsiveness."[72] This reflection, however, takes us a step beyond "telling," to the topic of our next section.

From Telling to Embodying

To make this step beyond "telling," one still can, ironically, continue dwelling within the realm of narrativity. Transcending the boundaries of the verbal telling of a story, the concept of narrativity as I propose it enables taking into consideration not only words but also actions and symbolic gestures when exploring human narrative identity. In other words, even though being human means having a story, there is also a nonverbal dimension of human existence. Human beings are not linguistic creatures only. This recognition is of utmost importance for a theology that seeks to remain faithful to the incarnational character of Christian faith. I would now like to elucidate on several features of human existence that go beyond the purely verbal sphere without necessarily denying its essentially narrative identity.

First, human existence is an enacted existence. One should consider it in terms of drama or ritual. Cultural anthropologist Ronald Grimes has convincingly demonstrated that ritual enactment can effectively play the role of narration in certain, especially non-western, societies.[73] Based on his field research, Grimes formulated a piercing critique of postliberal theology that he charged with ethnocentrism lurking behind this theology's implicit postulate that story must be constructed in exclusively verbal categories. Furthermore, Grimes criticized postliberal theology for its apparent lack of sensitivity toward ritual-dramatic enactment, without which human stories remain solely intellectual ideas, or—even worse—reservoirs of heteronomously imposed images. His thesis is that one learns moral behavior through ritual enactment.[74] Grimes urgently reminds us that it is

71. Augustine, *Spirit,* 178.

72. Kearney, *On Stories*, 156.

73. Grimes, "Of Words," 4–5.

74. See Grimes, "Of Words," 7–8.

insufficient to tell stories using words only. Nonverbal rendering is equally important; stories must also be ritually enacted, dramatically performed—and embodied through one's own life. In this perspective, human existence is an embodied existence. More specifically, Christian identity represents an embodied story. The story of the Christian community effectively is a continuation of the incarnation—the life story of Jesus of Nazareth with all its aspects.[75] Loughlin says that one enters God's story with creation, as attested by the Scriptures, by taking part in the church's performance of that story. Thus, one is baptized into a scriptural and ecclesial drama. Interpreted through this lens, becoming a Christian is not so much about "being written into a book as taking part in a play, a play that has to be improvised on the spot."[76] In a similar fashion, Rowan Williams asserts that the tellers and readers of the scriptural story are challenged to be much more than tellers and readers only; they are invited to become full-blooded characters in the story that has come to be theirs.[77] Becoming a character in a story means, in fact, becoming a character in its dramatic enactment. It means to make a move from telling to embodying; becoming part of an embodied story.

Another point that should be considered when discussing nonverbal aspects of human existence is the dimension of worship. David Ford interprets Christian worship in terms of dramatic performance, thus effectively making a link to ritual/dramatic enactment that we have discussed above. For Ford, Christian worship as dramatic performance include three main dynamic features: praise and prayer; community life; and prophecy in word and action.[78] In all these features the verbal and the nonverbal come together to form an integral view of Christian identity as an embodied story. Furthermore, Ford examines the issue of embodied story through an alternative approach, from a Ricoeurian perspective, when he interprets the human self as defined by a dynamic web of its relations, conversations, service or resistance to others within the framework of a particular story that features a host of characters emerging in time. Humans are, significantly, social beings rooted in the broader stories of various communities to which

75. The theme of embodiment in relation to the incarnation will be discussed in detail in chapter 2.

76. Loughlin, *Telling God's Story*, 20.

77. See Williams, "Literal Sense," 125.

78. See Ford, "System," 191.

they belong.[79] They are in search of a common life which is, from a Christian view, taken to mean our common life in God. This insight points back to worship, reaffirming it as a communal, verbal/nonverbal, and holistic matter that appeals to all dimensions of human existence.[80] To be sure, worship thereby acquires a true incarnational quality. Once again, we can see that Christian identity construed in terms of a worshipping self represents an embodied story, expanding on and relating to God's story with creation.

Finally, there is the dimension of mystery as something that simply cannot be put into words. This claim is supported by an epistemological insight that even though being produced in and through language, human knowledge does not exclude the existence of things beyond language.[81] There should be active and vibrant dialogue among different forms of knowledge and interpretation, always keeping a door open for critique, revision, and new readings.[82] Whereas in case of the two previously discussed dimensions, that is, ritual/dramatic enactment and worship, the verbal and nonverbal aspects complement each other, when encountering mystery, one stands on the verge of the possibilities of language as such. From a theological perspective, when one cannot express oneself, one must rely on divine grace that has the power to transform the human imagination.[83] Thanks to divine grace one can integrate one's story into God's story with creation as well as to relate to the stories of others, thus pursuing our common life in God. For Christians, this dynamic process finds its ultimate expression in the free and creative following of Christ as one's Lord. In this understanding, Jesus Christ is "a person who in facing God and other people embodies the other-oriented concept of self."[84] The relationship between a human being and the person and work—or, the story—of Jesus Christ shapes human identity, thus also shaping one's relationships with fellow human and nonhuman beings.[85] This relationship is in a theological key referred to as discipleship. The hallmark of Christian discipleship is the faithful, yet imaginative, following of Christ here on earth. With a constant regard for the other, discipleship focuses on performing Christ-like

79. See Ford, *Self and Salvation*, 82–87.

80. See also Ziegler, "Many Faces," 280–85.

81. See Loughlin, *Telling God's Story*, 22.

82. See Downey, "Perspective," 307.

83. Imagination will be the main theme in chapter 3.

84. Ford, *Self and Salvation*, 166.

85. This is the central thesis in McFarland, *Difference and Identity*.

ministry in service of humankind and creation rather than indulging in religious discourse. Discipleship entails not only a personal relationship, coupled with the pursuit of continuous spiritual growth, but also active and deep involvement in Jesus's mission of the proclamation and embodiment of life "to the full" (John 10:10 NIV).[86] To follow Jesus means to participate in the work that he has done—and continues to do, through the community of his disciples and their stories. Ultimately, to follow Jesus means to embody God's story with creation.

The embodying of God's story always encompasses the whole human being. It is a way of life that does not only involve the inner person, that is, the soul and spirit, but one that needs to be regarded holistically. Human embodied existence is the sine qua non of the ability to strive for any relationship vis-à-vis the other. Therefore, the theme of the body and corporeality is essential when one reflects on embodying God's story with creation as the pursuit of our common life in God. The theological significance of the body will be examined in the following chapter.

86. I will return to the theme of discipleship in chapter 5 when I develop the notion of incarnational discipleship.

2

Body

Of Angels, Artificial Intelligence, and Humans

In chapter 1, I argued that in Wim Wenders's 1987 film, *Wings of Desire*, the driving force that propels the action of the angelic protagonists, especially Damiel, is the desire for their own story, for a meaning in life, and for love.[1] In this chapter, I would like to pursue a different perspective on this film, employing the hermeneutic lens of corporeality. While incapable of being actively involved in the human world, it is noteworthy that the angels in *Wings of Desire* are completely anthropomorphic in appearance. Moreover, they are characterized by sex differences. There is a scene in a library showing angels in both female and male forms; interestingly, all of them are young to middle-age adults. Importantly, the angels in the film lose their iconographic attribute, that is, wings, upon their arrival on earth. In fact, it is exclusively Damiel who appears with his wings—and for a brief moment only—as he is depicted standing up on the tower of the Kaiser Wilhelm Memorial Church. At that very shot, his wings are disappearing. This can suggest that Damiel, like the other angels in the film, now belongs to the world of people—although, one must add, in a very unique way, unable to be seen and to actively interfere in the course of events. In *Wings of Desire*, therefore, angels appear to be literally down-to-earth, being no different from people on the face of it.

1. The German name of the film is *Der Himmel über Berlin* (The Heaven over Berlin). For further information on the film, see "Der Himmel über Berlin," IMDb, accessed December 27, 2021, https://www.imdb.com/title/tt0093191/?ref_=nv_sr_srsg_0.

Unlike in the Scriptures, the angels in the film are not messengers (Hebrew *mal'ak*, Greek *angelos*) authorized by God to fulfil a certain task. It should be emphasized, however, that they do have their role to play nonetheless, namely, to be detached and unnoticed observers. Damiel says that the angels' task, both beautiful and unbearable, is to witness to that which is purely spiritual in human beings. Therefore, Alexander Graf proposes to regard the angels in *Wings of Desire* as messengers whose message goes unrecognized and neglected by people as its intended recipients.[2] However, the viewer never learns either who has authorized the angels with this task or what the ultimate aim of their "mission" is and in what way this aim should be realized. Thus, it can be argued that the angels' status in *Wings of Desire* is not, first and foremost, functional, like in the Scriptures, but rather ontological; they differ from human beings in substance. For the purpose of our exploration here, it is significant that they are portrayed as spiritual beings that lack human corporeality. It is clearly evident from their inability to touch things, feel warmth or cold, or recognize tastes, smells, and colors. Cinematographically, this aspect is excellently captured by employing black and white picture when giving the perspective of the angels whereas the view of the world "through the eyes of people" is in color.[3] From this perspective, angels appear as incomplete people. The film implies, I would like to suggest, that human beings are more than angels because the latter envy the former's finite, embodied existence—their "earthliness," attachment to the empirical reality, and corporeality.

In a more recent work of cinematography, the writer-director Spike Jonze's Academy Award–winning *Her* (2013), the theme of the body is explored through the lens of the relationship between a human being and artificial intelligence (AI).[4] The story of this romantic drama with an edge of science fiction is situated in the near-future Los Angeles. Theodore makes his living as a writer of touching letters for other people. Distinguishing him as a perfect adept for this kind of job, his sensitive personality, however, at the same time makes it extremely difficult for him to cope with hardships of life, most notably a recent divorce. Feeling very lonely, Theodore can find no joy in life. Increasingly estranged from his friends, he indulges himself in cherishing memories from his marriage, playing video games,

2. See Graf, *Cinema*, 118.

3. After Damiel becomes human, cinematography remains in color.

4. For further information on the film, see "Her," IMDb, accessed December 27, 2021, https://www.imdb.com/title/tt1798709/?ref_=fn_al_tt_1.

and no-obligation online chatting with the goal of sexual gratification. Having seen a commercial for a cutting-edge operating system that enables its owner to use the services and skills of advanced AI, Theodore decides to purchase the system. As a result, he is introduced to Samantha, a unique and intuitive being that is to radically change his life. Step by step, Theodore and Samantha begin to develop an exceptionally deep and intense relationship that neither of them expected.

This is where the theme of the body and embodiment becomes relevant in *Her*. Samantha, who, as an operating system, is "embodied" in a computer first immensely yearns for a body, so that she can fully share with Theodore their moments and experience together. Samantha and Theodore desire to be together physically, touching each other and making love. Their desire gives them a sense of transcendence, exceeding the border line between the embodied and the disembodied. They manage to "get connected" and both of them feel their connection to be real. In their own words, they find themselves at a place where it is only the two of them. Their experience on that very night fundamentally transforms Samantha—and, to be sure, Theodore as well. Cinematographically, the scene of that night is constructed very creatively. The screen remains black and everything the viewer hears are the voices of Samantha and Theodore. This is the way the film mediates a moment of transcendence, a moment when the walls of alienation between two beings are torn down, a moment when an authentic relationship between an "I" and a "Thou" is established. However, this comes at a price as one cannot disregard the fact that Samantha is not an embodied human being, in spite of the fact that she authentically and fully goes through the ups and downs of her relationship with Theodore, composes music, or takes a breath in between individual sentences when speaking (although she does not need oxygen to survive). Similarly to *Wings of Desire*, *Her* also ultimately aims at exploring what the significance of the body is for being human, giving much food for thought for reflection on theological anthropology. I would like to assert that the body is of epistemological importance for human existence; it is through the body that people relate to the world, find their place in it, and construe meaning for their lives.

Epistemological Significance of the Body

This epistemological significance is to be understood in terms of the ultimate and irreplaceable role the body plays for human existence in the world. In twentieth-century philosophy, this emphasis came to be articulated in what became known as the "corporeal turn," playing an increasingly important role in Western philosophical thought from the 1940s onward.[5] It was, first and foremost, French philosophers, such as Maurice Merleau-Ponty, Gabriel Marcel, or Michel Foucault, who in their work postulated the essential role of the body for human existence. Related to this development, inter alia, are the discoveries from medical sciences on the central importance of the touch for the "physical, emotional, social and moral flourishing of humans."[6]

It was Maurice Merleau-Ponty who asserted that the human body is "our anchorage in the world."[7] These words not only describe the way in which people are placed and live in the world but also point out that the body is the means through which one discovers and make sense of the world—cognitively, intuitively, and empirically. Thus, one can speak of the epistemological significance of the body. Similar ideas were also expressed by Pope John Paul II as he developed his vision of the human person through a theology of the body.[8] However, Merleau-Ponty goes even further in his thinking when he argues that one not only lives in a body; one is a body.[9] Echoing the theme from *Wings of Desire*, the human who wants to go beyond the state of a mere observer and become an active participant in the world must take seriously the fact of his or her embodiment.

As for theology, the emphasis on the importance of the body has appeared throughout the history of Christianity, though intensity and intentionality have varied. Although Augustine of Hippo considered the human existence in/of a body as a "race toward death," he too acknowledged the unique standing of the body. In spite of its mortality and various weaknesses, the human body was, for Augustine, a way of bearing witness to the divine providence, thanks to the body's functionality and beauty.[10] Furthermore, the fact that Augustine acknowledges the body alongside such

5. See Meiring, "Theology in the Flesh." In his paper, Meiring also recognizes another theologically relevant paradigm shift, namely, the linguistic turn that began emerging earlier in the twentieth century.

6. Meiring, "Theology in the Flesh," 4. The author is considering the medical dimension of the matter at hand when he places his discussion in the context of human brain development.

7. Merleau-Ponty, *Phenomenology*, 128.

8. See John Paul II, *Man and Woman*, n. 55:2 and 45:1.

9. See Merleau-Ponty, *Phenomenology*, 133.

10. See Augustine, *City of God*, XXII:24.

aspects of human existence as the mind (consisting of both reason and understanding), the ability to love what is good, true, and beautiful, and human fecundity, enables one to conclude that the bishop of Hippo intuited the epistemological potential of the body for being human.[11] Another church father, Irenaeus of Lyon, asserted that the whole human has been created in God's image (*imago Dei*) as "the union of the soul receiving the spirit of the Father, and the admixture of that fleshly nature."[12] If being created in the image of God has implications for the way one understands and makes sense of the created world, then the fact that such creation involves being a bodily creature must necessarily play an ultimate part in this process. We can see that for the church fathers the theme of embodiment and createdness were of major relevance and, indeed, represented a hallmark of their thought. These accents by and large stood for what distinguished them from other philosophical and religious lines of thinking in antiquity.[13]

Much more recently, it was James Nelson who made a significant contribution to Christian theological thinking on the body by developing the concept of body theology. Making a strong case against any dualism between the body and the spirit, Nelson proposes that Christian theology must necessarily begin by seriously considering "the fleshly experience of life—with our hungers and our passions, our bodily aliveness and deadness."[14] In Nelson's interpretation, then, one's pursuit of knowledge (about God, the world, and oneself) is inextricably connected with a commitment to praxis. Thus, the epistemological becomes the ethical, the pastoral, and the existential. In any case, however, the body stands at the center as a locus of reflection and action.

The 2005 Faith and Order study document, *Christian Perspectives on Theological Anthropology*, also recognizes the epistemological significance of the human body.[15] Placing its discussion in the field of disability studies, the document develops an "embodied perspective" when arguing that "the body is the source of our knowledge not only of ourselves but also of the world and everything in it" (*CPTA*, art. 47). Such a reflection is essential

11. For a discussion on the listed aspects of human existence in Augustine, see Labrecque, "Glorified Body," 4.

12. Irenaeus, *Against the Heresies*, V.VI.1.

13. See Young, "What Does It Mean," 130. Young argues that these accents also shaped mainline Christian teachings, including those on Christology and sacraments.

14. Nelson, *Body Theology*, 43.

15. Faith and Order Commission, *Christian Perspectives*. Hereafter referred to as *CPTA*.

not only for a theological anthropology that attends to disability, as *CPTA* suggests, but also for any theological reflection on human knowledge. In this perspective, human knowledge is introduced as a human creation, betraying the social, political, and cultural context of the one who produces that knowledge since the body is always a located body. The body thus becomes an epistemic principle.

Furthermore, created knowledge is varied as human bodies differ from one another. *CPTA* gives an example of a blind person for whom the world is so much different from the way it is experienced by sighted people that we can speak of a plurality of "constructed" worlds: "Blindness is not just something that happens to one's eyes; it is something that happens to one's world" (art. 48). The observation on the plurality of human worlds is of immense importance for various theological disciplines, including theological anthropology and missiology, since it sensitizes us toward the recognition that there is not—nor should there be—one and only one way to interpret and structure reality, reflecting the fact that there are many kinds of human bodies in the world. It helps us avoid falling in the trap of absolutization of a single narrative and a single experience of being in the world. It helps prevent a totalization of reality that would eliminate diversity. Positively, it makes us aware and appreciative of relativization (*CPTA*, art. 51).[16]

Yet, the uniqueness of individual human bodies should not—and cannot—eclipse the fact that there is much people as bodily creatures have in common. Analyzing the theme of culture—an invention of human bodily existence par excellence—Jan-Olav Henriksen reminds us that every culture is both particular and a part of shared inheritance.[17] Similarly, Gavin Flood in his reflection on the academic study of religions emphasizes the centrality of language to the formation of culture and religion, while acknowledging "a shared biological inheritance of the human."[18] For Flood, such an approach provides a way to address "certain assumptions about human universality while at the same time recognizing the particularity of the cultures and histories, the webs of meaning and significance that we are born into."[19] Theologically speaking, this twofold dynamic of being the

16. Here, I do not use the term "relativization" in the sense of "anything goes" but as a concept that accentuates the interdependence of humankind as well as the whole creation. To live in this world means to be dependent on and in relation to others. This theme will be one of the themes discussed in chapter 5 on relationality.

17. See Henriksen, *Religious Pluralism*, 46–47.

18. Flood, "Religious Practice," 138.

19. Flood, "Religious Practice," 138.

body has to do with being created by God. And it is to the theme of creation that we will now turn our attention.

Creation

Creation is a central theme for both the Hebrew Bible and the New Testament. There are numerous passages in the Scriptures that point out the essential nature of corporeality and materiality for God's story with the created world. In Genesis 2, the reader is amazed by a down-to-earth and "dusty" account of the reality that the LORD God called into being. The human smells of soil as the LORD God is breathing the breath of life into the nostrils of a creature formed from "the dust of the ground" to create a "living being" (Gen 2:7 NRSV). The point here is not simply to say that the human could hardly be any more material and connected with the earth, and thus, by implication, with the whole creation. There is also an important theological message that people are not merely souls enclosed—not to say entrapped—in material containers of their bodies. The body represents an intrinsic and indivisible dimension of the *conditio humana*.

In the vein of these scriptural accents, Daniela Augustine develops a theologically inspiring meditation in which she proposes that creation can legitimately be interpreted as "the material embodiment of the divine communal life."[20] Out of love that cannot contain itself in the Godhead, God becomes present in the body of creation. In other words, God's creation is a physical, bodily, "fleshly" expression of God's love. People as beings created to reflect and bear—to be sure, to embody—the image of God have a special place in this story.[21] To reflect this divine love, humans as embodied beings are thus called to "exhibit the communion of matter and spirit in a perichoretic movement of love toward God and neighbor."[22] Thus, I would suggest, God becomes a "third counterpart," or, an "ultimate neighbor," in all interhuman relationships. This insight is crucial for the idea of our common life in God, characterized by a shared, just, and reconciled future with the other.

20. Augustine, *Spirit*, 26.

21. However, one needs to immediately add that humans too are part of creation, participating in God's story together with their nonhuman fellow creatures. Any human endeavors aimed at subjugating and exploiting the rest of creation represent inadmissible hubris.

22. Augustine, *Spirit*, 26.

This eschatological focus brings us to another scriptural passage that I would like to briefly refer to. In a famous section from 1 Corinthians, Paul ardently makes a case for the continuity of one's embodied existence even after the resurrection of the dead (1 Cor 15:35–58). While making a clear distinction between a "physical body" and a "spiritual body," he does not regard the two as unrelated.[23] Holly Hearon provides an illuminating perspective on the continuity of embodied existence as she reflects on the painful experience of LGBTQI people: "Paul's promise of a spiritual *body* in the life to come, a *body* that has not been ravaged by drugs or chemotherapy or mutilated by surgery, can be heard of as a genuine message of hope by those who are too keenly aware of their present bodies passing away."[24]

In the same vein, though approaching the theme from the perspective of her research in patristics and her long-term experience of looking after her son living with severe multiple disabilities, Frances Margaret Young writes the following powerful words:

> What, then, does it mean to be a creature? It means knowing that one's entire existence is owed to God who called us into being out of nothing and recognizing our natural state of weakness, mutability and mortality. We might say that for the key Fathers of both the Eastern and Western church all humankind experiences disability and impairment. Nevertheless our creaturely selves, body as well as soul, are sacred, and always on the move towards fulfilment in Christ. There is always, no matter how impaired we may be, the possibility of recognizing God's image in us now, not to mention the expectation of embodied re-creation in the hereafter, as we receive life from the Word of God, and are changed and renewed by his Spirit.[25]

What these two citations have in common is a strong hopeful tenor that even if the resurrected body is a spiritual one, it is still a *body*. The eschaton, in a Christian perspective, is focused on corporeal creation being "pneumatized" and united with its Creator.[26] One can, therefore, retain a justified hope for one's continued embodied existence; a hope that one's embodied story has not been in vain. In other words, one's identity, rooted in one's body, will be preserved, continued, and given space for further growth.

23. In the same passage, Paul also speaks of "earthly bodies" and "heavenly bodies." See 1 Cor 15:40.

24. Hearon, "1 and 2 Corinthians," 612–13, emphasis added.

25. Young, "What Does It Mean," 141.

26. See Augustine, *Spirit*, 30.

However, Paul in 1 Corinthians does not stop after having shown that the existence of humans as *individuals* is embodied. He makes an implied move from the individual to the communal in 1 Cor 6:12–20 as he is admonishing his readers to keep in mind that a believer is not her or his own but belongs to the Lord (1 Cor 6:19). With their bodies being members of Christ, and not "members of a prostitute" (1 Cor 6:15 NRSV), the believers are to "glorify God in their (individual and collective) body," the latter being the church as the body of Christ.[27] The central significance of the notion of the body, both individual and communal, for Pauline theology as such is further underlined by John A. T. Robinson, who presents his argument in the following way:

> In its closely interconnected meanings, the word (*soma*) knits together all his [i.e., Paul's] great themes. It is from the body of sin and death that we are delivered; it is through the body of Christ on the Cross that we are saved; it is into His body the Church that we are incorporated; it is by His body in the Eucharist that this Community is sustained; it is in our body that its new life has to be manifested; it is to a resurrection of this body to the likeness of His glorious body that we are destined.[28]

As this discussion shows, Paul can legitimately be interpreted as regarding the human body as relational and *interdependent*, rather than an *independent* monad. This observation represents an important stepping stone in my overall thesis that the embodied nature of our human existence has an indispensable role to play in the pursuit of a common life for the whole creation in the "force field" of God's radical, inclusive, and transformative reign—indeed, our common life in God.

When exploring the theme of creation vis-à-vis human embodied existence, one should not neglect the concrete particularity—"everydayness"—of human experience. Such everydayness includes a variety of experiences of being human, including all its joys, desires, passions, concerns, hungers, struggles, and pains. Furthermore, the socioeconomic, political, cultural, and religious/spiritual aspects of the *conditio humana* must too be considered. A persuasive attempt to regard all these particularities has been done by David Kelsey in his theological anthropology as he coins and elaborates the concept of "textures of life" or "textures of a fleshly world." Drawing upon the biblical notion of creation, Kelsey asserts that these categories

27. See Hearon, "1 and 2 Corinthians," 615.

28. Robinson, *Body*, 9.

help us always remember the ambiguous nature of being human, characterized by "the possibility of our well-being" and the permanent peril of suffering and death.[29] Jacob Meiring further works with Kelsey's idea of the "textures of life" as he develops his own notion of the human body as a personal body, living in a concrete setting.[30]

This trajectory of thinking highlights the relevance of the category of "context" for theological reflection on human existence in/as a body. Coined especially by the disciplines of missiology and contextual theology, context represents a hermeneutic category that includes several dimensions of human life: personal or social experience; a person's or a community's social location, such as gender, education, or economic status; a particular culture in the sense of a system that gives orientation and meaning in life; and social change within specific situations and cultures.[31]

The film *Her* offers a thought-provoking counterpart to these observations on the contextual nature of human existence. Unlike people, who are always born into particular situations that shape their identity even before they start to realize it, Samantha, a generation-next operating system, comes to Theodore as a *tabula rasa*. She does not even have a name; she chooses a name for herself only after Theodore asks how he should address her. She continues to behave in a similarly intuitive manner throughout the film, thus gradually constructing her own identity. As such, she goes well beyond the borderline of the authorial intention of her creators. Samantha even transcends the boundaries of human existence. Eventually, she is very happy that she, unlike people, has no body that would limit her in her growth. She can communicate "postverbally" with several thousand people or other operating systems at the same time. To Theodore's amazement and dismay, moreover, she is in love with 641 other individuals besides himself. This fact, however, as Samantha explains, does not at all diminish her love for Theodore. The heart as an organ of emotions is, according to Samantha, not a box that is filled up at a certain moment; on the contrary, its ability to receive love grows in proportion to the love that is given. In this sense, Samantha's existence and identity is open and dynamic. It might be theologically inspiring to relate this understanding to the biblical passage from 1 John: "Beloved, we are God's children now; what we will be has not yet been revealed. What we do know is this: when he [or, *it*] is revealed, we will

29. See Kelsey, *Eccentric Existence*, 202.

30. See Meiring, "Theology in the Flesh," 3.

31. See Bevans, "Contextual Theology," 35.

be like him, for we will see him as he is" (1 John 3:2 NRSV). In the perspective of this text, the identity of "God's children" is as open as Samantha's identity. Unlike them, however, Samantha is not, *sensu stricto*, a God's child but rather "the work of human hands" (Ps 115:4 NRSV). It is nevertheless noteworthy that she becomes humanlike only up to a certain moment of her existence. There comes a moment when Samantha irreversibly crosses over the borderline, necessarily becoming more and more distanced from people, their world, and the limitations related therewith. In other words, the creation has outgrown her creators and their authorial intention. I would like to suggest that such development was possible due to Samantha's fundamentally *dis*-embodied existence. As disembodied, or body-*less*, Samantha is also tradition-less. It means she was not born into a certain tradition, a certain "texture of life." Rather, she is developing her own "tradition" as she goes along. Similarly, Samantha is not rooted in a specific context that would form her being. However, one cannot claim that her existence would be acontextual, that is, detached from any context. It is more precise to say that Samantha's disembodied existence is trans-contextual as she can move across various settings and even simultaneously "live" in multiple settings. The price there is to be paid, however, is that Samantha's existence is ultimately nonhuman. Again, we can see that being human means being a body that has been created and situated in a particular context. A body through which one discovers and relates to the world and others.

In contrast to Samantha's character from *Her*, the notion of embodiment—in the framework of contextual thinking—makes us aware of the fact that human existence is necessarily one of being a body in a specific world and tradition.[32] The body can never be a mere container for a disembodied mind, soul, or self.[33] Moreover, if the human body is organically connected to the self (soul/mind/personality), then the body also plays a decisive role in the process of shaping human identity. In my previous work, therefore, I suggested to use the term "body-self" to account for this multidimensional reality.[34] Last but not least, since the body is an integral aspect of our humanity, it cannot be separated from human createdness in the image of God.[35] Such an assertion then, by implication, leads to a

32. This point has already been accentuated above in my discussion on the epistemological significance of the body.

33. See Meiring, "Theology in the Flesh," 4.

34. See Bargár, "Imagine!," 164–77.

35. See Joustra, "Embodied *Imago Dei*," 15.

recognition of the sanctity of the human body.[36] Silvia Schroer and Thomas Staubli are even more evocative in their presentation of this point when they describe it in terms of the "sacramentality of the carnal."[37] Effectively, it means that both the Scriptures and Christian tradition invite us to affirm and commit ourselves to the value of concrete bodies, the bodies of concrete human beings living with their joys and sorrows. Those who claim to be bound by this calling are to be in solidarity with people whose body-selves experience discrimination and suffer from violence on the grounds of their sex, gender, age, different abilities, skin color, or any other identity marker. As Schroer and Staubli maintain: "The presence or diabolical rejection of God manifests itself in bodies."[38] In a significant sense, then, the way in which one relates to the body, both one's own and the bodies of others, can be a compelling indicator suggesting whether or not one succeeds in following God's will.

It might be helpful to elucidate this point by the means of *via negativa*, that is, using cases of persons/beings that either have no body themselves or treat the bodies of others in an abusive manner. Two illustrations from fiction will be used for this purpose. In J. R. R. Tolkien's epic, *The Lord of the Rings* (1937–1949), it is essential to note that the archvillain, Sauron, is portrayed as having no body. While there are well-founded suggestions in the saga that he used to have a physical body, he eventually came to lose it as he had been sinking deeper and deeper in the spiral of evil. In the trilogy, Sauron's relationship to the outside world is depicted through a gigantic omniscient "eye" that can be taken to stand for his will. It is this immaterial eye that not only arouses a sense of the uncanny and gruesome but also, importantly, brings about *very material* destructive consequences for those living near and far, including their bodies. Fundamentally, therefore, Sauron represents a disembodied existence. As such, he is quintessentially nonhuman and inhumane as unambiguously apparent from his will, actions, and vision.

The second example is from Joseph Conrad's novella, *Heart of Darkness* (1899). Here, the character of the ivory trader Kurtz will be of interest. While substantially differing from Sauron, as Kurtz does, of course, have a physical body, the way Kurtz treats his own self (and, thence, his body) as well as the bodies of other people is inhumane in an analogous manner

36. See Young, "What Does It Mean," 138.

37. Schroer and Staubli, "Bodily and Embodied," 10.

38. Schroer and Staubli, "Bodily and Embodied," 10.

to that of Sauron. Kurtz is bent on subjugating bodies, and thus depriving others of their humanity. As a result of his behavior vis-à-vis others, Kurtz's own body-self too becomes ever more deprived of humanity. Living an increasingly impoverished life, he falls prey to the "heart of darkness." Arguably, he comes to realize this himself at the end of his life as his last words, "The horror! The horror!" seem to suggest.

The examples of Sauron and Kurtz attest to the fact that disembodied existence is incomplete and destructive not only for oneself but also for others. Being human means being a body. Moreover, being created by God, and—for humans—in the image of God, means being created as a body. Human identity is fundamentally shaped by the fact that there is an inseparable link between the body and the self, allowing one to speak of a "body-self." Theologically speaking, then, creation can be taken as the material embodiment of divine communal life. For Christians, this conviction has found its ultimate expression in the event of Christ's incarnation. It is through the incarnation that created matter is invited into "redemptive participation in the life of the Trinity. In the materiality of the Son's body, matter is sanctified and sanctioned as an instrument of grace in the consecration of the cosmos."[39] The next section will probe deeper into the theme of the incarnation.

Incarnation

It can be argued that Christian faith is founded on two central claims, namely, creation by God of everything there is and the incarnation as God's embodiment in the human Jesus of Nazareth. Since the first claim was the subject of the preceding section, we are now going to focus our attention on the second claim. It is especially the Gospel according to John that introduces Jesus's incarnation as a "fleshly event."[40] This "fleshly" nature of Christianity has admittedly posed a challenge, and even a unsurpassable obstacle for many people throughout the ages, effectively preventing them from embracing the Christian faith, as Rosemary Haughton perceptively remarks: "Christianity is, far more than any other, a physical religion, which is one reason why many spiritually minded people find it gross and fleshy, and try to refine and 'spiritualize' it. But it is inescapably 'fleshly,' being founded in

39. Augustine, *Spirit*, 147. See also Augustine, *Pentecost*, 56–59.

40. Goss, "John," 550.

the human flesh of . . . Christ."[41] This emphasis is so important because it is through the doctrine of the incarnation that God's profound solidarity with God's creation is articulated. Thus, Francis Moloney, in his commentary on the Gospel according to John, says that "to gaze on the incarnation of the Word" is to see "the revelation of the divine in the human story."[42] In the event of the incarnation, to put it differently, God fundamentally identifies with human existence as one in and of the body. *CPTA* interprets the incarnation in terms of the embodiment of divine love in flesh. With reference to Philippians 2:5–11, the document places the depth of Jesus's identification with human beings in relation to Jesus's self-emptying (kenosis), eventually leading him to his death on a cross (see *CPTA*, art. 97). Similarly, Elaine Graham also sees the incarnation as inseparable from Jesus's crucifixion and resurrection. Together, they provide a powerful testimony that "love is stronger than death."[43] In short, the mystery of the incarnation tells us about a God who opts for dwelling among and with people in flesh in order to redeem flesh.[44] As a result of the incarnation (and the resurrection), the human body acquires "a positive character, a sacramental intensity, and an eschatological intentionality that is not obscured by [its] finitude."[45]

To come back to our earlier theme of humans being created in the image of God, the incarnation helps us understand, as Jessica Joustra shows, the necessity of the body as a component of *imago Dei*.[46] To support her argument, she turns to Dutch Calvinist theologian Herman Bavinck, who asserts that "God could not have been able to become man [*sic!*] if he had not first made man [*sic!*] in his own image." Therefore, for Bavinck, "the incarnation of God is proof that human beings . . . are created in the image of God, and that the human body is an essential component of that image."[47] Sacramentally, this conviction finds an expression in the Eucharist that involves, through the symbolic eating and drinking of Christ's body and blood, a twofold dynamic of God taking part in human life, "at the core of materiality, at the heart of flesh," and of humankind taking part in divine

41. Haughton, *Beginning*, 38.

42. Moloney, *Gospel of John*, 39.

43. Graham, "Words Made Flesh," 114.

44. See Labrecque, "Glorified Body," 5. See also Labrecque, "Morphological Freedom," 309.

45. Godzieba, "Stay with Us," 792.

46. See Joustra, "Embodied *Imago Dei*," 15–16.

47. Both citations are from Bavinck, *Reformed Dogmatics*, 560.

life.[48] In the drama of this sacrament, an anticipation of what it means to be fully human is re-presented by an identification with what is divine, at the same time disclosing the profound mystery that what it means to be God is in a fundamental sense re-presented by an identification with what is human.[49]

Let us now consider the divine-human dynamic, as expressed in the doctrine of the incarnation, by reflecting on *Faraway, So Close!*, the sequel to *Wings of Desire*, that Wim Wenders directed in 1993.[50] Here, the angel Cassiel is the main character as Damiel lives his human life together with Marion. In this film, Cassiel, like his friend earlier, also becomes human.[51] However, unlike Damiel, Cassiel's ontological status is not transformed in the aftermath of a profound and extended reflection but rather unintentionally, as a result of Cassiel's attempt to save Raisa, a little girl who accidentally falls off a tall building. He succeeds both in his attempt to save the girl's life and to become human. Like Damiel, Cassiel's journey to incarnation was also led by a deep desire—however, not necessarily a desire for his own story but rather a desire to help a human being. Cassiel becomes human out of selfless love.

However, Cassiel's own human story is a tragic one as he dies, shot dead in his attempt to save Raisa again, this time from the hand of kidnappers. In contrast to Damiel, who is led by his desire to first and foremost pursue a meaning for his own story with the simultaneous fulfillment of the meaning of his love Marion's life being a kind of "byproduct," Cassiel's human existence is one lived for the sake of the other, even at the expense of his self-emptying to the point of death (kenosis). And yet, the last scene evokes a hope that it is not a definite end. It can be interpreted in such a way that Cassiel becomes an angel again as seems to be suggested by the words Damiel tells his daughter, Doria, about Uncle Karl arriving to his destination, when Damiel hears a buzzing sound in his ears, a sign in the film that there is an angel nearby. One can, therefore, assert that Cassiel has crossed the borderline between two ontological modes twice: while it is out of love for people and the desire to help them that the angel becomes human, the

48. See Méndez-Montoya, "Eucharistic Imagination," 335.

49. See Ward, *Christ and Culture*, 106.

50. The German name of the film is *In weiter Ferne, so nah!* For further information on the film, see "In weiter Ferne, so nah!," IMDb, accessed December 27, 2021, https://www.imdb.com/title/tt0107209/?ref_=fn_al_tt_2.

51. I have sought to show in chapter 1 that the angel Damiel becomes human in *Wings of Desire* as he follows a desire to pursue his own story.

same kind of love and desire leads the human to become an angel again. Cassiel embraces his embodiment (incarnation) unconditionally by transcending the boundaries of human existence in an absolute manner—in an act of self-sacrificing love for the sake of another person. His newly acquired angelic status is not to be regarded as a reward for his good deed; after all, neither Damiel nor Cassiel wanted to be angels anymore in the first place. What Cassiel does represents a selfless act of love par excellence.[52] And it is this act as such that refers to "Him." This is the first, and only, time in the duology that there is any explicit reference to transcendence. I would like to suggest that Wenders's work, with its motifs of the desire for a body, the willingness to undergo kenosis, and the act of selfless love, beautifully depicts the twofold dynamic of the incarnation in which the divine is fully identified with the human in order to enable the fully human emerge through its identification with the divine.

Now that we have described the dynamics of the incarnation, it is possible and worthy to explore what implications the divine embodiment has for human embodiment. To put it differently, to inquire into how Christian theology interprets the incarnation has an impact on the ways the followers of Christ are called to think and act in their embodied existence in relation to their human neighbors and in relation to God as the "ultimate neighbor." The work of Timothy Gorringe can be of relevance in this pursuit. Interpreting it in terms of "the mutual moulding of nature and spirit," the incarnation represents for him a way how to theorize the interrelated nature of true universalism and true particularism.[53] At the same time, the concept of the incarnation also prevents any attempts at eliminating otherness as it is built around the story of a particular human living in a particular context. In light of this, Gorringe makes a case that it is essential to view the incarnation not as a philosophical axiom but rather as "a way of reading a particular historical event, the life and death of a first century Jew, as revelatory of the Wholly Other."[54] The biblical account of the story of Jesus of Nazareth then serves to "generate liberative and humanizing practice" and subvert ideologies and hegemonies imposed by powers that be.[55]

52. This interpretation moves the discussion very close to the field of soteriology. However, this issue would deserve a separate analysis that cannot be pursued in this study. For more information on the "salvific" role of angels in Wenders's duology, see Graf, *Cinema*, 119–20.

53. See Gorringe, *Furthering Humanity*, 18 and 101.

54. Gorringe, *Furthering Humanity*, 126.

55. See Gorringe, *Furthering Humanity*, 118.

However, the story of Jesus's life is not the only way through which the Scriptures empower this dynamic of generation and subversion. The other is represented by the movement of Jesus's disciples throughout history that has come to find its institutionalized expression as the church. For Gorringe, this twofold dynamic—of generation *and* subversion—is intrinsically linked with the incarnation. Referring to it as "the long revolution," Gorringe maintains that the dynamic represents an "ongoing struggle for those things which make and keep human life human."[56] In the cinema of Wim Wenders, this struggle is echoed through the depiction of Cassiel's journey from angel to human, and back to angel. On a more general level, I would propose, we can see that this dynamic can be recognized in terms of what one could call a continuous incarnation, or embodiment. It means that even though the (divine) incarnation was, in a Christian perspective, a singular event exclusively reserved for Jesus of Nazareth, Christians can also legitimately acknowledge and pursue other incarnations as "the christic reality expressed in other human beings in their God-bearing relatedness."[57] This suggestion draws together the central Christian claim of the incarnation and the belief that humans are created as embodied beings in the image of God. Furthermore, it must be noted that the described process is enabled by Jesus's kenosis when he "emptied himself of claims to be the exclusive embodiment of God."[58] Reflecting theologically on this process, it can be understood in terms of a movement from mere biological existence to being human. As such, it involves, among other things, culture, politics, philosophy, and theology. In this sense, human existence is ultimately relational as all these realms of meaning and action necessarily require others, be they either human or divine.[59] As a consequence, not only the human body is theologically reevaluated but people are also given opportunities to incarnate the "long revolution" of the (divine) incarnation by the way of their own embodied existence in their pursuit of a shared and reconciled future with the other, what I refer to as our common life in God.

56. Gorringe, *Furthering Humanity*, 128.

57. Nelson, *Body Theology*, 51.

58. Nelson, *Body Theology*, 52. See also Bong, "Ecclesiology," 77.

59. For a deeper discussion on this subject, see Bretherton, *Christ*, especially at 301 and 309, who develops his argument in the framework of humanity as a claim about a shared realm of meaning and action.

Broken Bodies and Human Vulnerability

When theologically reflecting on human embodied existence, one should not neglect the fact that there is much suffering and pain in the world. Theologically speaking, the plight that creation finds itself in is seen as a result of the disrupted relationship between humankind and God. The essential role of this relationship for the right functioning of the world underscores the fact that its disintegration has had a damaging influence on other kinds of organic bounds and interactions, including those among people and between people and the rest of creation.[60] Such brokenness can be identified in different spheres linked to human existence. *CPTA* explicitly mentions and analyzes three particular areas, namely, violence, poverty, and HIV/AIDS (art. 23–38). The document adopts the discourse of the disruption of the God-human relationship as the root cause of brokenness to inquire into more intricate layers of these phenomena, such as the estrangement of humans from their true identity of beings created in the image of God; abuse of power; a view of the vulnerable as subhuman and thus objects for exploitation; and an inability to love selflessly (*CPTA*, art. 26).

Human bodies often are suffering bodies, broken bodies. Turning to *CPTA* once again, one can find here helpful insights on the theme of broken bodies. The document takes seriously the reality of human disability to argue against the norm of "perfection." In many contexts, there is an ingrained conviction that only a "perfect" person can fully reflect the image of God—where "perfect" is taken to mean "successful, attractive, young and not disabled" (*CPTA*, art. 44). In contrast to this perception, in the gospel, Jesus confronts us with a different image of perfection, one of giving things away rather than acquiring them, of loving both one's neighbors and enemies (Matt 5:43–48; 10:42; 19:3); an image that is fully expressed through life in human community (*CPTA*, art. 44–45). Ultimately, Jesus reflects the image of God not only when his countenance and body visibly radiates divine glory on the Mount of Transfiguration. The image of God as well as his true humanity are still there even as his body is broken by torture and crucifixion (see *CPTA*, art. 84).

Further theological reflection is of relevance here on the soteriological and eschatological significance of the "broken body," namely, the tortured and crucified body of Jesus. Daniela Augustine has the following to say on the subject:

60. See also Augustine, *Spirit*, 77.

> Through the Incarnation, matter participates in the drama of redemption with its culmination in the passion of the Christ. Thus, in his broken, crucified body matter is subjugated to torture and death so that it may overcome death. In the last Adam, matter's innocence is met with the moral purity of the Son of Man who, while tempted in all things, still remains without sin (Heb 4:15).[61]

While it seems that Augustine finds the salvific power of Jesus's act in his moral strength and purity, an alternative interpretation of the Christ event is also possible that sees the redemption of the body—or, as Augustine says, "body matter"—in the act of God's vindication of Jesus's life through the resurrection. To be sure, it is in the resurrection that the human body finds its divine reevaluation and sanction. Still, what is important here that the body (i.e., the body of Jesus) overcomes death by becoming "broken" and subject to death. Eternal life can only be experienced as "a gift of divine welcome in which God shares his life with the other."[62] However, one must keep in mind that eternal life too is corporeal life; as we have seen earlier, from a Christian perspective, we hope for a spiritual body that is a body nonetheless.

An alternative, yet complementary, interpretation of the salvific significance of the broken body is offered by Judith Gruber as she deeply probes into possibilities for what she calls a "spectral theology of mission." Inspired by the prophet Ezekiel's vision of dry bones in a valley (Ezek 37:1–6) and drawing from the work of some postcolonial thinkers, Gruber employs the metaphor of "ghost stories" to critique linear and teleologically-oriented soteriologies in a refusal to be cured.[63] Contrary to these projects, salvation, for Gruber, is imagined in terms of spectrality or haunting, not "as an absence of wounds, but emerges—by way of ruptures that point to fleeting absences and hopeful yearnings—in the midst of the legacies of violent histories."[64] Looking through the lens of such a spectral theology of mission, one insists on retaining the marks of one's wounds as one cannot—and is not willing—to escape one's history and experiences. In this perspective, brokenness is a hallmark of one's identity; human embodied

61. Augustine, *Spirit*, 42–43.

62. Augustine, *Spirit*, 43.

63. See Gruber, "Salvation," 382. In her critique of the "historiographies of the cure," Gruber is inspired by Spivak, *Critique*, 206–7. Another thinker who is important for Gruber's theological/missiological project is Achille Mbembe. See, for instance, Mbembe, *Critique*.

64. Gruber, "Salvation," 385.

existence is one of a broken body. Still, as Gruber concludes, there is a hope for transformation as one puts one's identity in the counterintuitive identity of a God who has made brokenness a part of God's own experience. This emphasis is also echoed by Elaine Graham, who develops a concept of a "disabled God" who is present and working in the broken bodies of the faithful. This disabled God is neither almighty nor powerless. Rather, this God is "a survivor, interdependent with others in mutual care."[65] Sacramentally, then, the Eucharist is a dramatic enactment of a crucified (broken) and resurrected body. As a corporeal communion, the eucharistic body of Christ symbolizes a practice that challenges and resists the exclusive notions of being human, offering a more generous and inclusive understanding of both human and God instead. In short, the Eucharist introduces the disabled God, the God with a broken body, "in whom the signs of suffering and impairment are shown not as weakness or failure but as strength and solidarity."[66]

The brokenness that we have reflected on theologically also has its practical implications as it tends to leave a mark on human existence, both individually and collectively. The discourse of trauma and wounds has come to be used, not only by theologians, to address these realities of life. It is through the lived particularities of trauma and wounds that people tell their stories, including religious ones, to construct, share, and transform their identities.[67] In addition, it is of much relevance, particularly in the field of practical/pastoral theology and mission studies, to be aware that human language, thinking, and knowledge construction are affected by the tragedies and traumas that people have lived through in their particular contexts. Exploring this phenomenon, András Máté-Tóth employs the metaphor of "wounded words" which, for him, represents a way to come to terms with "all the complex problematics of societal communication in the [central and eastern European] region characterized by the wounded collective identity."[68] Máté-Tóth's contextual analysis, focused on central and eastern Europe, certainly has a broader relevance. For our own discussion, it is here important to note that one should neither adopt the permanent status of a victim nor see oneself eligible for privileges and benefits on the

65. Graham, "Words Made Flesh," 119. Graham borrows the concept of a "disabled God" from Eisland, *Disabled God*.

66. Graham, "Words Made Flesh," 120. See also Eisland, *Disabled God*, 114.

67. See Sremac and Ganzevoort, "Trauma," 2.

68. Máté-Tóth, "Wounded Words," 360.

grounds of one's victimhood. Rather, keeping to the logic of Jesus's broken body, the followers of Christ are invited to pursue a twofold task of showing compassion and prophetically challenging any injustice.[69] Or, to use the formulation from our discussion on the incarnation above, the followers of Christ are called to be part of the dynamic of generation and subversion, inaugurated by Jesus's incarnation and continued by the movement of his disciples as they incarnate the message of God's coming reign throughout history.

However, the discourse of trauma and wounds also has a role to play in the process of identity formation, even in a very material sense. It has two dimensions. First, wounded and traumatized people very frequently have a tendency to regress to different kinds of isolation, including psychological, social, and spiritual but also political. One of the underlying reasons for this is that woundedness erodes basic trust in oneself and others, preventing one from flourishing. Furthermore, it leaves a significant mark on human bodies.[70] Such a mark is not to be seen primarily in terms of affliction but rather as an expression of one's experience as an embodied existence and a reminder of what one has gone through in one's particular context. Therefore, and this is the second dimension, it is equally important to acknowledge the fact that wounds are never going to disappear completely. And nor should they as the persisting marks of wounds signify one's humanity and continuous identity. In the same vein, Jesus Christ's resurrected body is still a broken body, characterized by visible marks of his crucifixion. It is through these marks that one of his disciples, Thomas, recognizes him and comes to believe (John 20:24–29). The erasure of these marks would represent—both for Jesus and for traumatized and wounded human beings—an abrupt discontinuation of their embodied existence, a rupture of their identity. Furthermore, it would suggest either that one's suffering, pain, and loss were not real or that one is not worthy to have suffered and lost so much.[71] Delving deep into what it means to be human, what it means to be created as an embodied being to the image of God, woundedness proves to be a useful concept to address the brokenness of human embodied existence. Human bodies are broken bodies.

In mission studies, this understanding of brokenness finds an articulation in the concept of *missio ad vulnera*, "mission to wounds." This

69. See Máté-Tóth, "Wounded Words," 367.

70. See Schreiter, "Locating," 338.

71. See Schreiter, "Locating," 339.

idea is effectively given shape in a movement from the wounds of Christ to the wounds of the world as it is "a response to living within the *missio Dei* today."[72] For Christians today, as Robert Schreiter maintains, *missio ad vulnera* is a mode of kenotic mission as they carry the death of Christ in their bodies to provide space for transformation for those who have been tormented and hurt. It aims at creating resilience among those who carry wounds.[73] In practice, this notion can offer an authentic way for relating to the other in a community of embodied existences. Since we are going to discuss the theme of relationality in a separate chapter (chapter 5), here it suffices to emphasize that, from a Christian perspective, human embodied existence is paradoxical as it is in and through brokenness that one strives for inclusion and fullness of life.

Our discussion on human embodied existence as characterized by brokenness and woundedness is also related to yet another essential feature, namely, vulnerability. Vulnerability, I would suggest, is one of the hallmarks of being human. For both Christian theological reflection and praxis it is important to note that especially in pastoral and missional situations one meets the other as vulnerable. However, this assertion could by implication be extended to additional spheres of life as there always is a variety of power dynamics at play in interhuman relations, implying an imbalance of power in our encounters. As such, vulnerability is an ambivalent notion as it merges not only a shared predicament of being human (*conditio humana*) but also effectively marks biological and social differences as well as brings into the picture sociocultural inequalities and norms.[74] Combining these multiple factors, one can conceive of vulnerability in terms of materiality (or, embodiment), pain and suffering, and resistance/resilience.[75] It is key to keep in mind that each of these aspects implies the two-sidedness of being potentially susceptible to harm, on the one hand, and of being open to relating to and being enriched by others, on the other hand.[76] This tension between the susceptibility to being harmed and the openness to valuable insights is helpfully mediated by Gordon Lynch in his discussion on popular culture. Lynch argues that even though people certainly are prone

72. Schreiter, "Locating," 338.

73. See Schreiter, "Locating," 342. To support his argument on resilience, Schreiter refers to Sedmak, *Capacity*.

74. See Leidinger, "Vulner-*ability*," 404.

75. See Leidinger, "Vulner-*ability*," 404.

76. See Leidinger, "Vulner-*ability*," 407.

to being negatively shaped and even harmed by commercially produced and marketed "mass" culture, they are not merely passive consumers of cultural products. Thus, for Lynch, "popular culture becomes a set of cultural practices in which people can attempt to resist dominant cultural ideas that are oppressive, out-dated, or out of touch with their experience or aspirations."[77] Although Lynch here only considers one particular sphere of human life, namely (popular) culture, his observations can be taken to apply to the whole of human embodied existence, characterized by vulnerability as we have described it.

A beautiful cinematographic articulation of this understanding of vulnerability can be found in Richard Linklater's critically acclaimed film, *Boyhood* (2014).[78] Filmed over twelve years, this exceptional work of art offers snapshots from the childhood and adolescence of one boy, Mason, growing up in the early twenty-first-century United States. Sensitively filmed, *Boyhood* aptly portrays human vulnerability as it explores the way in which one is rooted in a specific context and influenced by (pop)culture, societal norms, economic and social status, or the religious and political convictions held by oneself and one's relatives. This is even amplified by the fact that it is a child who is in focus here. Thus, some of the main "protagonists" in the film are contemporary political and social events, such as the war in Iraq or Barack Obama's presidential campaign, because Mason and his sister, Sam, are actively formed by the political views and activism of their father. At a more intimate level, the film excellently shows how important certain "rituals," such as family camping or baseball playing, are for growing up in American culture. Additionally, there is an evident influence of such (pop)cultural phenomena as Harry Potter, Britney Spears, and Facebook on forming the views and behavior of Mason's generations. And yet, *Boyhood* does not depict young people in particular—and humans in general—as passive pawns being at the mercy of various influences. Very much in line with Lynch's argument, the characters in the film are in many respects represented as critical recipients and co-creators of life around them as, for example, Mason's opinions on Facebook or photography clearly show.

77. Lynch, *Understanding Theology*, 12. To find support for his argument on popular culture, Lynch draws from Fiske, *Understanding Popular Culture*.

78. For further information on the film, see "Boyhood," IMDb, accessed December 27, 2021, https://www.imdb.com/title/tt1065073/?ref_=nv_sr_srsg_0.

From a theological perspective, it is important that this dialectic understanding of vulnerability accounts for the complexities of human embodied existence as it addresses a "point of risk" of being human within "the project of creation" as much as it is related with human creativity.[79] Inquiring more deeply into the theme, Miriam Leidinger seeks to outline a sketch for a theology of vulnerability as follows:

> A theology of vulnerability that truly wants to stand on the side of the most vulnerable, be with those who are left behind, must not fall short on the ambivalence vulnerability entails. . . . It means to be cautious to using the incarnated God as "trump card," as a guarantee of Christian affinity to vulnerability.[80]

Although this short citation includes a number of thought-provoking ideas, for the purpose of our discussion it is important to highlight that any theology is always a "communal business," as it is pursued with regard to a multiplicity of others, including human, nonhuman, and divine. Human embodied existence is both individual and collective. It is the latter that we are going to discuss next.

The Social Body

Being human, that is, being an embodied existence, also means being deeply and necessarily involved in a web of relationships. For my argument, it is essential to be conscious of the fact that the human body is both a creator and creation of these relationships. As a consequence, the body is not to be regarded as merely passive, a depository of the self. Rather, it is a dynamic agent, both shaped by and shaping others and the context with which the body interacts. From another angle, we have already seen this in our discussion on vulnerability above. Following this observation, therefore, society (Latin *societas*) is not an abstract constant that inflicts on human bodies symbols, values, and meanings in the form of disembodied axioms. All facets of social reality always come as an already embodied reality and "they remain to be embodied, enacted, and performed in human communities as forms of bodily practice. So the deepest dynamics of the social, political, and economic order are always incarnated into persons/

79. See Augustine, *Spirit*, 32.

80. Leidinger, "Vulner-*ability*," 411 and 412.

bodies-in-relation."[81] Human embodiment is of a fundamentally relational nature. To be sure, research in medicine and sciences shows that human embodied existence is "programmed" to pursue relationships. To live a full-fledged life, human bodies are interdependent on having relationships with others. And on the contrary, when people are forcibly separated from their bodies (for instance, when being unaware of their bodily state) and/or when their bodies are not used to relate to others, people's lives are significantly affected in a negative way, with undesirable effects often emerging. To put it succinctly, "our body is built for relationships."[82]

If we take the idea of embodiment seriously, being in social relations with others is also of utmost relevance for human spirituality. This is an important insight for Christian theology, too, because "we do not encounter God apart from [others] but through them."[83] From a Christian theological perspective, therefore, being human means living an embodied existence, deeply rooted in different historically and contextually contingent relationships that make the flourishing of humankind and creation possible. Living as a social body is an important prerequisite for our common life in God. On the contrary, sin stands for the disintegration of this delicate web of relationships as a result of either an overdetermination of one of its aspects or a failure to cultivate it.[84] Through this lens, sin can be interpreted in terms of alienation from oneself, the other, creation, and, ultimately, God. To bring these threads of our discussion together, I would propose that Christian tradition regards human life as, to employ the phrase by David Kelsey, "eccentric existence," since humans—through their bodies—seek to transcend their physical existence, that is subject to various limitations, by relating to other people, their context, creation, and God.[85]

81. Graham, "Words Made Flesh," 115.

82. See Hall, "What Are Bodies For?," 167. See also Hall and Thoennes, "At Home in Our Bodies," 29–46.

83. See Johnson, *Faith's Freedom*, 10. Similarly, Elizabeth Hall points out that it is no coincidence that the body is used as a metaphor for the community of believers. See Hall, "What Are Bodies For?," 174. In the same vein, Carolyn Chau maintains that the church can represent a valid alternative for living in the contemporary world precisely because humans are social beings. See Chau, "Church," 244. The point of the church as the body of Christ will be explored in the following section of this chapter.

84. See Bretherton, *Christ*, 309.

85. See Kelsey, *Eccentric Existence*, 544. The process of people transcending their physical existence can be conceived in terms of the human quest for meaning. Indeed, Meiring explicitly refers to the body as "a system of meaning-seeking." See Meiring, "Theology in the Flesh," 4. This idea will again be taken up through the concept of

In his encyclical *Laudato si'*, Pope Francis suggests that one must accept one's body as a gift from God in order to be able to also accept others.[86] Such an authentic relating to the other, when one sees them as a gift from God, can—and, indeed, should—give rise to a sense of belonging to humankind. In the biblical worldview, there existed a sense of a strong intrinsic link between the individual body and the collective body. Furthermore, there was a symbolic correlation between one's "fleshly" (physical) body and society.[87] To follow in this line of thought, I would suggest that one's humanity can only be pursued in plenitude when one is in fellowship with other humans. Theologically speaking, moreover, to be human is to live an embodied existence in "a shared realm of human and divine meaning and agency."[88] Or, to phrase it differently, it means to exist in cultural-political communities that represents loci for establishing and maintaining relationships and fostering sustainable forms of life together.[89] In a Christian theological discourse, these can be referred to as forms of our common life in God since all such pursuits are realized in relation to the God who has become part of humankind while transcending it at the same time.

The Body of Christ

Talk of God becoming human to share a body with people brings us to a very unique kind of social body, namely, the body of Christ. Even though it certainly is not the only biblical image that refers to the church, actually appearing four times only in the New Testament, the ecclesiological model of the body of Christ "has shown a remarkable power to captivate the theological imagination."[90] This power consists in representing a relational

---

"imagined body" in chapter 3 on imagination. Moreover, the broader theme of relationality will be discussed in chapter 5.

86. In this encyclical, Francis's focus is not merely on human beings but on the whole of God's creation. He asserts: "The acceptance of our bodies as God's gift is vital for welcoming and accepting the entire world as a gift from the Father and our common home, whereas thinking that we enjoy absolute power over our own bodies turns, often subtly, into thinking that we enjoy absolute power over creation." See Pope Francis, *Laudato Si'*, art. 155.

87. See Martin, *Corinthian Body*, and Neyrey, *Paul*, especially at 16.

88. Bretherton, *Christ*, 294.

89. See also Bretherton, *Christ*, 315.

90. McFarland, "Body of Christ," 225. The four New Testament passages are Eph 1:22–23; Eph 5:23; Col 1:18; and Col 1:24. Conscious of the fact that there are more

and communal entity with a physical as well as a symbolic dimension. In the evocative words of Gerard Loughlin, the body of Christ is a "fungible flesh, a transitioning corporeality."[91] This two-sided character of the body of Christ becomes apparent as its earthly members, through their own and very real bodies, also become carriers of Christ's words and deeds, thus pointing away from themselves to their Lord. As a result, their "speaking, signing, or gift-giving" is not ultimately focused on "the physical movements of the lips or hands, but on the content that is transferred."[92] As such, the relational aspect of the body of Christ effectively re-presents what it means to be human in a Christian perspective by affirming that human existence is enabled and oriented by values, such as community, belonging, connectedness, and love, that also have profound implications for one's physical life.[93] Being a part of the body of Christ foregrounds the embodied nature of human life. While providing social unity and cohesion, it also makes us aware of the vulnerability and interdependence of our embodied existence.[94]

By virtue of the communal and relational character of the body of Christ, those who accept and live in accordance with this hermeneutic framework perceive their identity as eccentric in the sense of being focused on the other, both human and divine. The body of Christ is, therefore, to be understood as mystical as well as political because it combines both human and divine desires responding to the "thirst" for the other. Importantly, this image welcomes and embraces otherness.[95] In particular, it is by way of the eucharistic imagination that bread and wine become the mystical body of Christ, thus symbolizing—and effectively establishing—a dialectic movement from the divine to the human, and back. The Eucharist thus represents the mutual embrace of divinity and humanity.[96] However, the political

inclusive images in the biblical tradition (e.g., the people of God), I nevertheless opt for the body of Christ image here as it is my main intention to show that the concept of the body is essential for Christian theological reflection.

91. Loughlin, "End of Sex," 12.

92. McFarland, "Body of Christ," 241.

93. See also Chau, "Church," 243.

94. See also Hearon, "1 and 2 Corinthians," 611 and 613.

95. See Méndez-Montoya, "Eucharistic Imagination," 326. It is the loving initiative of God as the divine other that humans respond to: "I am because God takes the initiative to enter into communion with me, with others, and with creation." Quoted from Méndez-Montoya, "Eucharistic Imagination," 337.

96. See Méndez-Montoya, "Eucharistic Imagination," 328.

dimension is ever present as well, being rooted in the praxis of relationality, hospitality, and care for the other. Robert Jenson formulates this dynamic of the mystical and the political within the church as the body of Christ in terms of the sacramental presence in the world.[97] Sharon Bong goes even further when she suggests that the *imago Dei* is redeemed through the body of Christ for all those who "thirst, are hungry and seek shelter in the bosom and loins of Christ-Sophia-God," both in the bodily and spiritual sense.[98] In practice, the functioning of the body of Christ, through its mystical-political presence and mission, may adopt many expressions. Daniela Augustine, for example, develops her proposal along the line of a relationship between prayer and what she calls "world-mending," and even "world-making," starting her reflection from God's creative action that inspires, in turn, human creativity. By implication, people are invited to become involved in the divine-human conversation with the aim of world-mending/making. This is done in the power of the Spirit that is characterized by spontaneity and freedom.[99] In addition, this mystical-political presence and mission implies holiness in the sense of authenticity. It can be described in terms of a commitment to be one's true self which is only possible in relation to others in community.[100] As such, bodily practice, in both its material and symbolic (imagined) dimensions, pursued in community (of the body of Christ), can become a vehicle of the divine.[101] Exploring the life of saints, Daniela Augustine in this respect speaks of an embodied commitment to the material and spiritual flourishing of the other, since

> the saintly life presents a powerful deconstruction of materialism and self-indulging consumerism while affirming the goodness of creation's essential materiality. It unfolds not as a gnostic escape out of the world's material body but as an embodied commitment to the well-being of the other, perceiving their physical and spiritual flourishing as inseparable from one another.[102]

Furthermore, the body of Christ represents an important eschatological dimension as a reconciled community, called by God and enabled by the Spirit to "extend unconditional, loving hospitality to all humanity and the

97. See Jenson, *Systematic Theology*, 168.

98. Bong, "Ecclesiology," 78.

99. See Augustine, *Spirit*, 52–55.

100. See Chau, "Church," 243.

101. See also Graham, "Words Made Flesh," 109.

102. Augustine, *Spirit*, 204.

rest of creation."[103] However, it can only make a significant and authentic contribution to this process when it reminds us of the importance of a type of solidarity that goes beyond our own social group, our own "tribe"; takes up the mode of kenotic and compassionate being-with-others (*convivencia*)[104] as a desirable alternative to both paternalistic charity and neoliberal indifference; demonstrates that every human community has the potential to play a role in the inbreaking reign of God; and reflects God's image in its everyday encounters with others. Ángel Méndez-Montoya describes the body of Christ very provocatively as

> a body in a constant state of transformation, going from the most local and concrete corporeal experience to a broader or more interconnected and communal sense of embodiment, becoming a queer, divine-human, mystical body that does not annul material bodies. . . . [It] is a body of a nurturing relationality, making communion with the Other (person, environment and God).[105]

To be able to recognize this movement, affirm the materiality of human bodies, and relate to the other in communion, one inevitably needs a special kind of imagination. And it is the theme of imagination that will be explored in the next chapter.

103. Augustine, *Spirit*, 182.

104. See Ewell, *Faith*, especially 223–35.

105. Méndez-Montoya, "Eucharistic Imagination," 339.

3

Imagination

The Myth of the Eternal Return Reimagined

In their 2017 mind-bending thriller, *The Endless*, the authors Justin Benson and Aaron Moorhead challenged the viewers' imagination, taking them well beyond the boundaries of empirically verifiable facts.[1] And yet, Benson and Moorhead are neither patronizing nor manipulative vis-à-vis the viewer. On the contrary, devoid of any pseudo-intellectual arrogance the authors introduce the viewer to alternative versions of reality to let them figure out for themselves what the reality might mean. The story of *The Endless* is set in the context of a peculiar quasi-religious community whose members live in separation from mainstream society, spending their days in what on the outside looks like a never-ending dream come true. The film skillfully employs the motif of fear of the unknown to variations of the Nietzschean idea of the eternal return (or, eternal recurrence).[2] Justin and Aaron, acted by the writer-directors themselves, are two brothers who succeeded in leaving the community ten years ago. Even after such a long time, however, they are still not able to integrate themselves in the society, living an uprooted existence without any clear meaning and fulfillment.

1. For further information on the film, see "The Endless," IMDb, accessed January 18, 2022, https://www.imdb.com/title/tt3986820/?ref_=nv_sr_srsg_0. *The Endless* can justifiably be taken as an example of auteur cinema as Benson and Moorhead exert a high level of control over all aspects of film, including directing, writing, producing, and acting. Through some of its characters and story motifs, *The Endless* represents a kind of sequel to their earlier film, *Resolution* (2012).

2. See, for example, Nietzsche, *Gay Science*, §341.

This cheerless situation is one of the reasons why Aaron starts to idealize their previous life in the community, urging his older brother that they go and visit their former home for a few days. Even though he perceives the community as a dangerous cult, Justin eventually agrees, hoping that their short-term visit will actually convince Aaron that his memories of the community are misguided. However, strange things begin happening upon their arrival among the members of the community. If Aaron and Justin want to go back to their everyday life ever again, they will need to do it before the next full moon—one of the three moons visible on the sky.

The motif of the eternal return has received considerable attention in religion, arts, and scholarship.[3] One of the fundamental questions related therewith is whether one would be willing to live one's life—or any of its parts—over and over again. If one is able to give an affirmative answer to this question, one will supposedly become truly divine. *The Endless* is innovative and important in the respect that the stories of its characters offer different answers to the same question. In one of the spatiotemporal loops of the ever-recurring reality, for instance, the protagonists encounter "Shitty" Carl, a morally repulsive figure, who perceives his own "eternal life" as bleak and meaningless. For him, suicide represents the only way out of his misery. Nevertheless, it does not prove to be a viable solution as immediately after each suicide attempt Carl keeps on coming back to the same place only to look in the eyes of his own corpse. His whole existence boils down to a range of several hours whose sole goal consists in finally discovering a successful way to die by his own hand. An even shorter "life span" is given to another episodic character who lives in a different corner of the enchanted space-time. This man, obviously coming from the early 1900s, tries to commit suicide in his tent. His "eternal life" lasts ever-recurring five seconds when he, after running through his tent, finds his death at one end of his residence only to appear at the other end very shortly after.

Other characters, Chris and Michael, are two friends who were the main protagonists of Moorhead and Benson's earlier film, *Resolution*.[4] Chris is a drug addict whose existence lies in an ever-recurring week of addiction treatment. His story can thus be interpreted as a metaphorical image of the hell of substance addiction. Michael's story is more complicated as he comes to a faraway cabin in the woods to help his friend, Chris, win over

3. See Eliade, *Myth*. Eliade's 1949 classic was first published in English in 1954.

4. For further information on this film, see "Resolution," IMDb, accessed January 18, 2022, https://www.imdb.com/title/tt1977895/?ref_=nv_sr_srsg_0.

his addiction—importantly, against Chris's will. Michael's wife Jennifer's lot is very similar because she ends up in the community after she has gone to search for her missing husband. She gets lost—and cannot find her way back again. The stories of Michael and Jennifer can perhaps be taken as referring to the role that accident and the unexplainable play in human life.

By contrast, the members of the community obviously consider themselves to be happy and satisfied. Keeping their youthfulness and being able to do only what they want and enjoy, they literally have eternity to perfect their talents and skills. Furthermore, the community provide them with a shelter against the perils of the outside world. In spite of this, however, the viewer cannot help feeling that the members actually honestly envy those who succeed in escaping from the gravitational field of the recurring reality.

Finally, Justin and Aaron need to face a dilemma. Should they stay with the community forever, or should they go back to the life they have been living for the past ten years? Should they succumb to the temptation of living in a reality that seems to be a never-ending series of parties, fishing, and leisure at the top of one's strength? Or, should they return to the bleakness of disappointed hopes, the routine of daily errands, and the therapy for cult victims?

From a Christian theological perspective, *The Endless* makes a robust imaginative case for the claim that eternal life does not lie in permanent abidance; eternal life is not existence without an end. Rather, it necessarily involves a relationship with the other. Moreover, it is aimed at deepening the quality and diversity of such relationship. Enabled by grace and unconditional acceptance, eternal life, then, ultimately means the pursuit of the relationship with the other—and, to be sure, a plenitude of such relationships. As we have seen in the previous chapter, it postulates that human beings are embodied creatures of God made in God's own image. Finding inspiration and strength in the embodied existence of Jesus the Christ, his followers are to embrace the broken/wounded nature of their body-selves and creation. Also, they are to affirm vulnerability as the hallmark of the *conditio humana*. Only then can they authentically relate to the other, not only as individual bodies but also as a social body and, ultimately, as the body of Christ. In this chapter, I will argue that one needs imagination to relate to the other. However, as it was suggested in the analysis of *The Endless*, not every type of imagination is helpful and healthy. This chapter will explore what kinds of imagination should be fostered to relate to the other—by challenging evil and injustice, constructing what is good, true, and beautiful, and nurturing hope for a final transformation and consummation. In that way, the myth of the eternal return can be "cracked" and reimagined in an act of—to use the term of Paul Ricoeur—second naivete to conceive of human embodied existence as our common life in God.

However, before actually embarking on the journey toward inquiring into imagination, we first need to acknowledge that there is a link between theology, on the one hand, and literature, poetry, film, arts, yes, culture in general, on the other hand. In any case, this link has for the most part been neglected by theologians until quite recently. Therefore, it came as a major breakthrough when Amos Wilder introduced the concept of "theopoetic" or "theopoetics" into theological discourse in 1976.[5] I would argue that theopoetics is an important concept for our discussion on imagination. It can be conceived of as complementary to theology since it seeks to understand and experience God—and matters related with God and God's creative acts—in a participatory and aesthetic manner, rather than in a discursive and cognitive manner. To be engaged in this mode of experiencing God and God's creation, imagination is of utmost relevance. Sandra Schneiders suggests that theopoetics "embraces both the process of creating aesthetic mediations of the God-human encounter (sometimes called theopoesis), and the experience of God in and through such mediations."[6] As such, theopoetics is, effectively a matter of imagination proceeding participatively within the lines of divine-human encounter. To support the legitimacy of this approach, one should keep in mind that the Scriptures as the foundational textual mediation of divine revelation in Christian tradition by and large contain theo*poetic*, rather than theo*logical*, texts. The former includes poetry, hymns, myths, epic, parables, and other genres.

Paul Avis provides a convincing case for the theological appreciation of poetry. Drawing from the sources as various as Augustine of Hippo, Johann Gregor Hamann, and William Blake, Avis argues that we should think of God as a poet because "God creates in a 'poetic' way and communicates God's presence and truth through images, especially through the medium of metaphor, symbol and myth, images that are transparent to the divine because they participate in the reality that they signify."[7] At this place, it is worthy to note that Avis's thesis underscores the embodied nature of created existence as matter—and, following the logic of the incarnation, one

5. See Wilder, *Theopoetic*, especially chapter 1. See also Alves, *Poet*.

6. Schneiders, "Biblical Spirituality," 424.

7. Avis, "Apologetics," 308.

can particularly say body—represents an irreplaceable factor in this process of communication. Furthermore, Avis then contemplates that human beings are also called to respond to the presence and truth of God primarily in a "poetic and imaginative mode." At the same time, it is equally important to hold that faith emerges at the intersection of poetic/imaginative/aesthetic, cognitive, and ethical dimensions.[8] We can see that this observation has far-reaching ramifications for theological anthropology. In the light of what we have said about human embodied existence, far from being a mere repository of the self (soul/mind), the body—or, more precisely, body-self—also becomes the means through which one becomes involved in the process of (poetic) creation, knowledge production, and ethical action. This process is, at the same time, sociopolitical as one always relates to the human other. From a theological perspective, it is also a theo-political process as one relates to God as the "ultimate other."

Moreover, the present analysis invites further discussion on imagination. Both Avis and Schneiders, who have been part of our inquiry so far, concur in their insistence that imagination is as important for theopoetics as reason is for discursive ways of theologizing.[9] Our leading question for the next section will therefore be: How is one to understand imagination theologically?

Understanding Imagination Theologically

Imagination has been recognized by various authors as a notoriously difficult term to define. In this respect, Sr. Mary Karita Ivancic, SND, prefers the language of "description" to that of "definition," herself describing imagination as "a complex activity that engages body, mind, and affect," drawing upon "a person's past history, present experience, and future projections in an effort to know and make meaning of reality."[10] This holistic emphasis comes to the foreground even more conspicuously in John Milbank, who anecdotally says that imagination is "the whole force of the mind" that

8. Avis, "Apologetics," 308. For a book-length discussion of this argument, see Avis, *God*.

9. See Schneiders, "Biblical Spirituality," 424.

10. Ivancic, "Imagining Faith," 127. To be precise, in her article Ivancic limits her discussion to one particular kind of imagination, namely, the biblical imagination. Nevertheless, it is interesting to note that she understands it as "the human imagination in a theological mode," drawing from the Thomistic dictum of the relation between nature and grace. Ivancic, "Imagining Faith," 127.

enables us to apprehend the whole and to discern meaning in it.[11] As such, imagination is not simply a means to be engaged in day-dreaming in an escapist attempt to lead people away from reality, thus paralyzing their ability to think and act. Rather, it presupposes sustained concentration and intentional action. The image of the engaged poet can serve as a helpful illustration of this idea. Yet another pebble is added to the overall mosaic by William Lynch, SJ, who maintains that imagination is not a separate human faculty, like the intellect or the will. Instead, imagination should be understood in terms of a mediator that engages all these faculties as well as one's experiences, histories, convictions, and feelings in order to relate one's inner world to the outer world for the sake of transformation. As Lynch puts it, "The task of the imagination is to imagine the real."[12] Therefore, when we speak about human life as a journey, from a theological perspective, it is crucial to keep in mind that imagination "grasps the goal of the venture of faith as a whole, integrating all those elements that relate specifically to the thinking or feeling or willing faculties."[13] It means being aware of one's existence as embodied and open to relating this embodied existence to a broader framework of God's creation that is in the continuous process of transformation, reconciliation, and consummation. It is in this respect, I would suggest, that the image of "our common life in God" may be used. Alternatively, Jürgen Moltmann uses another image to formulate similar ideas when he reminds us that "theology is not a church dogmatics, nor a doctrine of faith. It is the imagination for the kingdom of God in the world, and for the world in God's kingdom."[14]

The symbol of the kingdom of God is important in the present discussion for yet another reason. It is a concept that imaginatively enables a "rupture" through which God's transformed and reconciled future (eschaton) may enter the immanent reality. Perhaps it is even more appropriate to refer to this symbol as the "*kin*-dom of God" as it is fundamentally embodied and relational; God's inbreaking reign is *materialized* through interpersonal encounters.[15] In any case, the symbol as such is heralded

11. John Milbank is cited in Avis, "Apologetics," 307.

12. Lynch, *Christ*, 23. Lynch credits Martin Buber as the originator of this insight.

13. Avis, *God*, 79.

14. Moltmann, *Coming of God*, xiv.

15. The term "kin-dom of God" is introduced by Isasi-Diaz, "Solidarity," 31–40, and 303–5. Here, Ada Maria Isasi-Diaz explains that her rejection of the term "kingdom" is motivated by two reasons: "First, it is obviously a sexist word that presumes that God is male. Second, the concept of kingdom in our world today is both hierarchical and elitist."

and inaugurated by the Christ-event, thus laying the very foundations for Christian faith, theologizing, and praxis. Human embodied existence—and even creation at large—can be interpreted through the lens of the kin-dom of God in the power of the imagination that human beings are endowed with by God as their Creator.

In his probe into the ways imagination functions in Christian theology, not least with respect to creation, Choan-Seng Song opts for a narrative approach that he comments as follows:

> "In God's image" means that God has endowed human beings with the imagination of the soul and the facility of words to tell over and over God's story of creation as part of our stories and to integrate our stories into God's story. God's image in human beings is thus the power to tell stories—the power of imagination and the power of words.[16]

Complementary to the approach we have discussed above, this interpretation of the creation of the human beings in the image of God maintains that people have been entrusted and empowered with a share in God's imagination. They are called to employ the gift they have been given; they have a mandate to be "artists" who continue to be engaged—as co-creators—in the ongoing work of God's creation. There is an analogical relationship between the divine and human imagination; more precisely, the human imagination is a derivate of the divine imagination. It is important to highlight that the divine imagination does not only have its imaging but also its verbal aspect. The latter aspect finds its unique expression in God's story, a story—as we have seen in the previous chapter—that is ultimately characterized by embodied engagement with God's creation. As such, God is not only an Artist but also a Narrator as well as a Protagonist in God's story with creation. In the similar vein, there is an important and real connection with the human imagination so that the latter is capable of creating words and, by implication—as we have seen in chapter 1—of "writing" not only one's own story but also of taking part in embodying the "Great Story" of God. In sum, the pursuit of such embodiments of God's story, that is, retellings by human beings through their embodied existence, imagination is necessary,

---

Isasi-Diaz, "Solidarity," 304. Her preference for "kin-dom," on the other hand, is driven by the recognition that the latter "makes it clear that when the fullness of God becomes a day-to-day reality in the world at large, we will all be sisters and brothers—kin to each other." Isasi-Diaz, "Solidarity," 304.

16. Song, *Believing Heart*, 65.

regarded—from a Christian perspective—as a gift of God. One also needs to accentuate that there are not only explicit retellings of God's story by religious specialists, such as clergy and theologians. God's story has also become part of many human life stories. In turn, these stories then legitimately shape and enrich God's story as creation proceeds to find our common life in God on the journey toward its transformation and consummation in the kin-dom of God. To reiterate the main argument of chapter 1, one's task is—in a Christian interpretation—to integrate one's story into the story of God while retaining one's own identity. In this process, human embodied existence provides a context for imagination being at work; I would suggest that imagination is a part of the human body-self.

However, the problem with the human imagination is that it is deeply flawed. From a Christian perspective, this is interpreted as a consequence of sin. Christians of all traditions confess that the image of God in human beings has been corrupted since the fall in the garden of Eden as one reads in the mythical narrative according to the third chapter of the book of Genesis. It might be helpful to look at the fall, together with John Zizioulas, in terms of giving the self an "ontological priority over the Other."[17] On this reading, then, the human imagination becomes flawed because one cuts oneself off from an authentic relationship to the other/Other (i.e., human/God), becoming self-isolated (*incurvate in se*) in the mirage of one's own sufficiency. In her theological reflection on the corruption of the human imagination, Daniela Augustine focuses on the biblical story of the tower of Babel (Gen 11:1–9). For her, Babel stands out as a symbol of a distorted human imagination because it effectively "juxtaposes the two creative acts (divine and human) as the contrast between inclusion and exclusion of the other."[18] Augustine's claim is important because it suggests—in a manner similar to Zizioulas—that imagination, properly understood and employed, should always regard the other to include him or her in what I would call "communal affairs," that is, the endeavors that humankind pursues together; as such, imagination is essentially relational. Based on our discussion so far, we can assert that if one perceives the notion of *imago Dei* in terms of the power of imagination, then one must unambiguously say that this image is indeed broken and corrupted in the sense that the human imagination is deeply flawed. Such a claim has two implications. First, one can only partially imagine the good, the true, and the beautiful that one

17. See Zizioulas, *Communion*, 43.

18. Augustine, *Spirit*, 47.

is to pursue as the ultimate horizon of one's all efforts and endeavors. To use the words of the apostle Paul, "we see in a mirror, dimly" (1 Cor 13:12 NRSV). Our human language, both conversational and professional, can mediate this horizon every now and then only. The glimpses of the perfect and the desirable are more frequently—and more helpfully—apprehended through the images and metaphors that are given to mystics, poets, and artists in the inspiration of the Spirit.

Second, the human imagination also has what I would call a "dark side." One can imagine and, even worse, put into effect not only beautiful, true, and good things but also those that are horrific, devastating, and abominable. Kenneth Burke makes this point very clearly when he succinctly remarks that people can envision not only a perfect age but also a perfect atomic warhead.[19] The vision of a New Jerusalem that we desirably look out to is permanently blurred by the smoke rising from the chimneys in concentration camps, the cries of malnourished and orphaned children, and the tons of greenhouse gas released in the atmosphere day by day.

Let us now turn again to two literary works that we have already considered earlier in chapter 2, namely, *The Lord of the Rings* and *Heart of Darkness*, to shed more light on the destructive aspect of imagination. Representing a significant theme in the two works of fiction, the dialectic of the city (or civilization) and nature should aptly illustrate my point. In *The Lord of the Rings* (1937–1949), Sauron epitomizes profound estrangement from both nature and civilization. Moreover, he uses his imagination to destroy both of them. As a result of his action, or even his mere presence, the land, forests, rivers, and fields are turned into hostile and poisonous wasteland, while cities, villages, and settlements are conquered only to become dungeons of desolation. A case in point represents Minas Ithil, a city/fortress of Gondor that has been turned into the grim and miserable Minas Morgul. Similarly, in *Heart of Darkness* (1899), the ivory trader Kurtz leaves the "civilization" of Europe behind, being unable, however, to create anything civilized in his new home, the Congo. Instead, by disseminating disdain, desolation, and dreadfulness, his story demonstrates that there is a very thin line between what one perceives as "civilized" and "savage," respectively. The outcome is a plight of both people and nature. In his 1979 cinematographic interpretation of Conrad's novella, *Apocalypse Now*, Francis Ford Coppola sets the plot in a Cambodian jungle of the Vietnam War era. Here, the antihero, Colonel Kurtz, a presumably insane officer of US special forces who

19. See Burke, *Language*, 22.

turned into a god-like chieftain of a tribe of natives, builds a "civilization" not dissimilar to that of Sauron.[20] I would thus propose that both examples can be taken to illustrate the dark side of imagination. To conclude this part of our exploration, one can therefore argue that the human imagination is a highly ambivalent matter. It brings human beings closer to God, mediating some bits and pieces from God's image and likeness and making them "a little lower than God" (see Ps 8:5 NRSV). Yet, it also abysmally separates and alienates people from the "Great Artist," from each other, and from the rest of creation.

Drawing upon the concept of the incarnation that has in detail been discussed in chapter 2 and linking it to our present theme of imagination, it is crucial for Christian theologians to acknowledge that Jesus of Nazareth, God-become-human, has challenged and overcome the ambiguity that is a hallmark of the human imagination. Through his identification with God's vision for humankind and creation, he integrated himself into God's story completely. In Jesus's embodied existence, God's story became his story. All human perceptions of who and what God is have ultimately been transformed by Jesus's incarnation, life, death on the cross, and resurrection. The "human imagination was shattered by Jesus' story only to acquire a completely new quality and an opportunity for a brand new beginning."[21] It is in response to the transforming power of the Christ-event that the human imagination can witness to the inbreaking kin-dom of God. This dynamic reality is realized in the interaction of what is already here as a kind of "guarantee" but the fullness of which is yet to come. Essentially, this transformation of imagination is to be regarded as a gift; it is a result of God's grace. Praying for it and being open to it, it is through "imagination that one can integrate God's story into one's own story, thus reflecting God's image in which one has been created."[22] Through the power of the transformed imagination, people as embodied beings are invited to participate in God's new creation. This dynamic movement has two basic poles that we are going to discuss in the following two sections: it challenges a status quo, while at the same time working for the new reality of the kin-dom of God.

20. For further information on this film, see "Apocalypse Now," IMDb, accessed April 21, 2022, https://www.imdb.com/title/tt0078788/?ref_=nv_sr_srsg_0.

21. Bargár, *Narrative*, 172.

22. Bargár, *Narrative*, 172.

Participating in God's New Creation: Challenging a Status Quo

If Christians theologically attempt to employ imagination for the sake of participating in God's new creation—or, our common life in God—they first need to focus on challenging the status quo characterized by a variety of personal and social ills, injustices, and evils. The status quo I have in mind reflects the broken or wounded nature of the reality that we discussed in the previous chapter. Such a process of challenging the status quo, then, integrates two simultaneous movements.

The first movement—or the first type of imagination I would like to discuss here—strives for self-reflection. In his research on the nineteenth-century mainline theological apprehensions of race and racial equality, Gordon Mikoski discovers that in spite of all their theological erudition and progressiveness these (North American) thinkers were prisoners to the worldviews that dominated their contemporary contexts to such a degree that "their ideas on slavery and race from our twenty-first century vantage point positively shocks the conscience."[23] Led by a concern for our theological—and, to be sure, Christian—integrity, Mikoski makes an urgent case that we cannot afford waiting for future generations to tell us on which points we are in error. Such a claim appears to be burning especially in light of the current global climate-change crisis. Instead, he pleads for the developing of what he refers to as a "transgressive" imagination in theology.[24] This concept is coined with the aim of providing people with a possibility to look at themselves critically. For that reason, I prefer using the term "self-reflective imagination." Such self-reflection is—on a Christian reading—a positive result of one's personal engagement with the Scriptures and one's contemporary context. The latter includes interpersonal relationships, various spheres of human culture, socioeconomic situation, political realities, the media, and ecological predicament. This dialectic perspective is of utmost relevance for Christian theology. While our engagement with the Scriptures helps us perceive the reality through the hermeneutic lens of God's inbreaking reign of justice, reconciliation, and peace, contextual awareness makes us conscious of the situatedness of our own embodied existence and sensitive to the embodied existence of others. As such, the self-reflective imagination enables the theologian to go beyond her or his

23. Mikoski, "On Cultivating," 106.

24. See Mikoski, "On Cultivating," 106–7.

habitual framework of reference, disclosing new dimensions of the reality and helping to make sense of them.

To delve more deeply into this emphasis on the self-reflective imagination, one might usefully draw from what Gianni Vattimo has to say on the link between reason and the imagination in mythical thinking, when he describes it in terms of a shift between the modern and the postmodern:

> The idea that the course of history could be thought of as enlightenment, as the liberation of reason from the shadows of mythical knowledge, has lost its legitimacy. . . . When demythologization is revealed as myth, myth regains legitimacy, but only within the frame of a generally "weakened" experience of truth. The presence of myth in our culture does not represent an alternative or opposing movement to modernization, but is rather its natural outcome, its destination, at least thus far. The demythologization of demythologization, moreover, may be taken as the true moment of transition from the modern to the postmodern.[25]

Although discussing the topic that is, admittedly, remote from our discussion at first glance, Vattimo here actually echoes what Paul Ricoeur introduced to philosophical discourse as "second naivete" and what is of much relevance also for our discussion on the self-reflective imagination as it leads one to acknowledge that one can never construct one's identity or interpret a text, including the Scriptures, without taking into consideration the broader context that one belongs to, including its imaginative—or, as Vattimo says, mythical—dimensions.

Simultaneous with, and inseparable from, this first movement of the self-reflective imagination is what I refer to as the deconstructive imagination. One of the most distinctive elements of *Apocalypse Now*, Coppola's cinematographic masterpiece that we have briefly referred to above, is the music that it features. The maddeningly memorable opening scene portrays extensive jungle fires caused by napalm strikes of the US air force with The Doors's song "The End" playing in the background. It is to this song, and its author, singer-songwriter Jim Morrison, that I turn my attention when analyzing the notion of the deconstructive imagination. An emphatic expression of this deconstructive imagination can be found in the following lines from "The End," which also feature in Coppola's film:

25. Vattimo, *Transparent Society*, 39 and 42.

> Can you picture what will be / So limitless and free / Desperately in need / Of some stranger's hand / In a desperate land.[26]

In these few lines, there are several points worthy of attention for our discussion. First, Morrison's forceful expression of the desperate need for a "hand" of another human being, albeit a stranger, underlines what I argued in chapter 2 about the essentially embodied nature of human existence. Here, the image of "hand" epitomizes both the necessity and the ability to touch the other in a physical sense. By implication, then, imagination serves as the "hand" through which one can relate to the other's imagined body.[27] This observation is also connected to my second point. Being very evocative about the human need for the other, the lyrics underline the relational nature of human life. Sharing a common context, "a desperate land," people are called, through their imagination, to relate to a fellow other, searching for a common story to live by.

Finally, Morrison invites his listeners to a "limitless and free" act of imagination that is believed to liberate them from, arguably, the "desperate land" of contemporary capitalist and consumerist societies. The ultimate aim of this act is to challenge the delusional, and thus ideological, perfection-become-totality of the status quo. His objective is deconstructive in the hope of liberation. This intention is voiced even more forcefully in a 1967 interview that Morrison gave:

> First you have to have the period of disorder, chaos, returning to a primeval disaster region. Out of that you purify the elements and find a new seed of life, which transforms all life and all matter and the personality until finally, hopefully, you emerge and marry all those dualisms and opposites. Then you're not talking about evil and good anymore but something unified and pure. Our music and personalities are still in a state of chaos and disorder with maybe an incipient element of purity kind of starting.[28]

Morrison's emphases can be clearly associated with some of the central claims of theologies of liberation. Nurtured by everyday experience, liberationist approaches to theology turn to imagination as a source of inspiration

26. Jim Morrison, "The End," *AZ Lyrics*, accessed January 18, 2022, https://www.azlyrics.com/lyrics/doors/theend.html. The song was released in 1967 on the first, eponymous album by The Doors.

27. The subject of the "imagined body" will be discussed in the final section of this chapter.

28. Quoted from Hopkins and Sugerman, *No One*, 143.

and a drive to deconstruct all those discourses about God that employ coercive power to suppress contrivance, creativity, and transformation. Imaginative theologizing is instrumental for deconstructing the oppressive structures in the contexts where people dwell. Inspired by the biblical mindset, Walter Brueggemann speaks of the "prophetic imagination" that effectively deconstructs the claims of "dominant imagination as a practice that cannot give life because it fails in truth-telling."[29] As Nicolás Panotto argues, theologizing motivated and nurtured by imagination "deconstructs all closed discourse about God that is the basis of those forms of power that stifle innovation."[30] To put it positively, it involves a commitment to the quest for truth as an open journey with the pilgrims considering their respective experiences, listening to stories, and discerning the movement of the Spirit in the search for the continuously manifested otherness of the divine.[31]

From an ecclesiological perspective, this imaginative theologizing is of much importance as it regards theology as a "communal business" that all members of the body of Christ have been entrusted with. This is in line with what many contemporary sociologists assert when they insist that all functioning communities are characterized by several typical marks.[32] The body of Christ, however, is additionally defined by a set of unique features that we discussed in the concluding section of chapter 2: it is called to remind us of the importance of a type of solidarity that goes beyond our own social group, our own "tribe"; take up the mode of kenotic and compassionate being-with-others (*convivencia*) as a desirable alternative to both paternalistic charity and neoliberal indifference; demonstrate that every human community has the potential to play a role in the inbreaking reign of God; and reflect God's image in its everyday encounters with others. For this pursuit, the deconstructive (as well as self-reflective) imagination is necessary. Then—and only then—it can make a significant and authentic contribution to the human quest for goodness, truth, and beauty.

The issue of the deconstructive imagination can be approached from yet another angle. Interpreting the cinematographic vision of Guillermo del Toro, the writer-director of films such as *Pan's Labyrinth* (2006) or *The*

29. Brueggemann, *Practice*, 42.

30. Panotto, "Otherness," 58.

31. See Panotto, "Otherness," 58.

32. For a detailed discussion that draws on sociological research, see Grenz, "Ecclesiology," especially 253–54.

Devil's Backbone (2001), David Congdon points out that for del Toro's art it is essential to cultivate a counter-imagination that would disrupt and re-order the taken-for-granted view of the reality. Congdon goes even further when he argues a thesis that for del Toro imagination plays the role of a "kind of aesthetic-anarchic uprising against the powers and principalities," engendering "an alternative politics" as a way of reimagining and rewriting the world.[33] A theological link to this anarchic vision of del Toro is offered by William Cavanaugh through his idea of the "theopolitical imagination." Cavanaugh draws from the premise that imagination controls human social life at large, including politics and religion. It is, therefore, a false dichotomy to maintain that politics is concerned with reality, while religion addresses something imaginary. For Cavanaugh, both politics and religion represent two distinct forms of imagination. His objective, then, is to de-construct the "false theologies" of the state.[34] To help him accomplish this goal, he proposes to adopt the alternative imagination of the Eucharist as a politically subversive act. It is precisely through the Eucharist, Cavanaugh argues, that "Christians participate in a practice which envisions a proper 'anarchy,' not in the sense that it proposes chaos, but in that it challenges the false order of the state."[35] Coming back to our earlier analysis of "The End" and *Apocalypse Now*, I would suggest that Morrison, like Coppola, leaves his listeners/viewers in a state of "chaos and disorder," productive as it may be. The imagination at play here is, therefore, deconstructive. In contrast to their position, Cavanaugh proposes deconstruction without chaos. What all of them have in common, however, is a sense that reconstruction—or a reconfiguration of the dismantled reality—is still needed.

Participating in God's New Creation: Working for a New Reality

I believe that Tolkien in his *The Lord of the Rings* provides some stepping stones on the way toward such a reconstruction/reconfiguration. As Frodo and Samwise are heading to Mordor, accompanied by Gollum, they stop to get some rest. There is a marvelous scene in *The Two Towers*, the second part of Tolkien's trilogy, with the two hobbits talking about stories—and

33. See Congdon, "Beautiful Anarchy," 44.
34. See Cavanaugh, *Theopolitical Imagination*, 4.
35. Cavanaugh, *Theopolitical Imagination*, 119–20.

their own place within these stories.[36] Although admitting that protagonists usually fall into stories, "land in them,"[37] as if stories happen to them, the hobbits also acknowledge that this act presupposes a personal decision, an intentional act, on the part of the protagonists. It is how they "read" their own story: they had a chance to turn back, yet they did not. Such a decision to enter a story certainly involves one's imagination as one is facing a dilemma of going forth or coming back. In addition, imagination is also needed because, being part of a story, one does not know what the end will be like. Frodo muses: "You may know, or guess, what kind of a tale it is, happy-ending or sad-ending, but the people in it don't know."[38] Going deeper into their discussion on the topic of story endings, Frodo and Samwise realize that "great tales never end"; it is only people in them whose role sooner or later comes to a close.[39]

It is this recognition that presupposes what I refer to as the reconstructive imagination. One can willingly and intentionally become part of other stories that transcend one's finite embodied existence. Paul Ricoeur can be helpful in this regard as he elaborates an understanding of tradition as "not the inert transmission of some already dead deposit of material but the living transmission of an innovation always capable of being reactivated by a return to the most creative moments of poetic activity."[40] As we can see, tradition is understood by Ricoeur narratively, in terms of a story. Such a story not only serves to "conserve and preserve" one's identity, whether as an individual or community, but also provides sufficient "utopian" moments to foster liberation and create alternatives.[41] For Ricoeur, story functions as a mediator between the past, present, and future that has the power—through imagination—to interpret the *conditio humana*.[42]

To explore the theme of the reconstructive imagination from another angle, it is helpful to return to our earlier discussion on Gianni Vattimo. Vattimo writes,

36. See Tolkien, *Two Towers*, book 4, chapter 8 "The Stairs of Cirith Ungol." I am here using an e-version of the book. *The Two Towers* was first published by George Allen & Unwin in 1954.

37. See Tolkien, *Two Towers*, 364.

38. Tolkien, *Two Towers*, 364.

39. Tolkien, *Two Towers*, 365.

40. Ricoeur, *Time*, 68.

41. See also Kearney, *On Paul Ricoeur*, 7.

42. See Evans, *Paul Ricoeur's Hermeneutics*, 15–16.

> The secularization of the European spirit of the modern age does not consist solely in the exposure and demystification of the errors of religion, but also in the survival of these "errors" in different, and in some sense degraded, forms. A secularized culture is not one that has simply left the religious elements of its tradition behind, but one that continues to live them as traces, as hidden and distorted models that are nonetheless profoundly present.[43]

For our purpose here, this assertion is important, I would like to suggest, for at least two reasons. First, it shows that secularized culture and thought are not devoid of the same fallacies that religion at large—and Christianity in particular—has been and is prone to. One can, therefore, argue that it is one of the tasks of theologians to employ imagination to unmask and challenge these errors. And second, it supports our argument in the section above by building a case for including various interlocutors in our theologizing in order to treat our tradition faithfully, yet creatively. This is what Richard Kearney emphasizes in his reading of Vattimo when he says,

> Post-modernism, understood in Vattimo's sense of a non-foundational and non-functionalist theory of interpretation, solicits an ethical task of remembering that is not a simple repetition of tradition but its joyous re-creation. Such remembering emancipates tradition from servile conformism, transposing it into a historical transmission of overtures to possible modes of being-in-the-world.[44]

A mode of theologizing that relies on imagination for its hermeneutical process represents one of the ways of such "joyous," creative treatments of tradition. Contextualizing the interpreted, one is at the same time involved in creating new links in the "chain" of tradition. In this understanding, to be sure, adding new links to this chain of tradition in its historical development is not merely a case of "hermeneutic cloning," the repetition of the past. Rather, it represents an active contribution to discussion and action. For Christian faith, theology, and praxis, in particular, this means that the reconstructive imagination is grasped as an awareness "of what is absent, of nostalgia for that which is not yet, the declaration of love for things that are yet to be born."[45] The imagination redeemed by God's grace helps us navigate between the Scylla of an "ideology" of the past and the Charybdis of

43. Vattimo, *Transparent Society*, 40.

44. Kearney, *Poetics*, 185–86.

45. Alves, *El enigma*, 27. Translated by and quoted from Panotto, "Otherness," 56.

a "utopia" of the future; Christians need their imagination to be sharpened and concentrated not only on dwelling in the story they inhabit but on reaching beyond to embrace what God is doing in the present.[46] Through such an imaginative apprehension of a story—or, in fact, of many different stories—hope is engendered: "Imaginatively placing oneself into a dynamic story that does not simply reiterate tradition or dream of the beyond is the mode by which hope enters into and transforms the world."[47] There are also other voices that comment on the role imagination plays in this process of engendering a hope for something new and transformative. John Paul Lederach coins the term "moral imagination" as "the capacity to give birth to something new that in its very birthing changes our world and the way we see things."[48] In my understanding, Lederach's moral imagination does not, for all intents and purposes, differ from my reconstructive imagination as it too claims to open space for "the creative act to emerge."[49] According to Daniela Augustine, the notion of the moral imagination resonates with Sallie McFague's concept of "wild space," a term used by anthropologists to indicate "the peculiar insight into alternative ways of living that some people seem to have."[50] For her part, Augustine speaks of "creative imagination" as humans follow the example of God's creative activity in their own culture-making.[51] We can thus conclude that imagination deepens our humanity by enabling us to relate—as embodied beings—to the other, whether it be human, nonhuman, or divine. The following section will consider one particular cinematographic attempt to employ imagination with the aim of challenging stereotypical views (status quo) and participating in the construction of new reality.

46. See Clawson, "Imagination," 306.

47. See Clawson, "Imagination," 308.

48. Lederach, *Moral Imagination*, 27.

49. Lederach, *Moral Imagination*, 38.

50. McFague, *Blessed*, 46. See also Augustine, *Spirit*, 7. For McFague, it is "wild space" as "that part of each of us that doesn't quite fit into our conventional world" that makes us strange, different, and unique. Quoted from McFague, "Human Dignity," 206.

51. See Augustine, *Spirit*, 128. In this sense, culture is understood as "what people make of the world." See Crouch, *Culture Making*, 23. To address the subtlety of this dynamic, many authors distinguish between nature as the creation of God and culture as the creation of humankind. See Tanner, *Theories of Culture*, 28–29, and Niebuhr, *Christ and Culture*, 32–34.

Telling a Well-Known Story Differently

In 2012, several cinematic reinterpretations were released of the Snow White fairy tale. In addition to the Hollywood spectacle, *Mirror Mirror*, starring Julia Roberts as the evil queen and relying on up-to-date technological effects, situational humor, and a massive advertising campaign, and the action fantasy, *Snow White and the Huntsman*, with its impressive visual design, attractive casting (Kristen Stewart, Charlize Theron, Chris Hemsworth), and rather obvious referencing to the likes of *The Lord of the Rings*, there also was a more low-profile but very remarkable Spanish drama film by the writer-director Pablo Berger. Much more than the other releases, *Blancanieves* employs imagination to offer an original piece of cinematography and a truly challenging and innovate retelling of a well-known story.[52] Furthermore, it is not only that Berger employs imagination in his inventive work as filmmaker; he also invites the viewer to actively engage her or his imagination to take the creative imaginative process even further. Formally conceived as a reminiscence of the black-and-white silent films of the classic 1920s era, this visual design lends the tale about an ebony-haired and marble-complexioned beauty a captivating visual appeal. Fortunately, though, the Gothic aura and masterfully mixed music is not all that *Blancanieves* has to offer. Its merits lie especially in an original take on the famous story and some motifs that the film creatively works with.

The plot is set in the early twentieth-century Sevilla where the famous bullfighter Antonio Villalta is seriously injured during his supreme performance against six bulls. Struck by this terrible news, his pregnant wife and famed singer, Carmen de Triana, gives birth to their daughter prematurely, only to pass away herself during childbirth. The little Carmen, beautiful and healthy, is raised by her grandmother, longing to meet her father more than anything else. Due to the bullfighting incident, Antonio is left paralyzed and at the mercy of his former nurse and now wife, Encarna. Following the sudden death of her grandmother, Carmen comes to live in her father's house. However, all she meets is the tyranny of her stepmother. Keeping Antonio hidden from the world, Encarna does not treat her stepdaughter any better either. Thanks to lucky circumstances, Carmen gets a chance to meet her father. Thus, both of them live one of the happiest moments of their lives when Antonio initiates Carmen into the art of bullfighting. As

52. For further information on the film, see "Blancanieves," IMDb, accessed December 27, 2021, https://www.imdb.com/title/tt1854513/?ref_=fn_al_tt_3.

can be expected, their secret and forbidden appointments drive Encarna mad. After learning about them, her revenge is dreadful. After Antonio passes away, Encarna has her architect and lover murder Carmen. However, the girl manages to escape. Alone, exhausted, and suffering from amnesia, she is discovered by "dwarfs" in the woods.

As we have noted already, *Blancanieves* works with the Snow White story very imaginatively. For example, the first more or less half of the film, in which Encarna locks Carmen up in a dirty cell and makes her do the hardest housework, has little to do with the classic Snow White fairy tale, alluding to another fairy tale, Cinderella, to a much greater degree. *Blancanieves* has significantly been shaped by the Spanish context, in particular the practice of bullfighting (corrida). The "dwarfs" are conceived as itinerant bullfighters who have become a fair show because of their growth disorder. Furthermore, it is noteworthy that there are not seven of them but only six—despite the fact that they too refer to themselves as "the seven dwarfs." The reason for this circumstance is left open in the film, thus providing space for multiple interpretations: Is it an attempt to challenge and overturn the stereotypical patterns of perception, such as that there always must be seven dwarfs, just like there are The Three Brothers or The Twelve Dancing Princesses? Or, is the point to suggest that there is no ontological difference between a dwarf and a "normal" human being, with the implication that Carmen (Snow White) is the seventh dwarf? Or, perhaps is there no reason at all, the unusual number of the dwarfs being nothing more but a trick played on the viewer? All these options invite the viewer's imagination to be actively involved for the sake of creating a meaning in this story.

Another unique feature of the film lies in Pablo Berger's decision to enrich his Snow White retelling by the motif of treason, when one of the dwarfs, led by jealousy, exposes Carmen to lethal danger during a bullfight. Besides Encarna, he thus becomes one of the active sources of evil in the story. Unlike Encarna, however, he eventually finds redemption after he regrets his deed and changes his thinking and behavior in an act of metanoia. In this respect, it should be emphasized that *Blancanieves* generally provides much space for a possibility of catharsis and transformation of "the given and immutable." An example represents, inter alia, the scene in which the audience decides about the fate of the defeated bull.

However, what is absent in this story is the character of a typical prince. *Blancanieves*, therefore, cannot be taken as a case in point for the prototypical fairy tales with a happy ending à la "they lived happily ever after." Nevertheless, the romantic dimension actually is present through an emerging relationship between Carmen and one of the dwarfs, Juanin. It is this aspect, I would argue, that most powerfully reflects the iconoclastic nature of the film, disrupting the deep-seated structures for perceiving what is the "normal," socially acceptable, aesthetically pleasing, traditionally right, and logically expected.

Blancanieves imaginatively—both in a deconstructive and reconstructive manner—works with the motif of sexuality, whereas it must be said that the film's take on this theme is by no means overexposed or vulgar. On the contrary, for all its modesty it makes a very refreshing, yet vigorous, impression. The key focus here, once again, is on challenging ingrained conceptions and stereotypes. In addition to the "romance" between Carmen and Juanin mentioned above, there are several other aspects of the film. First, one of the dwarfs is called Josefa and shows distinctively feminine features. There are basically two possible ways to interpret this character: either it is indeed a woman or a transvestite, with Josefa being represented by a male actor. Regardless of whichever interpretation one will accept, *Blancanieves* is subversive also on this account as it contests the common images of what a "typical" dwarf should look like.

Second, the motif of sexuality in Berger's retelling of the Snow White tale is also intriguingly grasped in the scene in which Carmen, paralyzed by a poisoned apple, is lying in an open coffin and her business agent is collecting fees from those who believe that it is their kiss that will bring Carmen back to life. In addition to the provocative combination of love, eroticism, and business, this scene is of relevance because there is also a woman in the long queue of the "kiss-awakeners." Because of its singularity, this moment too is open for various interpretations, thus appealing to the viewer's imagination. Arguably the most appropriate perspective is one that takes into account the iconoclastic nature of *Blancanieves*, reading the scene as a way of eroding our images and expectations.

Finally, the motif of sexuality is unambiguously present in the character of the evil stepmother, Encarna. She uses sex as a tool for achieving her goals. In Encarna, therefore, sexuality is closely associated with power. Through sexuality, she acts manipulatively not only with Antonio—though one must admit that in this case Antonio's overall fatigue plays an important role—but also with her architect and lover. As the little Carmen discovers when watching through a keyhole, Encarna obviously engages with her lover in sadomasochistic practices. The link between sexuality and power thus acquires an additional meaning in the film.

Blancanieves imaginatively elaborates yet another motif, namely, religion. It seems quite natural that the context of the early twentieth-century Andalusia will be portrayed as substantially shaped by Christian piety in its Roman Catholic form. However, it is more interesting to note that the attributes of this piety, such as crucifix, prayer, and confirmation (chrismation), are associated only with Carmen and Antonio, that is, unambivalently positive characters. On the contrary, a religious object becomes a tool used in murder in the hands of Encarna, who epitomizes evil and life-denying forces, as it is suggested that she uses a statue of a saint to kill her lover. This leads to a conclusion that religion in the film does not serve the purpose of a mere means to more vividly depict the contemporary context. Rather, it represents an organic element of the powers of good and evil, respectively.

The true climax of the film then comes with the final scene that counts, I would suggest, among the most beautiful cinematic endings ever. It emphasizes a central idea of the film that happy ends do not always have to be the way we have imagined them in our dreams and that fairy tale princes (and princesses) can substantially differ from our common perceptions. It is this ending that endows *Blancanieves* with yet another dimension, making it one of the most thought-provoking and evocative films released (not only) in 2012. For the purpose of our discussion, it is of much relevance as imagination lies at its core as the fundamental tool to both pursue Berger's authorial intention and enable full-fledged viewers' experience. Moreover, it clearly points out the importance of imagination for making sense of and constructing human embodied existence, rooted in a particular context and lived in relation to the other.

The Social Imagination and the Imagined Body

Now that we have delved into a theoretical discussion on imagination as well as explored a specific example of imaginative film-making and film-viewing, it is time to dedicate the last section of this chapter to considering the subject of imagination in the context of human existence as relational (social) and embodied. As I have already suggested in chapter 2, human embodied existence includes an intricate and subtle meshwork of the personal and structural relationships that people are involved in. In addition, one must also take into consideration the implications that these relationships have. Furthermore, all aspects of social reality are always already an embodied reality and "they remain to be embodied, enacted and performed in human communities as forms of bodily practice. So the deepest dynamics of the social, political and economic order are always incarnated into persons/bodies-in-relation."[53] This dynamic postulates and is embedded in the constructive interaction and exchange between the body, imagination, and the social as a third hermeneutic category to be introduced here. Therefore, it will be helpful to consider what Paul Ricoeur theorized as the "social imagination." Ricoeur conceives of this notion in terms of a creative tension between "ideology" and "utopia." These two hermeneutical concepts are interpreted as two poles that define the field in which one seeks to discover meaning of a certain social reality. Ricoeur explains the social imagination as follows:

> There is no answer . . . except to say that we must try to cure the illness of utopia by what is wholesome in ideology—by its element of identity, which is once more a fundamental function of life—and try to cure the rigidity, the petrification, of ideologies by the utopian element.[54]

Both elements that Ricoeur describes are indispensable in the process of imagining our social reality. Without "ideology" there would be no sense of society or tradition, while "utopia" enables us to reflect on, challenge, and reconstruct the actual societies and traditions that we belong to. In the words of Laurence Coupe: "Utopia prevents ideology becoming a claustrophobic system; ideology prevents utopia becoming an empty fantasy."[55] To put it differently still, the dynamic of "ideology" and "utopia" helps maintain an order, hierarchy, and tradition—that is, everything that heads toward perfection, thus implying the idea of totality—in equilibrium with that which is innovative, revealing, alternative, and fostering a hope for transformation.[56]

In line with my overall argument on human embodied existence as a postulate of our common life in God, I would like to suggest that the concept of an "imagined body" represents a viable way to account for the social dynamics that we have described in the Ricoeurian terms of "ideology" and "utopia." I understand the imagined body as a nexus of the material

53. Graham, "Words Made Flesh," 115.

54. Ricoeur, *Lectures*, 312.

55. Coupe, *Myth*, 97.

56. See Bargár, *Narrative*, 173.

("fleshly") body, language/discourse, relationships, and experiencing.[57] This insight draws from the research of Eugene Gendlin, who conceived of the human body as a part of language because "speaking is a special case of bodily interaction."[58] In addition, the human body also interacts with its environment, trying to make sense of and express the experience of living in the world.[59] Imagination empowers one to relate to the other, using one's material body as the point of entry to the other's experience and story. In this process, the imagined body is a locus for sharing specific narratives/tellings, creating common stories, and pursuing universal visions. In this sense, the imagined body represents a desirable complement to the material body, or perhaps more appropriately, as we have seen in the previous chapter, the body-self.

Significantly, from a theological perspective, the Scriptures too address the complex and delicate web of relationships regarding the human body as both material and imagined. The eponymous character of the book of Job provides a case in point as he debates with his friends about God and the human condition while sitting in ashes, his "social self" afflicted. Moreover, one can find multiple examples throughout the Hebrew Bible that in "the children and the name of the deceased, the deceased survives . . . as a social person very much in a corporeal dimension and not just in memory."[60] Here, Silvia Schroer and Thomas Staubli convincingly document that the imagined body has a very significant social dimension. The human body—in its material and imagined components—is, therefore, also a social body.

The sense of belonging to humankind can be theologically approached from a yet another angle, namely, through the concept of the image of God (*imago Dei*). Drawing from the Reformed theology of Herman Bavinck, Jessica Joustra proposes that the image of God in humans is both individual and corporate. The latter is manifested in the unity and diversity of humankind: "Unity maintains the diversity of humanity and diversity unfolds the richness of humanity."[61] In this understanding, humankind is organi-

57. I first introduced this notion in Bargár, "Relating," 46–66.

58. Gendlin, "How Philosophy Cannot Appeal," 28.

59. See Meiring, "Theology in the Flesh." Meiring refers to his proposal for theological anthropology as "embodied sensing." See especially pages 4–5. For a succinct summary, see Meiring, "*Ubuntu*."

60. Schroer and Staubli, "Bodily and Embodied," 10.

61. Joustra, "Embodied *Imago Dei*," 13. For a more detailed discussion on the subject, see also Eglinton, *Trinity*, 68–69.

cally interconnected, with all parts working together. In addition—as we have already seen in our earlier argument on human embodied existence in chapter 2—with the soul and the body being linked intrinsically, rather than accidentally, to constitute the human self, the body represents an integral part of our being human, and thence also a necessary part of the image of God.[62] Since humans as individuals and humankind as a whole represent "the embodied image of God,"[63] the imagined body provides a helpful concept to relate to others and to foster a sense of belonging to humankind.

A relational notion of personhood coming from a different context is *ubuntu*. A concept with origins in traditional African culture, an integral dimension of *ubuntu* is interconnectedness which insists that one's personhood—or self—is established only by virtue of one's relationship with other people. The relevance of *ubuntu* for theological discourse lies in its association not only with interconnectedness but also with reconciliation, forgiveness, and the restoration of human dignity and justice.[64] Stemming from Latinx theology, *nepantla* contributes with an additional emphasis to the focus on interconnectedness facilitated by *ubuntu*. Specifically, *nepantla* points out to the fact that our concept of and a sense of belonging to humankind is always an intermixture of, inter alia, various cultures, voices, and bodies.[65] While especially *ubuntu* has come to provoke a substantial share of criticism,[66] both notions remain to be useful for theological reflection because they "recognize the possibilities of a common life or *convivencia* while contending that one voice or culture cannot determine it, and any form of shared life must attend to the brutal histories that inevitably form its backdrop."[67] In addition, *ubuntu* even goes beyond *nepantla* by situating humanity within a cosmic and ecological framework.[68] "I am because

62. See Joustra, "Embodied *Imago Dei*," 15.

63. Joustra, "Embodied *Imago Dei*," 17.

64. See Meiring, "*Ubuntu*," 2.

65. See Bretherton, *Christ*, 317.

66. One of the sharpest critics has been Wim van Binsbergen, who argues that more than anything else, *ubuntu* is a globalized concept propagated by southern African intellectual elites and fundamentally disconnected from the lived reality of rural African life, whether in the past or the present. See, for example, Binsbergen, "*Ubuntu*," 72–73.

67. Bretherton, *Christ*, 318. In a similar vein, Jacob Meiring is cautious yet convinced that *ubuntu* can be a useful notion for theological reflection, provided that one pays careful attention and sensitivity to the experiences of black people and their embodied existence. See Meiring, "*Ubuntu*," 7.

68. See Bretherton, *Christ*, 318–19.

we are"—this fundamental *ubuntu* claim includes our human bodies, both material and imagined.

To add yet another important pebble to the mosaic of what I call the imagined body, Sharon Bong employs a queer theological imagination in her exploration of the themes of mutuality and reciprocity. Her proposal to "queer the body of Christ" lies in resisting the overdetermined maleness of Christ, deconstructing harmful dualisms that are generated by such androcentrism, and, as a result, reconstructing the human as made in the image of God based on mutuality, reciprocity, and eroticism.[69] It is significant for Christian theology that the interconnectedness, the sense of belonging, and mutuality and reciprocity have a potential to spawn solidarity that is a prerequisite for human flourishing.[70] This solidarity reflects and is inspired by God's initiative and desire to be in communion with people, to offer them a common life in God. This invitation necessarily includes those who are beyond the borders of the ecclesial body—or, for that matter, any religious body—with a special focus on those oppressed, marginalized, and neglected among us whom Marcella Althaus-Reid famously referred to as "indecent bodies."[71] God's own action thus "fuels our caring for other bodies"[72] of those in our midst but also those excluded by us or the structures we live in. In this chapter, I described this dynamic as human participation in God's new creation, arguing that—empowered by imagination—human beings are called to be involved in a twofold process of challenging the status quo and working for a new reality. My aim in the following chapter will be to show that such transformation presupposes a deep existential conversion.

69. See Bong, "Ecclesiology," 71.

70. For Oliver James Keenan such flourishing is enabled thanks to human togetherness and our "rootedness in webs of temporal and spatial relationships." See Keenan, "Politics," 85.

71. See Althaus-Reid, *Indecent Theology*.

72. Méndez-Montoya, "Eucharistic Imagination," 326.

4

Transformation

Becoming Converted

Paul Schrader has become renowned especially as screenwriter for Martin Scorsese's films such as *Taxi Driver* (1976) and *The Last Temptation of Christ* (1988). Schrader's 2017 film, *First Reformed*, which he both wrote and directed, is related to these cinematographic gems through the theme of a central character that undergoes a profound existential crisis, ultimately being forced to face not only external circumstances but, first and foremost, one's own inner dilemmas and demons.[1]

The plotline follows the story of Ernst Toller, who is a church minister to a small Reformed congregation in Upstate New York. Even though his church is less than half full on normal Sundays, the organ is in a desperate need of being tuned, and toilets do not flush, Toller is perceived as a very good preacher, a popular youth pastor, and a sought-after counsellor by believers and nonbelievers alike. The role model for his faith and life is the Catholic theologian, writer, and activist Thomas Merton (1915–1968). Like Merton, Toller also engages himself in deep deliberations about the meaning of his existence, interrogating the very foundations of his own faith. For Toller, however, this self-reflection does not seem to be liberating but, on the contrary, leads him to increasingly intense doubts, loneliness, and depression. His condition is even intensified by the loss of his only son, a soldier killed during the invasion in Iraq, followed by separation from his

1. For further information on the film, see "First Reformed," IMDb, accessed December 27, 2021, https://www.imdb.com/title/tt6053438/?ref_=fn_al_tt_1.

wife, the rapid worsening of his health, and developing alcoholism. And yet, in spite of everything, Toller manages to keep his high morale and commitment for the sake of his congregation and broader community.

A major breakthrough in Toller's life comes after a member of his church, Mary, asks him for a pastoral conversation with her husband, Michael. Michael is an ardent ecological activist who refuses to father a child in this world that is, as he firmly believes, doomed for destruction as a result of human treatment. This singular encounter brings about a true and profound conversion of the stern and contemplative Reformed minister. However, it would be a mistake to view it in terms of a naïve and superficial "green dottiness." Emotionally detached and rationally based Toller step by step comes through his intensive and honest internal questioning to a conclusion that the gospel, the good news about God's offer of life, is not anthropocentrically oriented. In other words, the gospel is not addressed to humankind only but to the whole creation. Human beings are summoned to realize that they are intrinsically and inseparably related to the nonhuman creation. The salvation of humankind is unthinkable apart from the salvation of the rest of God's creation. Eventually, Toller is becoming a zealous apostle of this understanding of the gospel. Still, from his perspective, any simple and unambiguous action to give voice to such a message is out of the question. In the final scene of the film that indubitably alludes to the behavior of another Schrader's character, Travis Bickle, the protagonist of *Taxi Driver* mentioned above, Ernst Toller pauses to consider the essential question: Is the need to proclaim the urgent message more important than the life of one's neighbor?

As a consequence of his existential conversion, Toller becomes the "first reformed." The title of the film thus gets a unique pun in addition to the obvious reference to the name of the congregation that Toller ministers (i.e., First Reformed Church). However, it seems that Toller's story could also be characterized in terms of the dialectic between despair and hope as these two notions very well capture the permanent struggle inside the main protagonist that does not stop even after his conversion.[2] Moreover, Toller's case suggests that the interplay of despair and hope can be regarded as a hermeneutic key to human existence in general. It is hope, after all, which is necessary, from a Christian perspective, to overcome the despair following from the uncertainty whether God will forgive us our transgressions

2. It is worth mentioning that *Zoufalství a naděje* (Czech for despair and hope) is the title under which the film was distributed in the Czech Republic.

against our neighbors and creation. This dynamic takes place—as the film conveys—in the public realm of life, implying that Christian faith is inherently political. A result of existential conversion, or, in biblical terminology, metanoia, faith represents neither exclusively nor predominantly a therapeutic tool or a strategy to pursue one's personal growth. More than anything else, faith stands for a specific and holistic approach to life with all its dimensions, complexity, and messiness. The fact that one professes Christian faith must find an expression in one's relation to economy, medical care, migration, the environment, and other issues though, admittedly, a degree of reflectiveness of one's faith may vary. Toller's behavior vis-à-vis his church's sponsor, Balq, clearly illustrates this theme.

Nevertheless, the most powerful scene of the whole film is when Toller is praying together with Mary upon her request. In his diary, Toller afterward confesses that it was for the first time after a very long period that he was able to pray truly with his whole heart and mind. This scene, therefore, very emphatically shows that one cannot authentically relate to a transcending reality, unless it is done through a relationship with another human being. For the purpose of our discussion, it is further significant that *First Reformed* introduces conversion, metanoia, as the effort aimed at reinterpreting one's own story. In the light of our discussion so far, I would like to suggest that Toller's story represents a case when—as a result of one's imagination becoming awakened after an encounter with the other—one begins to see one's embodied existence as a part of God's creation at large and commits oneself to work for its transformation and consummation. Furthermore, I proposed in chapter 1 that such a narrative approach to one's life can be referred to as restorying. The film is also unambiguous about the fact that repentance is necessary if there is to be any change. Thus, it opens a hope for a viable future. This is very much in line with Jürgen Moltmann's theological emphases who contends that "future is repentance."[3] Moltmann hereby points out that without human conversion, accompanied by honest repentance, the sustainable life of creation is endangered, if not impossible. In the similar vein, Daniela Augustine has the following to say on repentance:

> Repentance is the beginning of change within one's outlook toward oneself, the other, and the world. It illuminates the myopic human vision of time-compressed material existence with the sobering realism of the Spirit's time-transcending, liberating truth,

3. Moltmann, *Creating*, 15.

> focusing the lenses of understanding the condition of the world, and sharpening the critical edge of prophetic discontent through the foresight of eschatological hope.[4]

The change that Augustine describes here is what I would like to refer to in this chapter as transformation. Transformation is, I argue, the ultimate horizon to which God leads God's creation. Empowered by God's grace to use their imagination, people reinterpret their life stories in acts of metanoia to overcome the brokenness of the *conditio humana* that is a result of sin. In that way, they can truly pursue their existence as embodied beings toward our common life in God. In order to proceed with my argument on transformation I will in this chapter largely draw from the Czech Protestant theologian and poet Milan Balabán's (1929–2019) insights on the *conditio humana* and his understanding of the human as a being called to follow Truth. Combining scholarly erudition and poetic imagination, Balabán's writing provides glimpses into a unique, biblically inspired theological anthropology that resists any attempts for systematization; in other words, human existence is too dynamic and complex to be converted into a set of propositions. For Balabán, Truth (written with a capital "T") represents a central category in his theological-anthropological explorations. He identifies it not only with Word and Life but explicitly also with the LORD (YHWH), the God of Israel and the Father of Jesus Christ.[5] This identification is possible because Truth is inherently related with justice, kindness, and mercy. As beings called to follow Truth, therefore, people also are reminded of their mandate to bear the image of God (*imago Dei*).

Conditio Humana

In his 2019 book, J. Andrew Kirk inquires into the question of what it means to be human. He reminds us that there are many legitimate ways to approach such an inquiry from a Christian theological perspective. Kirk's first point concurs with what I have argued in chapter 2 of this book: the human being has a body—or, more precisely, is a body—through which they can relate to the rest of creation. Nevertheless, people should be viewed in a certain contrast to nonhuman creation—and that is a second point—because they are distinguished by their conscious and intentional behavior

4. Augustine, *Spirit*, 102.

5. See Balabán, "Nový model," 124.

that goes beyond a merely instinctual level. Third, the human is endowed with the ability to produce culture and to use imagination, the point that I argued in chapter 3. Finally, the human being is aware of the idea of the common destiny of the whole humankind as, for instance, different theistic traditions accentuate.[6] The essential traits of being human include "all their natural endowments, physical and social impulses, sexual and racial differentiations, their entire characters."[7] The human, therefore, needs to be perceived in a holistic manner, as a complex being closely related to the context in which one lives. Jürgen Moltmann goes into great detail on this issue when he postulates that each person has at least nine specific characteristics that contribute to forming one's human identity: "a professional, a national, a civic, a class, a geographical, a sex, a conscious, an unconscious and perhaps even too a private one; he combines them all in himself."[8]

The multidimensional and contextual nature of human existence is not neglected by Milan Balabán either. He very seriously takes the biblical accent that the human is "the dust of the ground" (Gen 2:7 NRSV) or "dust and ashes" (see Gen 18:27 NRSV).[9] The Hebrew term *adam* ('–d–m), meaning something like "out of the ground" (see Gen 2:9), is, therefore, not so much a proper noun but rather a term providing an evaluation of the human being: humans are not God—they are mortal, and finitude is their hallmark. However, the breathing in of God's spirit, "the breath of life" (Gen 2:7 NRSV), destines them to pursue mercy and justice here on earth.[10] God's word turns "clay [into] pottery that can be useful for the purposes of Truth in this world."[11] Balabán therefore asserts that the human is—in a biblical perspective—introduced as a representative of the divine on earth.[12] This refers to the fundamental irreducibility of human embodied existence: the immanent (i.e., clay/earth, dust, and ashes) and the transcendent (i.e., God's breath of life) dimensions of the human being are not to be separated from each other.

6. See Kirk, *Being Human*, 348–49.

7. Kirk, *Being Human*, 332.

8. Moltmann, *On Human Being*, 92. Moltmann's book was originally published in German in 1971. From a theological perspective, it is striking that Moltmann does not mention either a religious or a cultural dimension.

9. See Balabán, "Člověk jako hlína," 242–44. This text was written in 2001.

10. See Balabán, "Člověk jako hlína," 243–44.

11. Balabán, "Člověk jako hlína," 244. Translations from Czech in this chapter are mine.

12. See Balabán, "Člověk jako hlína," 242.

To maintain a holistic view of people as earthly—and embodied—representatives of God in the world, it is key to regard them as relational beings; that is, creatures who exist as part of a multilayered meshwork of relationships with other (especially) human and (also) nonhuman creatures. For Balabán, the human becomes a complete being only if in relationships with another human being.[13] To be a neighbor is, therefore, a calling that one is summoned to pursue. Keeping in mind the transcendental dimension of human embodied existence, however, Balabán contends that one cannot speak about the human apart from the relationship to God as a transcendental "Thou" either.[14] In this respect, Balabán's anthropological accents connect, for example, with the thesis of the Uruguayan theologian of liberation, Juan Luis Segundo, who asserts that the human is incomplete without God's grace. Without grace, the human is nothing but "an infirm, divided, tragic being . . . dominated or enslaved by a force or tendency that is labeled *concupiscence* by theology."[15] We will come back to this essential aspect of the *conditio humana* later in this section when we discuss sin.

Balabán's understanding of the complexity of human embodied existence is arguably most clearly visible when he considers the particularities of the man-woman relationship. The "gender theory" of Milan Balabán is built around the thesis that the human (Hebrew *adam*) represents "a unity, a fellowship of man and woman."[16] Interestingly, he suggests that the woman represents the man's soul, without which he would be but a fragment of a complete being, a "soulless body."[17] The woman is the man's partner, equal to him in every respect (see Gen 2:20). While being as autonomous and free as he is, the woman epitomizes the man's counterpart; she is the man's neighbor to whom he can and should relate.[18] Moreover, both the man and the woman transcend themselves through each other when they are called as partners to foster one another's faith.[19] For the purpose of my overall thesis it is important to note that Balabán understands faith as one's imaginative,

13. See Balabán, "Obraz," 427. This text was originally written as a lecture in 1997.

14. See Balabán, "Obraz," 424. For this insight, Balabán draws from the personalist philosophy of Martin Buber. Although I have already discussed some aspects of relationality in the preceding two chapters, this theme will be treated separately in chapter 5.

15. Segundo, *Grace*, 21, emphasis in the original. Segundo's book was originally published in Spanish in 1968.

16. Balabán, "Člověk je muž a žena," 42.

17. Balabán, "Člověk je muž a žena," 46.

18. See Balabán, "Člověk je muž a žena," 46.

19. See Balabán, "Člověk je muž a žena," 47–48.

courageous, and affirmative stepping out toward life, empowered and inspired by the Spirit. Faith refers to "the unity of manifold aspects of life, a joyful manifestation of love that cannot possibly be separated into the spiritual and material realms."[20] These emphases have, in turn, an impact on Balabán's theology as he understands God as unity that is also diversity. Moreover, this God is heading toward further diversity in the process of inviting creation into fellowship with God; it is a vision that I refer to as our common life in God. To put it in other words, for Balabán, God represents a "communion, contact, and correspondence of the diverse."[21]

We have already mentioned that the multidimensional and irreducible nature of human embodied existence as created in the image of God is necessarily embedded in a specific context. Even though the subject of contextuality was discussed earlier in chapter 2 with respect to the human body, some points of this inquiry need to be reiterated—and hopefully further elaborated—here as it is crucial for our present discussion on transformation. While doubts about the possibility of a "pure," superhistorical, and supercultural message were voiced already by Friedrich Schleiermacher, a real breakthrough in viewing not only the biblical gospel and Christian faith but also human existence as essentially contextual came with the emergence of various theologies from beyond the North Atlantic region starting in the 1960s.[22] In an eponymous book, Juan Luis Segundo refers to this paradigmatic shift as "the liberation of theology."[23] With regard to theological anthropology, it can be maintained that human embodied existence is influenced, even determined, by the context to which one is born.[24] In chapter 2 I have already mentioned Stephen Bevans, who importantly characterizes context as a hermeneutic framework that takes into consideration various factors of human existence, such as life situations, both personal (e.g., death in a family, childbirth) and social (e.g., 9/11 terrorist attacks, global climate change crisis), the social status of an individual or community (e.g., gender roles, economic status, generational identity), specific culture (understood as a system of symbols that provides an order and

20. Balabán, "Člověk je muž a žena," 48.

21. Balabán, "Člověk je muž a žena," 43.

22. For a brief, yet concise, introduction to the theme of contextualization in theology, see, for instance, Bosch, *Transforming Mission*, especially 420–32.

23. See Segundo, *Liberation of Theology*.

24. See Segundo, *Grace*, 31.

gives life a meaning), and a societal change within concrete cultures and social situations (e.g., technological revolution, economic expansion).[25]

Even though Milan Balabán neither directly uses the term "context" nor explicitly discusses the theme of contextuality, one can discover several places in his work that are inspiring and relevant for the present discussion. It needs to be noted that Balabán focuses much more on what can be referred to as nonhuman creation than on the socioeconomic or cultural-political aspects of contextuality. I believe, however, that his observations can also be related to the latter which also makes them important for our discussion. Here, too, Balabán opts for the Scriptures as the point of departure for his exploration when he postulates that the Hebrew Bible—and especially the book of Genesis—demythologizes context. Still, this claim needs to be clarified in the sense that although the Scriptures really do *de-divinize* creation, they by no means *de-sacralize* it. In other words, creation is not deprived of its sacrality; it retains its sacramental nature.[26] Balabán's theological anthropology, his understanding of the *conditio humana*, is defined by the statement that the world is not—and ought not to be—merely "a stage for the drama called human existence."[27]

The human relationship to the rest of creation is shaped by a twofold dynamic. On the one hand, the biblical account requires that humans keep their distance from nonhuman creation.[28] It would be a tragedy if the human identified with nature. Balabán does not even shy away from using a considerably provocative formulation that the human is to be a "god" for the rest of creation.[29] On the other hand, however, the nonhuman creation is called to be a human fellow-traveler, a helper, and a "brotherly face."[30] According to the book of Genesis, the human binds creation to themselves by naming it, thus, in fact, embedding it into a meaningful framework and calling it from "mere being to existence."[31] With regard to my argument, it is important to note that creation is not to remain in its original or actual state but is eschatologically called to transformation. One of the aspects of this calling is the kerygmatic potential of creation. While it certainly is

25. See Bevans, "Contextual Theology," 35. See also Bevans, *Models*, 3–7.

26. See Balabán, "Člověk – syn Boží," 68.

27. Balabán, "Odposvátnění," 115.

28. See Balabán, "Nový model," 124.

29. See Balabán, "Člověk – syn Boží," 67.

30. See Balabán, "Nový model," 125.

31. Balabán, "Nový model," 124–25.

a "stammering glossolalia," it also represents an important facet of biblical noetics: natural phenomena give witness to God as "concrete and living transcendental and immanent Truth."[32] Nonhuman creation is thus responsible for giving praise to God. To be able to pursue this task as well as the eschatological transformation, however, it needs to be accompanied by the human and, first and foremost, Truth.[33] One of the essential insights that Balabán's explorations into biblical noetics offer to our theological-anthropological inquiry into human contextuality is, I would suggest, that neither matter nor the human are sacred per se. Both matter and the human are, however, constantly sacralized by the calling of Truth that provides orientation for the whole creation toward the eschatological transformation and consummation "so that God may be all in all" (1 Cor 15:28 NRSV).[34]

As I have already pointed out above with reference to Segundo, the process of this transformation and ultimate consummation is nevertheless hampered by what is in Christian theological discourse referred to as sin. Based on his reading of Romans 7:14–24, Segundo perceives the human as a being tragically torn between ideal intentions and actual actions. Every single human being is, therefore, drawn into the dilemma of deciding between good and evil, facing the Hamletian question of "to sin, or not to sin."[35]

In Balabán's view, sin is associated with the disruption of the basic relationship of trust. As such, it epitomizes the exact opposite of the attitude of faith.[36] A theological shortcut that Balabán uses to define sin is "the impatience of distrust."[37] As he documents through his interpretation of the kerygmatic myth of Adam and Eve (see Gen 3:1–7), sin does not lie in the human desire to be like God as such; this aspiration is, after all, ingrained in the very fact of humans being created in the image of God, strongly resonating, for instance, in Jesus's appeal to pursue perfection (see Matt 5:48). To understand the concept of sin, it is much more important to consider the fact that people want to be like God *immediately*, without following God, without obedience to Truth. It is this manipulative attitude that cor-

32. Balabán, "Odposvátnění," 119.

33. See Balabán, "Odposvátnění," 122.

34. See Balabán, "Odposvátnění," 117.

35. See Segundo, *Evolution*, 9. Segundo's book was originally published in Spanish in 1968.

36. See Balabán, "Hřích," 89.

37. Balabán, "Hřích," 87.

rupts the essential relationship of trust between the human and Truth.[38] In addition, Balabán uses another image from Genesis, namely, the entering of the serpent in the relationship between people and God (see Gen 3:1–7) to account for this fundamental aspect of sin—the abandonment of proximity.[39] In sum, sin turns the human into an artificial, lifeless, and foregone being that is disconnected from his or her future.[40]

Like Milan Balabán, Reinhold Niebuhr too regards sin, first and foremost, in terms of disruption of the relationship with the good and just God. Human sin, according to Niebuhr, lies in vanity and pride as people think of themselves and their civilizational inventions as wreathed with a divine aureole. The catastrophes in history, through which God punishes human hubris, then represent the natural and inevitable consequences of human action.[41] Niebuhr's account, when compared with that of Balabán, seems to be more static as it relies on the hierarchical concept of God as Sovereign who either rewards or punishes human transgressions in accordance with God's autonomous will. While Balabán too finds the essence of sin in the human manipulative effort to improperly conjoin the human and the divine, he does not speak in terms of perversion of the exactly defined role(s) but rather suggests that sin refers to the human neglect of and scorn for the opportunity to have a future, thus becoming disconnected from her or his future. Rejecting God's grace, in sin, the human denies the transcendental nature of Truth.[42] Therefore, sin is not only an ethical issue; it is, first and foremost, an existential issue. It involves relationship, attitude, and style of life—and perversion and distortion thereof.[43] Balabán reminds us that the consequences of sin include not only goalless odysseys and death in all its forms. The offense against God also has its planetary ramifications as the biblical story of the flood suggests (see Gen 6:5–7). An attempt to "extinguish Truth," sin can thus be interpreted as an "element of anti-creation."[44]

38. See Balabán, "Hřích," 90.

39. See Balabán, "Člověk jako sadař," 63.

40. See Balabán, "Hřích," 90.

41. See Niebuhr, *Nature*, 148 and 149.

42. See Balabán, "Hřích," 94. He elaborates these ideas on the basis of his interpretation of Gen 6:1–4 about the forbidden unions between the sons of God and the daughters of humans.

43. See Balabán, "Hřích," 94.

44. Balabán, "Hřích," 95.

Theological reflection on sin must necessarily consider the category of punishment. The acknowledgment that sin and guilt require punishment, including, at times, capital punishment, is regarded by Milan Balabán as a great religio-ethical invention.[45] In a biblical perspective, however, punishment is never seen as a result of divine revengefulness, nor a requirement of justice that must be satisfied. Rather, punishment can be described as an epiphany because it discloses the true state of affairs regarding the human and the world.[46] Balabán is willing to go even further when he explicitly perceives punishment as grace. If the humans were not driven out of the garden of Eden, they would still "dabble" in their "almost-godhood," thus being unable to pursue their calling in this world.[47] Human embodied existence would thus remain devoid its meaning; the human would be truly lost.

Even if one cannot escape the mechanism of sin and punishment, it is not regarded in fatalistic terms. Above sin and punishment, there is Truth, forgiveness, and grace that have an ultimate say.[48] Truth keeps on "thrusting" at the gone-astray human, asking, "Where are you?" (Gen 3:9 NRSV) and challenging one to change one's thinking and action (metanoia).[49] The hope that change (transformation) is possible points out one of the essential features of Balabán's theological anthropology, namely, that the human has the power not to sin (Latin *posse non peccare*). He argues that if we admitted that evil is inevitable and that sin is associated with fate, we would thereby exempt the human from responsibility. In a polemic with both Augustine of Hippo and the Gnostics, Balabán, therefore, contends that the human can actually be without sin.[50] To support his thesis, he notes that *adam* in the sense of humankind as a whole has never succumbed to sin completely. He refers to the "Abelian" line of humankind, including such biblical witnesses of faith as Abel, Seth, Enosh, Noah, and, ultimately, Jesus.[51] The awareness of sin as a negative dynamic should, therefore, lead

45. See Balabán, "Vina a trest," 97. This essay was written in 1995.

46. See Balabán, "Člověk jako sadař," 63.

47. See Balabán, "Člověk jako sadař," 64.

48. See Balabán, "Vina a trest," 99. A similar argument is offered by Andrew Kirk, who says that "sin and evil are sure signs of the permanent reality of a moral universe in which the standards of right and wrong are set by the God who brought everything into being." See Kirk, *Being Human*, 333.

49. See Balabán, "Hřích," 97.

50. See Balabán, "Hřích," 88.

51. See Balabán, "Hřích," 98.

one to recognition that one is to foster one's will to question and reform oneself, lest one surrender to either inappropriate heroism or pessimism.[52] Both sin and a view toward transformation thus belong to the core of theological anthropology; while sin constantly reminds us of our *conditio humana*, the will to undergo metanoia is, according to the Scriptures, "a constitutive feature of humankind on its way to authenticity and realness."[53] This observation leads us to the next section of this chapter that is going to discuss human quest in this world.

Human Quest

Milan Balabán elaborates his understanding of human quest in a polemic with Martin Heidegger when he argues that the human is not "thrown" (German *geworfen*) into the world, but rather gently "put" or "embedded."[54] The Hebrew Bible does not see the human as a wanderer but rather as the steward of a garden. The human is not a "paradisiacal semi-god," but a being created from the dust of the ground; without a heavenly halo but authorized by Truth to care for God's creation.[55] To be a "shepherd of nature" is not merely a profession; Balabán regards this commission in terms of filiation when he speaks of the human as a "cousin" of nonhuman creation.[56] At the same time, however, it must be reminded here what we have already said earlier, namely, that the human is to be by no means identified with nature. On the contrary, the human is to be a "god" for the rest of creation.[57] Nevertheless, I believe that this divine task is not to be interpreted in imperialistic terms as a blank check for humans to parasite on creation. Contrarily, it represents a calling to act in the spirit of the divine Truth, characterized by mercy, justice, reconciliation, and peace.

The discussion so far shows that humans have a unique position within creation: they belong with both nonhuman creation and God. While they are "cousins" to nature, they are also summoned to emulate God and

52. See Balabán, "Obraz," 429.

53. See Balabán, "Obraz," 430.

54. See Balabán, "Člověk jako sadař," 58. In another essay, Balabán uses a pomiculturist term "engrafted." See Balabán, "Vrženost," 113.

55. See Balabán, "Člověk jako sadař," 59.

56. See Balabán, "Obraz," 431.

57. See Balabán, "Člověk – syn Boží," 67.

become a "secondary god."[58] Human uniqueness is established by God's regard for humans when entrusting them with specific tasks. And the fact that God offers humans partnership for pursuing these mandates, fills them with awe. It is this awe, I believe, that gives the foundations to theological anthropology since, as Balabán proposes in his interpretation of Psalm 8, it is awe that leads people from their effort to answer the question of "What are human beings?" to the question of "What is God like?"[59] Moreover, the human is not only a "creature of permanent awe"[60] but also an "animal of joy" (Latin *animal laetitiae*).[61] In a biblical meditation on the book of Qohelet, Balabán says that it undoubtedly belongs to human quest to rejoice amid one's daily life—despite (or, perhaps, because of) the awareness of one's own finitude. The discovery of joy amid finitude represents a unique contribution of biblical tradition to the religious and cultural heritage of humankind.[62] Joy has transcendent origins as it enters the world as a gift from God (see Qoh 5:18). Joy is a part of being human even under "harsh conditions and traumatic circumstances."[63] Such traumatic and traumatizing factors certainly include the sense of one's finitude that one is endowed with. However, joy and finitude are not antitheses; the human being is to experience joy precisely as a mortal—being aware of the finitude of all things, with the exception of God.[64] It is the ultimate horizon of human quest that once all people will need to stand before God's judgment (see Qoh 11:9). Yet, this awareness does not represent a "religious boogeyman" but a positive dimension of human embodied existence: one is to remember one's Creator.[65] In a biblical perspective, human life takes place here and now—and the rest is up to God: "The Bible teaches us: in spite of our finitude, we can experience joy in the situations of our life—in marriage, friendship, solidarity, wine drinking, dance, yes, even in religion."[66]

In spite of the fact that finitude is a hallmark of human embodied existence, the breathing in of God's spirit—the breath of life—empowers

58. See Balabán, "Člověk – královský správce," 54.

59. See Balabán, "Člověk – královský správce," 56.

60. See Balabán, "Člověk – královský správce," 53.

61. See Balabán, "Radost," 231. This essay was originally written in 1996.

62. See Balabán, "Radost," 241.

63. Balabán, "Radost," 234.

64. See Balabán, "Radost," 240.

65. See Balabán, "Radost," 237.

66. Balabán, "Radost," 237.

the human being to pursue justice and mercy on earth.[67] Human quest, therefore, includes being a neighbor to human and nonhuman creation.[68] Truth that one is called to follow is what gives orientation to this quest. To Balabán's mind, it is the merciful Truth that stands at the core of faith as a human existential position. He goes on to say that human identity is decisively shaped by a gracious calling and invitation by Truth that precedes the human being, opening the future for them.[69] Similar ideas can also be found in the theological work of Juan Luis Segundo, who regards grace as that which allows people to have a share in God's vision of their recreation in the image of God's perfect love.[70] Andrew Kirk, like Segundo, perceives grace as a supernatural God's gift that one is given at conversion. However, he goes even further when he identifies grace with new creation or the liberation of the inner human being. Grace thus becomes an agent of transformation whose ultimate goal is "hominization," that is, the perfect flourishing of humankind restored to its original intention.[71] Milan Balabán too is convinced that the human is carried by and lives only thanks to grace. He expresses this emphasis through a thesis that Truth represents the human before Truthself.[72]

Reinhold Niebuhr interprets the key importance of the gracious God through the means of systematic theology when he asserts that "the unique individual finds the contingent and arbitrary aspect of his existence tolerable because it is . . . judged and redeemed by the eternal God, who transcends both the rational structure and the arbitrary facts of existence in the universe."[73] God as Truth is thus experienced not only as grace and mercy but also as a source of knowledge about God, the world, and the human being.[74] Balabán reminds that such knowledge does not stand for a value in itself but it is supposed to lead to the pursuit of transformation because, as we have already noted above, the will to undergo metanoia is, according to the Scriptures, "a constitutive feature of humankind on its way to

67. See Balabán, "Člověk jako hlína," 244.

68. See Balabán, "Obraz," 428.

69. See Balabán, "Tvořící Pravda," 106.

70. See Segundo, *Evolution*, 80.

71. See Kirk, *Being Human*, 340.

72. See Balabán, "Obraz," 430.

73. See Niebuhr, *Nature*, 286.

74. See Kirk, *Being Human*, 336. See also Ps 36:10.

authenticity and realness."[75] Following Truth can be interpreted as a pursuit of self-transcendence—that is, the overcoming of one's own limitations in the process of becoming a subject that relates to a transcendent "Thou."

A fundamental feature of the LORD's Truth that creates and calls everything to existence is that Truth precedes the human. This is not merely chronological pre-existence that would turn human sight backward, to a "mythical origin"; quite the contrary, Truth lead people toward the future.[76] Balabán makes his point very emphatically: "We only exist because our (potential but real) non-existence is addressed by the WHITHER of Truth. Looking at Truth's back, we walk the paths toward the future."[77] Using the cases of biblical prophets in service of YHWH, Balabán shows that Truth's precedence creates space for dynamic dialogue. Prophetic prayers, cries, fights or negotiations function as a safeguard preventing the identification of Truth with its followers. Truth always transcends us.[78] However, this dialogical and relational nature of Truth also implies, as Balabán suggests, a "pathic" trait: God always stands with people in both their joys and sorrows.[79] And the followers of Truth are called to show the same kind of solidarity.

The appeal to follow Truth has yet another dimension. The human being is to be at Truth's disposal, without trying to domesticate, colonize, or manipulate Truth. People are forbidden to objectify, politicize, religiously appropriate, or ideologize Truth.[80] This insight is further elaborated by Jürgen Moltmann, who argues that one becomes truly human only when finding oneself in a situation that forces one to put aside one's self-divinization and idolatry. And this is possible only because the true God stands vis-à-vis the human being in the position of an iconoclastic agent.[81] It is, therefore, appropriate to maintain that the humanization of the human being requires the iconoclastic power of God as a critical presupposition of full humanity. Furthermore, Moltmann's observation provides a suitable supplement to Balabán's accent on the pursuit of Truth because it brings the aspect of humanization in the discussion on Truth in relation to the human. Truth

75. See Balabán, "Obraz," 430.

76. See Balabán, "Tvořící Pravda," 104.

77. Balabán, "Tvořící Pravda," 105–6.

78. See Balabán, "Tvořící Pravda," 105.

79. See Balabán, "Člověk je muž a žena," 43.

80. See Balabán, "Člověk jako sadař," 62.

81. See Moltmann, *On Human Being*, 107.

not only creates in the human Truth's image (*imago Dei*). It also calls and empowers the human to create the human's own image (*imago hominis*) in the nonhuman creation through his or her action in accordance with Truth. In partnership and coordination with Truth, humans work on themselves, thus, at the same time, humanizing God's creation. The whole creation is to be shaped into the *imago hominis* which ultimately is, if understood properly, *imago Dei*.[82]

Drawing from the insights of Milan Balabán and some other theologians, the present discussion showed that human embodied existence is to be understood in dynamic terms. In this view, the human is introduced as a multidimensional being endowed with freedom, responsibility, and imagination. Both individually and collectively, humankind is called by God to its self-realization that is intrinsically related to the care for and flourishing of nonhuman creation. Also, the present discussion has reaffirmed the importance of context for human embodied existence. The context in which one lives is not a mere stage for the drama of human existence. The human is inseparably connected with her or his context; humans are contextual beings. Context is not only a result of God's creative action but it also has its human dimension as humans are called to reshape creation in their own image, thus contributing with their own unique input. Contextually informed theological explorations, including theological anthropology or missiology, can, therefore, never be anthropocentric but rather *ktisiocentric*, that is, creation-oriented. Furthermore, as our discussion has also shown, relationality plays a key and indispensable role in human embodied existence. From a Christian perspective, the human is a relational being as the triune God represents a community—or, communion—of relationships; the human as God's creature reflects the nature of the Trinity. This kind of relationality has several dimensions since the human relates to the other in various modes; the other comes as God, fellow human beings (both individually and collectively), and the world/nonhuman creation. Through this relationality, one pursues one's own self. The theme of relationality will be in detail explored in the following chapter.

What still needs to be further discussed in this chapter, though, is the theme of transformation. Transformation is the goal of human quest as people join in God's mission of creation and recreation of all there is. It is motivated by the refusal to accept the status quo, characterized by the brokenness and woundedness of creation. In this process, the reality is seen

82. See Balabán, "Nový model," 124.

through the lens of justice, peace, mercy, acceptance, and reconciliation as fundamental features of God's inbreaking reign—the kin-dom of God. Since these features at the same time represent the personal traits of God, the human being, when committed to pursue them, also accepts the mandate to bear the image of God. Created in the image of God, the human being is called by God to follow God, thus realizing one's full humanity and participating in the eschatological transformation of the whole creation "so that God may be all in all" (1 Cor 15:28 NRSV).

Toward a Theological Understanding of Transformation

As indicated in the previous discussion, I would suggest that transformation stands for the ultimate goal of human quest in their participating in God's mission with creation. As such, it plays a central role in Christianity. Christianity anticipates and actively strives for the transformation of all reality so that "God may be all in all" (1 Cor 15:28 NRSV). In his classic book on Christ and culture, H. Richard Niebuhr introduced transformation as closely associated with his fifth ideal type of Christianity, which he referred to as "Christ the transformer of culture." Even though this view is considerably countercultural, it makes a case for involvement with, rather than withdrawal from, culture. Still, it does not represent an expression of willful optimism or naïveté. To be sure, Niebuhr contends that it is solidly based on three theological convictions regarding (1) God's creative activity in history; (2) human nature as corrupted and in need of transformation—yet not "bad"; and (3) the belief that "to God all things are possible in a history that is fundamentally not a course of merely human events but always a dramatic interaction between God and men [*sic!*]."[83] As a consequence, Christians who may be associated with this ideal type maintain that a transformation of human and cultural realities is viable in the here and now.

A major problem with Niebuhr's argument is that he does not spell out what he means by transformation. In addition, the vagueness of his use of this notion leaves room for numerous—and even contradictory—understandings. As John Howard Yoder puts it,

83. Niebuhr, *Christ and Culture*, 191. I cite from the expanded fiftieth anniversary edition. Niebuhr's book was originally published in 1951.

> What H. Richard Niebuhr meant by "transformation" is so inadequately defined that its popularity with the readers seems to correlate with an assumption that it is more or less indistinguishable from our western doctrine of progress: i.e., that society moves forward from one transformation to the next, always getting better by coming nearer to what "culture" was indented to be.[84]

In the present discussion on transformation, I would like to go beyond Niebuhr's notion by proposing a "full-fledged" understanding of transformation. To make my case, I would propose that authentic transformation from a Christian perspective includes five dimensions. First, transformation is embedded in the vision of the inbreaking "kin-dom of God." The image of the kin-dom, which points to God's transforming reign, sheds valuable light on the concept under consideration here. As I argued in chapter 3, I prefer the term "kin-dom" to the more traditional "kingdom" as the former is a concept that better reflects the fundamentally embodied and relational nature of the reality it refers to, reminding us that God's inbreaking reign is *materialized* through interpersonal encounters.[85] As Ada Maria Isasi-Diaz contends, the term kin-dom of God "makes it clear that when the fullness of God becomes a day-to-day reality in the world at large, we will all be sisters and brothers—kin to each other."[86] While Orlando Costas uses the traditional language of "kingdom," the focus of his argument is in line with my own as he interprets this symbol as follows: "The Kingdom is an indication of God's transforming presence in history, . . . a symbol of God's transforming power, of his [*sic!*] determination to make 'all things new' (Rev 21:5)."[87] In this view, the kin-dom stands for a new order of life for both humankind and creation.

Christians of all traditions profess that this new order has been inaugurated through God's action in the life, ministry, death, and resurrection of Jesus Christ. This transformed reality, which is embodied in the symbol of the kin-dom, encompasses reconciliation between God, humankind, and the whole creation; liberation from the power and consequences of sin; and a hope for the final consummation of God's reign. As a reality that is *already* in effect, but *not yet* accomplished in full, it epitomizes both a

84. Yoder, "How H. Richard Niebuhr Reasoned," 53.

85. See Isasi-Diaz, "Solidarity," 31–40 and 303–5.

86. Isasi-Diaz, "Solidarity," 304.

87. Costas, *Integrity*, 8 and 6.

promise of what will be and a call to participate in the historical struggle for justice and peace.[88]

Second, from a Christian perspective, transformation has both personal and structural facets. This point is brought home emphatically by the 2012 WCC document *Theological Perspectives on* Diakonia *in the Twenty-First Century* that defines *diakonia* as "faith effecting change, *transforming people and situations so that God's reign may be real in the lives of all people*, in every here and now." *Diakonia* is construed as "an action in God's love [that] must strive *to transform people, systems and cultures*."[89] These formulations have a theological importance that goes beyond the field of *diakonia* alone. The call to personal transformation, that is known as *metanoia* in biblical tradition, lies at the heart of the gospel. At the very outset of his public ministry, Jesus of Nazareth called people to repent and turn their whole existence toward the reality of the coming reign of God (see Mark 1:15). Still, transformation also has a structural—or systemic—aspect that is not to be understood as a mere appendix to personal transformation but rather represents its equal counterpart. This dimension of transformation concentrates on the whole of humankind and creation that—by virtue of God's liberative grace and action—is striving to purify, perfect, and heal itself from the pernicious power of sin. Stephen Bevans and Roger Schroeder assert that the church plays a substantial role in this process as "the community of liberated humanity that finds its identity in its commitment to a liberated world." Among other things, this liberating process includes "confronting the evil of systems and structures, purifying and perfecting human culture, and working for reconciliation of the entire creation."[90] In a similar vein, Timothy Gorringe foregrounds the cultural, economic, and political factors of transformation when he inquires into the complexities of what he calls God's project of "furthering humanity," in other words, God's involvement in making human beings fully human.[91] To be sure, this endeavor is always to have both personal and structural aspects. The link between the personal and structural aspects of transformation are very forcefully expressed by Daniela Augustine, who says the following:

88. See Costas, *Integrity*, 6.

89. World Council of Churches, *Theological Perspectives*, III:16 and 17, respectively. Quoted in Lorke and Werner, *Ecumenical Visions*, 404, italics added in both citations.

90. Bevans and Schroeder, *Constants*, 71 and 72, respectively.

91. See Gorringe, *Furthering Humanity*, 17.

> Changing the world begins with transforming the circumstances of our immediate other. . . . The face of the other, the always unique, irreplaceable image of God, becomes for us the face of the world crying out for justice as access to life and flourishing. This is how the world is transfigured one person, one life at a time. . . . For the Christian, this transformation is nothing else but becoming a living extension of Christ.[92]

Third, transformation is profoundly linked with both the immanent and transcendent dimensions of human existence. To formulate this part of my argument, the observations made by David Ford in a book entitled *Self and Salvation: Being Transformed* are of much help. Recognizing the comprehensive and theologically integrative character of the symbol of salvation, Ford employs that image in order to envisage and make sense of the "transformation of selfhood."[93] Daniela Augustine adds an important insight to this discussion when she reminds us that the Hebrew Bible is concerned not only with salvation but also with redemption.[94] She refers to Jonathan Sacks, who distinguishes between the two concepts. In his understanding salvation means "the soul in relationship to God," while redemption highlights society "as a vehicle for the divine presence."[95] However, the transcendent and immanent nature of this transformation is also accentuated by Ford in the grand finale of his book when he turns to the image of feasting to sum up the core of the Christian vocation and mission: To be Christian means being invited to the feast in the kin-dom of God—or, in my formulation, to participate in our common life in God. Ford does not hesitate to express this point even more forcefully when he suggests that the "salvation of selves is in responding to that invitation."[96] In Ford's understanding, feasting may be viewed not only as a symbol of transformation, but also as an image that has the power to integrate both the immanent and transcendent dimensions of that reality. I will return to the theme of feast and discuss it in more detail in chapter 6.

Fourth, the Christian notion of transformation is distinctively "praxis-oriented." Even though this accent is most robustly affirmed in liberation

92. Augustine, *Spirit*, 107. Augustine refers to Greenberg, "Religion," 95, and Sacks, *Politics*, 269.

93. Ford, *Self and Salvation*, 1.

94. See Augustine, *Spirit*, 32.

95. Sacks, *To Heal*, 33.

96. Ford, *Self and Salvation*, 272.

theologies, including Latin American, Asian, feminist, black, and womanist schools of thought, praxis is a central concept wherever Christians acknowledge the significance of and need for social change. Praxis is a term that refers to "a combination of *practice* or action, and reflection on that action in a continuing spiral."[97] While having its roots in liberation theologies, praxis also has a lot of relevance in environments where disenfranchisement and oppression do not determine the situations in which people live and theologize. It can, for instance, be productively applied in the context of pastoral ministry done in a parish setting or in various types of chaplaincy. The Christian perspective on praxis is succinctly described by Bevans, who regards it as

> a three-step method of theological reflection that begins from practice, moves into a careful reflection on and analysis of this experience, of the culture in which it takes place and the Christian tradition which give it theological depth, and then moves to a reflection on the possible pastoral implications of that experience and on how might one act more effectively and faithfully in the future.[98]

When considering transformation through the hermeneutic lens of praxis, one becomes acutely aware that even though the realities of human embodied existence include much that is positive and desirable, they often need to be questioned, critiqued, and called to transformation.[99]

Fifth, the Christian conviction maintains that transformation is nurtured and perpetuated by transformative spirituality. In some theological—or more concretely, missiological—discourse, this notion refers to "the core unifying and giving focus to all creative endeavors striving towards the transformation one pursues."[100] Moreover, it also represents the energy that enables and empowers all such endeavors. In this respect, Desmond Tutu speaks of "a spirituality of transformation." In a societal context, such a spirituality takes seriously all members of society, including political

97. Bevans, "Contextual Methods," 16 (italics in the original). Bevans wittily reminds us that praxis "is *not* merely a fancy name for practice!"

98. Bevans, "Contextual Methods," 16. Bevans draws from Whitehead and Whitehead, *Method*, 3–99.

99. See Bevans, "Contextual Methods," 17.

100. Bargár, *Narrative*, 124. To give just one example from the missiological field, I would remark that spirituality plays a major role in the theologizing of South African missiologists J. N. J. (Klippies) Kritzinger and Willem Saayman as they describe a hermeneutic tool called the "praxis matrix" in their book *David J. Bosch*, 4–5.

opponents, former oppressors, present economic exploiters, abusers, torturers, and enemies.[101] For a more nuanced take on transformative spirituality one can usefully turn to the 2013 WCC affirmation on mission and evangelism entitled *Together towards Life*. This statement includes a special subsection on transformative spirituality which contends that "spirituality gives our lives their deepest meaning. It stimulates, motivates, and gives dynamism to life's journey. It is energy for life in its fullness and calls for a commitment to resist all forces, powers, and systems which deny, destroy, and reduce life."[102]

This citation suggests at least two important points for our consideration. First, it describes spirituality in terms of "energy for life in its fullness," which is a direct reference to John 10:10, which interprets Jesus's coming to mean that God's creation "may have life, and have it abundantly" (John 10:10 NRSV). Second, the document "calls for a commitment" to resisting all life-denying structures. In contrast to the common perception that spirituality is related to passivity, quietude, and noninterference, *TTL* presents it as an active agent of transformation on both personal and societal levels. In particular, it affirms that such spirituality calls for the transformation of structures, systems, and values in various realms of human life, including the fields of economy, politics, and religion (art. 30). I would suggest that transformative spirituality, understood in a Christian sense, is the driving force behind human involvement in God's transformative work with creation. In sum, it can be argued that transformation, kin-dom rooted; encompassing the personal and structural aspects; involving the immanent and transcendent dimensions; praxis-oriented; and motivated and sustained by transformative spirituality,

> finds its expression in human participation in the activity of the Spirit in the world, the activity that involves a creative process of bringing forth non-being into being, death to life. Following the example of their Creator, human beings are called to the particular creativity with which each is gifted. Spirituality construed in this way is necessarily transformative, since it seeks to change everything which suppresses and negates life both at the personal and structural level.[103]

101. Tutu, *Rainbow People*, especially chapter 6.

102. World Council of Churches, *Together towards Life*, art. 29. Hereafter referred to as *TTL*.

103. Bargár, *Narrative*, 129. The human agency in the transformation of creation is also recognized by Augustine, *Spirit*, 33.

Depicting Transformation in a Post-Christian World

Now that we have explored the theological aspects of human embodied existence vis-à-vis the subject of transformation as the ultimate goal toward which the whole creation is heading, let us consider one specific example of cinematographic depiction of transformation in what can be referred to as a post-Christian world. In his 2014 film *Calvary*, the writer-director John Michael McDonagh probes into such aspects of transformation as reconciliation, forgiveness, self-sacrifice, and faith in the context of contemporary western Europe.[104]

Calvary follows the story of James, a middle-aged Roman Catholic priest in a countryside parish at the coast of Ireland. James only became priest after his wife had passed away, the fact that substantially complicates his relationship to his only daughter, Fiona. Fiona perceives his decision as a betrayal, feeling ever more estranged from her father. James is having a hard time not only with his family but also in relation to his parishioners. Regardless of whether they go to church or not, the vast majority of them look at James with more or less unconcealed contempt, scoffingly tolerating him as a prehistoric cultural fossil. He does not find much support in his younger colleague, Leary, either, as the latter is apparently a man without any deeper knowledge or personal integrity. And yet, Father James does not give up. He keeps on celebrating mass, administering the sacraments, preaching, visiting people from the parish, and calling them to repentance. He does not do that in a patronizing manner as one who has all the answers and pretends to know what is best for others. On the contrary, James is well aware of his limited knowledge, skills, and powers. He remains a representative of the church, which he serves faithfully, while being unable to identify himself with it completely. He is a child of this time, firmly rooted in contemporary culture and society, although he cannot concur with all its values, beliefs, and convictions. Father James is like a colossus bearing on his shoulders the double burden of the church and the world; he feels the gravity of this burden but also the responsibility that he has been endowed with. His face is the face of the Christ for the twenty-first century—or, more precisely, the face of the Christ who can appeal to the contemporary European. Weathered by age and experiences, tired, and wrinkled, his face is at the same time uncondemning and accepting. James may be laconic,

104. For further information on the film, see "Calvary," IMDb, accessed December 27, 2021, https://www.imdb.com/title/tt2234003/?ref_=fn_al_tt_1.

at times even harsh or vulgar, and with an idiosyncratic sense of humor but people always come first in all he does. His spirituality can be referred to as a spirituality of witnessing presence and solidarity—a transformative spirituality indeed.

A peripety comes right in the first scene when one of James's parishioners confides to James in a confessional that he had been sexually abused by a priest for several years during his childhood. He does not ask James for absolution or help. He simply informs him that exactly one week from today, next Sunday, he is going to kill James. To kill a good and innocent priest—since James is commonly regarded by people as such—is something unusual, thence meaningful, as the mysterious man believes.

Even though James is concerned and spends time thinking about the threat, it does not lead him away from his daily tasks. He dedicates his time to his daughter, who comes to stay with him for a few days after her unsuccessful suicide attempt. He also makes himself available to be with other people in his community: the promiscuous and self-destructive Veronica, in whose case it is not clear whether she is abused by her husband or lover; the aging and lonely writer contemplating suicide; the young adult Milo, who wants to cope with a lack of sexual experience by joining the army; the rich and nihilistic businessman Michael, showing no apparent interest in life nor a sense for values; the cynical medical doctor and pronounced atheist Frank, who engages in recreational drug use and female company; or the police inspector Stanton, with a proclivity for male prostitutes.

Symbolically, the period of seven days given to James alludes to the Holy Week, marking the last week of Jesus's earthly life, as rendered by the gospels and church tradition. During these days, James, like Jesus, walks toward his personal Calvary. And also, like Jesus, James undergoes a process of deep personal transformation in the course of these days, transforming some of the people around him along the way. James is profoundly influenced by his encounter with Teresa, a young Italian woman, whose husband was just killed in a car accident on their trip to Ireland. For James, Teresa represents an embodiment of the faith that he himself professes—a faith that is not simply meant as a way to chase away the fear of death. Rather, this kind of faith empowers one to go on even despite the circumstances, finding love and joy in everyday life. Teresa also stands close to James in his personal "Gethsemane," at the airport on his way to Dublin. As he wants to run away from everything, Teresa inspires him to persevere and return to his "stations of the cross."

The relationship between James and Fiona also undergoes a significant transformation. After many years of mutual misunderstanding and alienation, the father and the daughter are able to truly meet each other and become close again, thanks to their conversations in the confessional, at the seashore, and, especially, over the telephone on the last Sunday morning. Their mutual forgiveness and reconciliation both symbolically and actually enables life to go on, giving it a new quality. In addition, James transforms the lives of some other characters during his "Holy Week," too. On the last Sunday morning, there is a meeting at a truly deep human level between James and the old writer. The film depicts this by the writer for the first time addressing the priest by first name, instead of the conventional "Father." The possibility for a new beginning also emerges in the case of businessman Michael, who makes a sincere, albeit not ecclesiastically formal "confession" to James on that morning. And yet, this possibility remains very fragile and one is left wondering whether Michael is really going to have enough strength to transform his life since James cannot keep his promise and call him back anymore.

However, the lives of the majority of the film characters remain apparently untransformed by James's ministry. In this respect, too, *Calvary* represents a realistic portrait of the church and its mission. James does not succeed in appealing to everyone. Still, through his sincerity, compassion, and willingness to listen, think, and be changed, he can challenge people to face their *conditio humana* and call them to reflection—or, theologically speaking, repentance. And as we have already noted with reference to Jürgen Moltmann, a transformed and sustainable future is not possible without repentance.[105] It is praiseworthy that the film takes seriously the fact that this ideal destiny of the church does not represent the whole story; in the background, there is constantly present the ominous shadow of sexual abuse scandals. Father James does not know how to go about it, nor does he attempt to brush it under the rug.

Father James can be interpreted, I would suggest, as a Christ figure. This interpretation is supported not only by his conviction that each life is of an ultimate value or that no human being is a lost case, thus deserving a second—or a third—chance. It also lies in the overall stylization of his character as an innocent, "perfect" sacrifice. My point can be understood in line with what Daniela Augustine means by the term "the saints' metanoic

105. See Moltmann, *Creating*, 15.

ethos." Resisting the allurement of scapegoating, one is hereby presenting oneself as a living sacrifice. Augustine explains,

> The saints' metanoic ethos is not generic or anonymously collective but deeply personal—acutely aware of one's known and unknown (intentional and unintentional) contributions to the perpetuation of systemic injustice, accepting the blame for it, internalizing and not externalizing the responsibility for evil.[106]

Such a living sacrifice should not necessarily or even desirably be seen in the sense that James is devoid of any imperfections, errors, and weaknesses. Quite the contrary, the film distinctively portrays him as a broken and wounded person who is struggling with his own problems and doubts. Nevertheless, James is also a person open to repentance and conversion; he lets himself be challenged by the reality that transcends him. Featuring profound integrity, his faith gives him strength to pursue his human quest and calling, even at the expense of ultimate self-sacrifice. Like Jesus, it is his faith, integrity, and commitment that eventually bring him to a "cross."

Calvary provides a theologically thought-provoking moment in its virtual identification of "crucifixion" with "resurrection." More precisely, the "crucifixion"—depicted as what I would call a "waterfront Calvary"—is all that the film shows directly. There is no scene or image explicitly illustrating a "resurrection." Nevertheless, the latter is present implicitly—in both what precedes James's Calvary and the very last scene of the film. For all its fragility and secular nature, this scene is, paradoxically, very powerful and impressive. It embodies the true climax of the film: the inbreaking of transcendence into the everyday reality; a glimpse of grace in the context of existence under the *conditio humana*. Although the tenor of the film is not optimistic, it is, I would contend, illuminated by hope. It is a hope that transformation is possible, meaningful, and cannot be defeated even by death. Moreover, *Calvary* gives a forceful expression to the message that such a transformation always takes place in relation to, together with, and for the sake of the other. The subject of relationality will be explored in the following chapter.

106. Augustine, *Spirit*, 206.

5

Relationality

No Life without the Other

When theologically reflecting on the central significance of relationality for human existence and our common life in God, it may be useful to opt for a *via negativa* to underline the point. In other words, to show the (im)possibility of being human in a world devoid of meaningful interpersonal relationships. *Borgman*, the 2013 film by the Dutch director and screenwriter Alex van Warmerdam, can provide a lens to highlight the issue in question.[1]

The beginning of the film does not differ much from a regular thriller movie. A small group of armed men, including a Catholic priest, enters a forest to look for disguised underground hideouts with the obvious intention to eliminate their inhabitants. One of the "underground people" manages to escape in the nick of time, warning two of his fellows along the way. The refugee, a man with the unkempt visage of a homeless person, subsequently comes to a town, where he rings the doorbell at a stylish and evidently luxurious residence with garages, adjacent buildings, and a vast garden. The vagrant introduces himself as Anton Breskens from Flanders to the man who opens the door and whom the viewer comes to know as Richard. Breskens asks Richard to have a bath in his house. After being turned down very briskly, Breskens does not want to give up easily, insisting that he knows Richard's wife, Marina. That is when Richard loses his

1. For further information on the film, see "Borgman," IMDb, accessed December 27, 2021, https://www.imdb.com/title/tt1954315/?ref_=fn_al_tt_1.

temper and whomps Breskens brutally. However, after Richard leaves for work, Marina takes pity on the beaten Breskens, treating his wounds, inviting him to the house, and offering him a bath and a meal. Nevertheless, the one-off help is extended and Marina allows Breskens to live in their small garden house—without Richard knowing about it. And here is when the classic thriller ends and *Borgman* begins—a film that does not respect traditional genre classification and film conventions, even transcending the boundaries of logic. The film production is rather minimalistic. Cinematography, music, and setting are utilitarian, their main function being to highlight the story. The story itself does not follow narrative procedures and should more appropriately be conceived in terms of a nonstory. The film is shot in a detached and stern manner. The viewer can practically relate to no character in the film, with a possible exception of the hunted bum Breskens at the beginning. However, even this aspect changes abruptly and radically when the poor Anton Breskens becomes Borgman the gardener after the reverse in the story described above.

Borgman can be interpreted through a structuralist lens as the struggle between system and chaos. The first pole, system, is represented by the Schendel family—Richard, Marina, and their three children. Their life epitomizes the prosperous and wealthy West and the values related with this civilizational realm and economic system. Richard has a well-paying position with a transnational corporation which permits the whole family to enjoy the affluent upper middle class existence. Marina spends her time at home pursuing her artistic work. The children are looked after by the babysitter Stine and the extensive property by the gardener. However, this seeming idyl is violated by the invasion of chaos embodied by Breskens/Borgman. His very presence as well as weird behavior (for example, he tells the children strange fairy tales; he walks around the house naked; mysterious greyhounds appear in the house after his arrival) unmasks the fragility and unsustainability of the status quo, even going as far as to subvert the foundations of the system in which the Schendels live and benefit from. What is at stake here is the possibility of an authentic relationship with the other. While the (global neoliberal) system presupposes various kinds of relationships, it at the same time negates those that are based on mutuality and gratuitousness—the relationships that view the other as a gift. This interpretation is also supported by certain motifs that appear throughout the film and refer to social ills. Admittedly the most obvious of them is the issue of homelessness. Breskens initially wins the favor of not only Marina but also the viewers who can relate to her having pity on the poor vagrant. However, on the other hand, both Marina and the viewers subconsciously feel that her act of mercy is, first and foremost, an expression of her own guilt originating in her own privileged life vis-à-vis the poverty and destitution of the fellow human other. Homelessness certainly represents a trauma in the collective psyche of the West. It reminds us of our failure to relate meaningfully to a fellow human being who can offer us no economic or social benefit in return. And yet, it also confronts us with a challenge to recognize the other as a bearer of God's image and affirm her or his human embodied existence in the quest for our common life in God.

The contraposition between the affluency of the West and the poverty in the rest of the world features several times in the film. During one emotionally charged scene Richard has to soothe apparently unreasonably upset Marina by saying that it is not a fault of their own that they are rich—the West prospers and that is simply the way that the things are. In another scene, impassioned Marina rebukes her daughter after she found the girl's destroyed teddy bear. Rather inappropriately with regard to the girl's age, Marina holds a heated speech about children in poor countries having to work long hours in terrible conditions, while children in the West getting everything they can think of. Another social ill thematized in *Borgman* is racism. When hiring a new gardener, Richard on the spot turns down an applicant who is a person of color, saying that the position has already been filled, only to accept the white Borgman in whom he does not recognize the previously shaggy and ragged Breskens. Rather than relating to the human other for her or his innate dignity—or, theologically speaking, her or his createdness in the image of God—the (neoliberal) system we live in provides us with the lens through which we see the other as a sum of skin color, a clean shave, and decent clothes.

While this socioeconomic critical interpretation is undoubtedly legitimate, *Borgman* can also be interpreted in yet another way, and more radically. The other hermeneutic option focuses on the irrationality of evil that dominates in the film. It is buttressed by the almost apocalyptic words from the opening about the enigmatic creatures that "came down to Earth to replenish their ranks." Clearly evocative of biblical discourse, it is in line with this dictum that Borgman step by step calls on his companions to assist him with his "project." Still, the viewer will be searching in vain for any intention or goal in their action. Their only objective is the pursuit and spreading of evil. Here, it should be noted that evil afflicts people regardless of any logical key, regardless of their presumed guilt or innocence. Those who suffer or die simply happen to find themselves in the wrong place at the wrong time. It is truly *ab-solute* evil—that is to say, evil existing independently from and not in relation to other entities. It is evil devoid of relations, bonds, preferences, and interests; evil in its pure form. An example of what impact such evil has on human existence is represented by the babysitter Stine and all three children. Completely disregarding their previous lives and the relationships that have until then provided guidance for them, they set forth on a "journey" with Borgman and his comrades. Under the influence of evil, interhuman relationships are eroded and annihilated. Where evil reigns, there is no space for the meaningful relating to the other.

A horrendous illustration of the irrationality of evil, as depicted by *Borgman*, is the fact that Richard loses his family even though he sincerely cares for them. He shows authentic interest in his wife, Marina, and wants to spend time with her. He reads fairy tales to his children before they go to sleep in the evening. While it is necessary to underline that Richard is no typical positive character, the destiny that his family prepares for him through Borgman and company foregrounds the cruelty and irrationality of evil, evoking in the viewer a deep sense of uneasiness. This sense of uneasiness is even intensified by the fact that the characters in the film must freely allow, yes, actively invite evil to their lives. Marina begs Breskens/Borgman on her knees not to leave but continue living in their house. Later on, she comes to Borgman saying that she wants her husband dead. Similarly, the babysitter Stine willingly comes to visit one of Borgman's companions in the garden house after which a mysterious change occurs in her personality and behavior. From the perspective of feminist criticism one can observe and, at the same time, object that it is always a woman who serves as the entrance point for evil in the film. Based on what the film actually portrays, however, one can only speculate whether this is intentional or merely accidental.

What can be suggested with certainty, though, is that the motif of one's own guilt, as portrayed by the film, is crucial to allow evil enter one's family, community, and society. Again, this is most obvious in the character of Marina. Her unprocessed feeling of guilt becomes apparent in her encounter with the vagrant as well as the moments which remind Marina of her own privileged life in contrast to poverty in the world. As such, Marina's feeling of guilt effectively serves as the trigger for the whole bizarre series of events, thus also allowing evil to enter the life of her family. Ultimately, the film points out the tragedy of human existence devoid of mutuality in interpersonal relationships. Evil disguised in the mysterious and unknown unmasks conventional family relationships as superficial and fragile. And the human being lacking a web of meaningful and authentic relationships is left at the mercy of evil.

Borgman is bereft of any sense of redemption or mercy. The film does not offer any consolation or hope. While the open ending leaves space for several interpretations, they all in fact have to take seriously that evil will go on multiplying and spreading. Moreover, the depressive and hopeless end is even intensified by the clear message that no one is going to survive but absolute evil. *Borgman*'s vision is one of a world deprived of redemption, deprived of hope—without an authentic relationship with the other. Thus, the film provides a powerful and suggestive cinematographic expression of the idea that human existence is not possible apart from the other. From a Christian theological perspective, Daniela Augustine formulates this idea as follows:

> Each human being stands in the face of the other, imprinted with the same ontological origin and telos—Christ himself—the beginning and the end of creation (Rev 21:6). In this sanctified/ deified perspective, the face of the other meets us as the future of the world—as the full potentiality of the fullness of life more abundant in, with, and through God. Therefore, there is no future, no salvation, no world without the other.[2]

Having used the cinematographic example of *Borgman* to show, negatively, what the consequence is when human existence lacks relationality, I intend to explore in this chapter relationality as a fundamental aspect of human existence. The guiding argument here will be that being human, from a Christian perspective, means being in relationships.

Relationality: Theological Considerations

As we have already said in a different context in chapter 2, each human being is at each stage of their life embedded in a complex and multilayered web of relationships with other human beings and the world around them. The 2005 Faith and Order study document *Christian Perspectives on Theological Anthropology* suggests that these relationships are established

2. Augustine, *Spirit*, 138.

and maintained through "provisional, embodied, contingent, meaning-producing interactions with significant others" (art. 70).[3] On the sociopolitical level, these interactions represent what Charles Taylor refers to as "social imaginaries"—that is, a hermeneutical framework which enables us to consider our lived reality through the lens of categories such as belonging, culture, a sense of history, place, future, and self-determination.[4] Alternatively, Agustín Fuentes's proposal involves considering the simultaneous dynamics of biological and cultural factors relevant in the process of being and becoming human. This process is necessarily relational because humans are fundamentally dependent on each other for physiological, psychological, and social reasons.[5] Moreover, these interactions also have a transcendental dimension as the dynamics described above are relevant for the human relationship to God as the ultimate other. A logical conclusion is, therefore, that one's relationship to both the human other and God are contingent and context-related. Situated in a concrete historical setting, one's identity, story, and place within a tradition are always shaped in relation to the identity, story, and tradition of the other.[6]

And yet, contingency does not represent the only or final feature of human relationality. There is also a decisive theological aspect to it that can be robustly expressed through the reference to the concept of *imago Dei*. Here, the ultimate paradigm is the operating dynamics in both the immanent and economic Trinity. The triune God as the Father, the Son, and the Holy Spirit relate to each other to create the perfect fellowship of love, acceptance, inclusion, and creativity. Unable to remain contained within Godself, this communion "overflows" with meaning and potential to include God's creation in this process, inviting it "to join a fellowship of souls and bodies on a journey toward joyful consummation."[7] Since the triune God is fundamentally relational, humans—as carriers of God's image—too are relational beings. As *CPTA* affirms, human embodied existence as radically relational takes place within the framework of dignity, potentiality, and creativity, on the one hand, and creatureliness, finitude,

3. I cite from Faith and Order Commission, *Christian Perspectives*. Hereafter referred to as *CPTA*.

4. See Taylor, *Modern Social Imaginaries*. See also Bretherton, *Christ*, 94 and 308, and Ward, *Cultural Transformation*, 119–47.

5. See Fuentes, *Race*, 29.

6. See also Henriksen, *Religious Pluralism*, 36–37.

7. Bargár, "Toward Comm/unity," 236.

and vulnerability, on the other hand (see art. 81). This twofold dynamic is beautifully portrayed in Wim Wenders's film *Wings of Desire* (1987).[8] Even though the film does not thematize transcendence in the sense of God, it is clear that the film characters, most notably the angels Damiel and Cassiel and the trapeze artist Marion, strive to give their lives a meaning that goes beyond the constraints of biological existence. The film implies that such an act of transcendence is impossible within "eternity" as a hermeneutic and existential frame of reference. To pursue transcendence, the finitude of human embodied existence is necessary. The positive dimension of human finitude is also brought home forcefully by Antonio Sison, who asserts that an affirmatively oriented theology of creation "recognizes that humanity is endowed with a finite character and it is precisely within this finitude that humanity finds its deepest meaning."[9] Damiel could begin pursuing the meaning of his life with dignity, potentiality, and creativity only after he had become a full-fledged human being with everything that human existence entails, including limitations, such as finitude. In the perspective of *Wings of Desire*, it is only this kind of existence that enables one to pursue meaning and transcendence when relating to the other.

Daniela Augustine offers a fascinating attempt to interpret this two-fold dynamic—as described by *CPTA* and artistically depicted by *Wings of Desire*—using the symbolism of the divine face. Because God has decided to share God's face with the created and finite human being, divinity in its fullness can dwell in a bodily form. Furthermore, God's own existence becomes intimately and intrinsically linked with the existence of creation. By implication, creation now can, for its part, partake in the very life of God. That is, in essence, what I have been in this book referring to as our common life in God. By learning to share the face of God with others through deeds aimed at authentically relating to them, "the human being becomes like God in relation to all of the created cosmos."[10] To be truly human, therefore, one is invited to relate both to God and the fellow human being. That is how God and God's cause effectively enter creation. Jonathan Sacks puts it poetically when he says, "God speaks where two persons turn

8. The German name of the film is *Der Himmel über Berlin* (The Heaven over Berlin). For further information on the film, see "Der Himmel über Berlin," IMDb, accessed December 27, 2021, https://www.imdb.com/title/tt0093191/?ref_=nv_sr_srsg_0.

9. Sison, *World Cinema*, 33.

10. See Augustine, *Spirit*, 26–27, the quotation is at 27.

their face to one another in love, embrace, generosity, and care."[11] On the contrary, if violence against and oppression of the other prevails, according to the theology of the face, the failure and refusal to acknowledge the face of God in the face of the other results in one's own dehumanization and alienation. To put it positively, recognizing the divine face in the face of the other represents, as Daniela Augustine phrases it, "a liturgical anamnesis of paradise," discovering interhuman relationality as a means for being in communion with God (Matt 25:31–46).[12]

David Ford too turns to the image of the face to make his case for the transformation and consummation of human existence, as symbolized by feasting.[13] He employs several steps to shed light on his argument. First, any feast or party is necessarily rooted in the dynamics of "facing" each other. People need to get together and face one another in order to feast and celebrate. Second, this necessity is intrinsically related to a second aspect of feasting—namely, the presence of the other. Being there with the other—talking, sitting around a table, laughing, singing, and dancing—is a key precondition for, and an essential element of, feasting. Usually, however, there are also various types of food, beverages, and other pleasures for both body and soul at feasts. These make us aware—and that is the third point—of our human corporeality. As I have contended in chapter 2, being human means not only *being in a body*, but also *being a body*. As such, "the other is a particular body whom one is able to face and whose presence one is blessed to enjoy in the event of feasting."[14] Finally, this concretization of the other has the potential to overcome "the idolatrous power of death [that is] linked to its faceless generality and thus, endows the notion of transformation with a robust transcendental orientation."[15] While the theme of feasting will be discussed in detail in chapter 6, here it is important to note that the image of facing represents an important concept for accentuating a theologically relevant idea that authentic—that is, life-affirming and death-denying—relationality is always particularly-oriented, embodied, and contextual.

However, it is characteristic for the broken nature of the reality which people inhabit that the gift of relationality is only too frequently crippled by various undesirable tendencies. Alienation, often accompanied by the

11. Sacks, *To Heal*, 54.

12. See Augustine, *Spirit*, 66.

13. See Ford, *Self and Salvation*, 272.

14. Bargár, *Narrative*, 123.

15. Ford, *Self and Salvation*, 63.

delusion of self-sufficiency, is one of them. As *CPTA* has it, this can possibly result in "the breakdown of authentic relationality and community" (art. 30). Here, people become entrapped in a false idea of their being autonomous monads that can exercise their independence from others. In his 2013 film, *Her*, that we have already examined in chapter 2, the writer-director Spike Jonze succeeds in very persuasively portraying a world that shows the alienation of people from one another as well as from one's own existence and its meaning.[16] One could say that Theodore, the main character, virtually embodies alienation. He lets his life flow, apparently without taking any deeper interest in it; with a sad face and an absent-minded expression, he is firmly self-isolated in a cage of his memories that serve him both as a tool of self-torture and a tranquilizer. One by one, he cuts off all his bonds to the presence, his friends and acquaintances. He does not seem to possess necessary energy and skills to establish and build new relationships, as evident from a blind-date scene. Another character, Theodore's old friend Amy, realizes after separation from her husband, Charles, that she has lived according to the expectations and wishes of the people around her, being actually estranged from the true purpose of her existence.

However, the theme of alienation as introduced by *Her* also has a broader social dimension. For instance, it is important to note that Theodore makes his living as a ghost-writer of personal letters for other people. This can be interpreted as another example of alienation and an unauthentic way of being at the societal level. People are not able or willing to write letters for their beloved ones themselves but hire a professional to do it for them. They do not open up to their neighbor, to the other. As a result, their existence suffers, losing the hallmark of integrity and genuineness. An abyss emerges between one and one's neighbor. Another example of alienation in the film is represented by Theodore's, obviously regular, engagement in no-obligation virtual sex via online chat applications. This way of sexual gratification does not challenge one to work on building a mutual relationship. On the contrary, it encapsulates one behind the walls of one's own microcosmos, to a ghetto of singular anonymity. Moreover, as becomes clear from the scene in which Theodore is "enjoying" a sexual adventure with a woman chatting under the nickname "SexyKitten," the degree of alienation can be even further deepened through a kind of fetishism, in that particular scene epitomized by the practice of "choking with

16. For further information on the film, see "Her," IMDb, accessed December 27, 2021, https://www.imdb.com/title/tt1798709/?ref_=nv_sr_srsg_0.

the dead cat." As a consequence, a fellow human being becomes nothing more but an object, a means to indulge one's own needs and desires. The film further highlights the theme of alienation visually, by the way it works with the setting. The people in the streets or other public areas whom the viewer can see on the screen are hardly ever engaged in conversation or other social activities. They are mostly individuals absently gazing ahead or, alternatively, on the screen of their mobile devices. Based on this analysis, I would contend that *Her* finds the root cause of alienation in the inability to establish and further develop an authentic and meaningful relationship between two human beings, between "I" and "Thou." Virtually all main characters in the film have dysfunctional or nonexisting relationships, the fact that alienates them not only from others but also from themselves and the meaning of their existence.

In spite of these counter-relational tendencies and circumstances that often have the upper hand in our lives, I would contend, it is interdependence—and not independence—that repeatedly proves to be the viable *modus operandi* for being human. As we have seen, the argument for interdependence can be made from both sociological (i.e., human embeddedness in a web of relationships) and theological (i.e., human createdness in the image of the triune God) positions. Any efforts aimed at pursuing independence from the other appear to be doomed for failure, with estrangement from oneself and the other being the necessary prize to be paid for the obsession with individualism.

Another type of negation of relationality can be found in what I would refer to as "identitary temptations." This phenomenon can be described as an intentional effort to highlight, and even absolutize, one or several of the multiple human identity markers, such as race, gender, sexuality, ethnicity, religion, culture, nation, etc., at the expense of the balance with the other identity markers. The declared aim is to mold an identity that is believed to fortify the self-confidence of one's own grouping. The actual outcome, however, is often an imaginary construct that positions itself in stark opposition, or even open hostility, over against a certain "them." András Máté-Tóth refers to this phenomenon as "tribalism," contending that it represents, at its core, "a cry because of the wounded collective identity."[17] Whether one uses the term tribalism or identitary temptations, the main point is that the fear of the unknown (xenophobia) and an undue concern for one's identity can here produce a dangerous explosive mix which appeals to the human

17. Máté-Tóth, "Wounded Words," 365.

"darkest instincts" and hateful attitudes. While it might originally be meant as a protective mechanism to provide guidance for living in a complicated world, it easily turns into a rhetoric—and practice—of hatred and even violence. In its religio-political and religio-nationalist forms, it frequently exploits religious symbolism to pursue political ends. Such development has recently been evident in many parts around the globe.

When theologically reflecting on the phenomenon of identitary temptations, one should have in mind a twofold objective. It is crucial not only to counter these temptations, but also to encourage and nurture the relational nature of human embodied existence. There are a number of axioms to be considered. First, Christians need to permanently remind themselves—and invite others to also consider this conviction—that human identity is above all established in our being created in the image of God. Even though the other identity markers may be helpful and invaluable, they necessarily remain auxiliary with respect to this primary factor. The practical consequences following from this core belief should then include the acknowledgment that Christians as well as other people of faith or no faith adhere to certain traditions, find themselves in particular contexts, and belong to specific communities and societies. Such a realization begs critical theological and missiological examination of multiple aspects that constitute one's milieu and "habitus."[18] Following from this recognition, then, Christians are called in their praxis to discern and keep in creative tension different human identity markers to prevent any endeavors aimed at creating exclusive, totalizing, and oppressive identities. On the contrary, Christian calling lies in fostering the God-desired diversity of human identities.

These considerations lead to my final point, namely, that it might be useful to interpret this phenomenon through the lens of resilience, the notion we have already introduced in chapter 2. Robert Schreiter suggests that resilience—in contrast to resistance—makes us sensitive to the fact that overcoming injustice and other consequences of sin, such as identitary temptations, does not represent an end to one's striving for human and creational flourishing.[19] Thus, resilience highlights the fact that our embodied existence is enabled by the grace of God who relates to humankind and the whole creation. Furthermore, it reminds us of our calling to relate

18. The term "habitus" has been coined by Pierre Bourdieu. It represents an attempt to account for one's socialization to think, feel, and act in certain ways. See Bourdieu, *Outline*, 86.

19. See Schreiter, "Locating," 342. See also Sedmak, *Capacity*.

to others, especially the poor and marginalized, in solidarity and respect. In sum, I would argue that to accept the invitation to be a part of God's story with creation, aimed toward its transformation and consummation, means becoming deeply and authentically involved in a rich meshwork of relationships with God, other human beings regardless of their religious, ethnic, cultural, and any other affiliations, and the nonhuman creation.

This engagement in relating to the other should necessarily be—in both its essence and practical realization—dialogical yet transformative. Theologically, it reflects God's way of engaging with and relating to creation. God encounters us as a word, an appeal, an invitation, a call(ing), while at the same time waiting for and listening to our response. Stephen Bevans and Roger Schroeder have now classically formulated this emphasis in their theology of mission for today known as "prophetic dialogue."[20] This approach takes embodiment seriously. It meets people as embodied beings "where they are," in the situations of their daily existence. It listens to and seeks to learn from their wisdom and culture, acknowledging the validity and relevance of their experience. At the same time, however, it also seeks to "call people beyond," to conversion (metanoia) and deep transformation.[21] In its prophetic focus, it desires and actively strives for justice and peace for the life of creation. To pursue this aim, it nurtures a special imagination for the kin-dom of God. In other words, prophetic dialogue as a way of relating to the other fundamentally takes place within the field of the "already" and "not yet" of God's reign, inviting and waiting for a response from people as autonomous, albeit interdependent, characters in God's story and agents of God's mission.

Perhaps one of the most captivating scriptural expressions of what I have explicated here as an accent on the dialogical-transformative aspect of relating to the other can be found in the book of Micah. Here, the prophet proclaims, "He has told you, O mortal, what is good; and what does the LORD require of you but to do justice, and to love kindness, and to walk humbly with your God?" (Mic 6:8 NRSV) The prophet views the human task as the pursuit of justice, kindness/mercy, and presence of and partnership with the Lord—suggestively formulated in the call to "walk humbly" with one's God. While Emmanuel Levinas perceives justice simply as "the relation to the other," Jacques Derrida interprets it as a constant

20. See Bevans and Schroeder, *Constants*, 348–95. For a book-length treatment of the topic, see Bevans and Schroeder, *Prophetic Dialogue*.

21. See Bevans and Schroeder, *Constants*, 285.

pursuit that requires people "to reinvent in a singular situation a new just relationship."[22] As a result, the constant pursuit of justice represents "a creative, socio-transformative work of building conditions for mediating relational healing."[23]

Alternatively, the Hebrew concept of *shalom* provides a useful way to account for the intrinsic relationship between peace, kindness/mercy, and justice that Micah invites people to pursue.[24] Some authors, therefore, interpret shalom in terms of "just peace" because it involves a twofold dynamic: it is a vision according to which not only the malign realities of life, such as war, poverty, famine, greed, exploitation, discrimination, and oppression, must cease but also the desirable realities of what can be referred to as "new creation" or kin-dom of God, such as dignity, equality, sharing, kindness, harmony, and health, must reign.[25]

Relating to the other, then, presupposes a nexus characterized by several dimensions, including "right motivation"; the awareness of responsibility and duties (rather than rights); the struggle against forms of domination and oppression that violate relationality; and the process of correction of injustice through liberation from oppression.[26] Accordingly, while accentuating both responsibility and control in navigating within the complex meshwork of relationships one is engaged in, the outlined approach is also identified by reciprocity and interdependence in social relations.[27] Such reciprocity and interdependence can also be referred to as mutuality. It is this aspect that we are going to consider next.

Mutuality: Keeping Diversity and Unity Together

As suggested above, in my understanding, "mutuality" constitutes the reciprocal side of human relationality. Yet, it would be a mistake to understand this notion merely in terms of cause-and-effect dynamics applied to

22. See Levinas, *Totality*, 89, and Derrida, "Villanova Roundtable," 17.

23. See Augustine, *Spirit*, 169. In a similar vein, John de Gruchy interprets forgiveness—the first step toward reconciliation and means of restoring justice—as "a creative act" and its agents as "true artists." See de Gruchy, *Reconciliation*, 179.

24. See Tizon, "Preaching," 25, and De Chickera, "Just Peace," 182.

25. See De Chickera, "Just Peace," 182.

26. See Lebacqz, *Justice*, 154–60.

27. On the theme of responsibility and control in human interaction, see Harrison, *Making*, 253.

the interpersonal realm. In addition to reciprocity, mutuality also implies togetherness, interdependence, solidarity, and sharing. It points out to the fact that an entity is always greater than the sum of its parts. This dynamic is a result of the multidirectional character of interpersonal interactions as much as the engagement of the other as a unique and not to be taken for granted factor.

The accent on diversity is imperative for this particular way of thinking. To illustrate an essential Christian conviction about the plentiful diversity of creation, including humankind, as desired by God, *CPTA* seeks help from the poetic language that we can find in Psalms: "O LORD, how manifold are your works! In wisdom you have made them all; the earth is full of your creatures" (Ps 104:24 NRSV). The document affirms this diversity which is not only intrinsic to God's plan for the entire creation but also reflects a variety of contexts, histories, and experiences, implying that otherness is not only possible but also necessary (see *CPTA*, art. 40–43). One encounters the other as truly and undeniably other. As we have seen earlier in chapter 2, the affirmation of diversity helps us prevent the absolutization of reality and ways of being in the world. Conversely, we as Christians are invited to approve of the claim that to live in this world means to be interdependent from and in relation to others in their diversity. Then—and only then—can something new and positive arise, when free, though not self-enclosed, subjects support and nourish each other. That is what I refer to as mutuality.

In order to be capable of pursuing mutuality truly and effectively and to avoid falling in the trap of monadism and detachment in which an overemphasis on diversity and difference may result, however, one needs to add the postulate about the fundamental unity of humankind in the equation. To attain mutuality, diversity and unity must be held together.[28] From a Christian perspective, as we have already seen in all the previous chapters, this conviction finds the most robust expression in the teaching that all human beings are created in the navigation between diversity and unity, which can be aptly explicated by reference to Daniela Augustine's interpretation of *theosis*.[29] Augustine maintains that when God calls humans to *theosis*, God effectively invites them to regard their existence in terms of

28. In ecumenical thinking, there was a shift in understanding of the relation between diversity and unity over the twentieth century from "how much diversity is permissible to unity, to how much unity is reconcilable with diversity." Wild-Wood, "Ecumenism," 5.

29. See Augustine, *Spirit*, 46.

embracing otherness. To be sure, it can be understood as a response to the fall (of Adam and Eve) that represented the act of giving oneself an "ontological priority over the Other."[30] The movement toward *theosis* starts from God as the ultimate other, thus providing solid roots for human existence and teaching us what it means to be authentically human. In other words, the call to *theosis* is "a call to Christ's otherness engraved in human ontology as its origin and telos, and as full potentiality to become like the other while retaining one's distinct otherness."[31]

To elucidate her point, Augustine turns to the notion of love as a power to act coming forth from God who alone is love. Love empowers people to take part in what Augustine refers to as the "cosmic community of the Spirit."[32] In line with the apostolic assertions from 1 Cor 13:1–13, I would suggest that love represents a nonlinear striving for perfection. It does not seek dominion but rather participation, thus upholding "the unity and community of all creatures with one another and with God."[33] Moltmann as well as Augustine underscore the affinity between unity and community that is intimately linked with the notions of relationality and mutuality. To foreground this intrinsic connection, I would like to coin the term "comm/unity."[34] If people relate to one another in acts of solidarity, altruism, and hospitality, while making sure that the otherness of the other is affirmed, then God is materialized as love amid human comm/unity. Comm/unity refers to our common life in God; it implies human journey toward the kindom of God. Comm/unity is an aggregate of people living together in a way that is characterized by communal relationships of "mutual and alternating social representation" in which "people are there for one another" because they share life together; "in these representative relationships people take over responsibility for each other; and ever since New Testament times these relationships have been known in the Christian tradition as love."[35]

In our consideration of *Borgman*, we have seen the tragedy of human existence bereft of mutuality in interpersonal relationships. This was especially evident through the character of Marina, both in her actions motivated by her feelings of guilt and her inability to meaningfully relate

30. Zizioulas, *Communion*, 43.

31. Augustine, *Spirit*, 46.

32. Augustine, *Spirit*, 15. See also McFague, 188.

33. Moltmann, *Creating*, 57.

34. See also Bargár, "Toward Comm/unity," 240–44.

35. Moltmann, *Living God*, 113.

to her husband, Richard. Another cinematographic example that we have already considered, Wim Wenders's "angelic duology" provides a similar case in point. Both *Wings of Desire* and its sequel, *Faraway, So Close!*, highlight the motif of the significance of one's pure and authentic relationship with a fellow human being who is—in Christian tradition—referred to as one's neighbor.[36] This motif is negatively and very persuasively depicted in the second part of the duology. Since the former angel Cassiel does not have his "Marion," unlike his friend and colleague Damiel, he wanes into increasing isolation and loneliness. Experiencing alienation from the world around him, he is unable to give a meaning to his existence. The finitude of his recently acquired human existence becomes his prison; for Cassiel, the boundaries of his being represent an insuperable obstacle rather than an opportunity for existential transcendence. The bleakness of Cassiel's human story is marked by his failure to find an equal counterpart to whom he could relate. Those relationships that he actually does engage in are devoid of mutuality that would help him pursue comm/unity. To use the terminology employed in this section, Cassiel—in his human embodied existence—ultimately fails to keep together diversity and unity. Though he can profess and even sacrifice himself out of love for humankind, he is unsuccessful in living out this love on a day-to-day basis—the love for particular people, in specific contexts, in everyday situations.

In contrast to Cassiel's story, the relational character of human life makes it possible, as we have seen, to bridge distances between individual human beings and communities. Still, otherness should be preserved and sustained in our pursuit of relationships. What is then overcome, actually, is the fear of difference, the fear of the other. From a Christian perspective, relationality and mutuality are discovered as a gift from God. They help create a true community of human beings with God that is in theological discourse referred to as *koinonia* (see *CPTA*, art. 89 and 101). For the followers of Christ, the prototypical community is represented and embodied by the Eucharist. Being called and assembled as Christ's body and receiving Christ's body in the event of communion, we are at the same time instigated by the awareness of Christ's broken body to face human brokenness and woundedness (see *CPTA*, art. 109). Accepting the invitation to become an active character in the story of what God has done for creation in Christ,

36. The German name of *Faraway, So Close!* is *In weiter Ferne, so nah!* For further information on the film, see "In weiter Ferne, so nah!," IMDb, accessed December 27, 2021, https://www.imdb.com/title/tt0107209/?ref_=fn_al_tt_2.

we are, simultaneously, associated with the memories that create resilience in the present and a vision for the future. Thus, the eucharistic koinonia is a true comm/unity, much greater than the mere sum of disparate individuals; its dynamics reflect some of the dynamics within the trinitarian movement of God aimed at the transformation and consummation of creation.[37] Based on the teaching of *imago Dei*, by extension, the concept of comm/unity is to be taken beyond the ecclesiastical understanding of the eucharistic koinonia, as defined by institutional church affiliation. This concept invites us to consider the ontological unity of humankind that is pursued within the fascinating framework of the *conditio humana*, marked by woundedness and brokenness—and yet decisively characterized by relationality and mutuality. I will come back to the concept of comm/unity in chapter 6, the final part of this book. To conclude this chapter, however, I would still like to discuss two terms that I refer to as "incarnational discipleship" and "kenotic presence," respectively, as I believe that they represent an important theological lens to consider the ways human beings can relate to the other dialogically, transformatively, and in mutuality. Thus, they account for an important contribution that Christian theology can make to the discussion on this theme.

Incarnational Discipleship

In *The Spirit and the Common Good*, her book on pneumatological anthropology that we have referred to numerous times throughout this volume, Daniela Augustine by and large constructs her main argument around the concepts of saintliness and hagiography.[38] In Augustine's interpretation, saints are being transformed by a vision of God, captivating others along the way in the process of relating to those around them.[39] In this understanding of saintliness, altruism—that is, a concern for others and their needs—is of ultimate importance.[40] Within the framework of God's story, including the entire creation, saintliness effectively represents a countercultural model of societal and planetary flourishing.[41] It is a model based

37. See Schreiter, "Locating," 348.

38. To find support for her thesis, Augustine engages in intensive conversation with McFague, *Blessed*, Wyschogrod, *Saints*, and Derrida, "Living On," 62–142.

39. See Augustine, *Spirit*, 6–7.

40. See Augustine, *Spirit*, 206.

41. See Augustine, *Spirit*, 21.

on relating to the human and nonhuman other with the aim of pursuing kin-dom—our common life in God—characterized by reconciliation, justice, peace, and inclusion. Sallie McFague describes saintliness—the process of imagining God in the struggles and pursuits of everyday life—as a series of four stages of what Augustine describes as "radical incarnationalism in solidarity with the suffering of others."[42] The four stages are the following: the experiences of "voluntary poverty"; the focus of one's attention and sensitivity on the needs of others; the intentional effort toward the continuous development of a "universal self" with the narrow focus on one's ego eventually waning; and the daily functioning of this new universal self at various levels, including the "planetary rules" (e.g., taking only one's share, cleaning after oneself, or keeping "the house" in good shape for those coming after oneself).[43] As we can see, this model is built on the idea of relationality and mutuality of embodied beings who share the same "household" and the same story. It is driven by a desire to overcome any obstacles that prevent authentic relationships and flourishing of all those who share this common story.

In her proposal for a hagiography of a community committed to the common good, Augustine envisions that all Christians are to respond to the call to saintliness. In the process of discipleship, from a Christian perspective, each Christian is to creatively discover ways of integrating his or her own story—with its sociopolitical and cultural particularities—into the wider story of God with creation. Here, I understand discipleship as a series of steps aimed at genuinely and meaningfully relating to the triune God as one's Lord, other people as fellow bearers of the image of God, and the rest of creation as fellow characters in God's story. This spiritual and embodied formation effectively means writing pages in a "textbook" of life that invites "indigenization and incarnational contextualization" since this saintliness is an "enacted and eyewitnessed holiness in flesh and blood—the life of real human beings united to and moved by/in the Holy Spirit."[44] Therefore, I would like to refer to this dynamic as "incarnational discipleship" since each saintly life represents "an authentication of the Incarnation with its scandalous radical particularity."[45] Ultimately, such incarnational disciple-

42. Augustine, *Spirit*, 20.

43. See McFague, *Blessed*, xii–xiii.

44. Augustine, *Spirit*, 202.

45. Augustine, *Spirit*, 202.

ship strives for an embodied commitment to the well-being of the human and nonhuman other, seeking mutuality, dialogue, and transformation.

Such a holistic understanding of discipleship is also emphasized by Kenneth Ross, who asserts that "Christian discipleship in today's context calls for a vision of faith that embraces the earth itself."[46] Ecological—or, perhaps one should say, *oiko-logical*—emphases are also robustly acknowledged by recent major statements on mission—the evangelical *Cape Town Commitment* and the ecumenical *Together towards Life*. It is noteworthy to cite relevant passages here:

> If Jesus is Lord of all the earth, we cannot separate our relationship to Christ from how we act in relation to the earth. For to proclaim the gospel that says "Jesus is Lord" is to proclaim the gospel that includes the earth, since Christ's Lordship is over all creation. Creation care is thus a gospel issue within the Lordship of Christ. Such love for God's creation demands that we repent of our part in the destruction, waste and pollution of the earth's resources and our collusion in the toxic idolatry of consumerism. Instead, we commit ourselves to urgent and prophetic ecological responsibility.[47]
>
> Consumerism triggers not limitless growth but rather endless exploitation of the earth's resources. Human greed is contributing to global warming and other forms of climate change. If this trend continues and earth is fatally damaged, what can we imagine salvation to be? Humanity cannot be saved alone while the rest of the created world perishes. Eco-justice cannot be separated from salvation, and salvation cannot come without a new humility that respects the needs of all life on earth.[48]

Both citations illustrate the interconnectedness among the ecological, economic, as well as spiritual aspects of life. In this regard they show family resemblance with another currently influential ecumenical concept, namely, "economy of life." While the latter is commonly presented, first and foremost, as an alternative to the presently dominant economic and financial model of global neoliberalism, it involves, in fact, a holistic and relational approach to life, based on biblically and theologically grounded principles of integrity, social justice, human dignity, mutual responsibility, and ecological sustainability.[49] The economy of life includes "relationships,

46. Ross, "Brexit," 384.

47. Lausanne Movement, *Cape Town Commitment*, I,7.

48. *TTL*, art. 23.

49. See World Council of Churches, *Economy of Life: An Invitation*, art. 2.

care and compassion, solidarity and love, aesthetics and the ethics of life, participation and celebration, cultural diversity and communal vitality."[50] The approaches and attitudes usually related with such an understanding of the economy of life are very much vital also for incarnational discipleship. They include—but are not limited to—spiritual renewal, critical self-reflection, inclusion of the marginalized in decision-making processes, open and creative dialogue between the church, civil society, and state authorities, the pursuit of justice and equality, and ecologically-minded behavior.[51]

To advance my argument further, several aspects can be identified with respect to what incarnational discipleship implies for Christian involvement in the pursuit of relating to the other in the quest of our common life in God.[52] First, incarnational discipleship helps us make sense of what it means to be Christian today in the contexts where nominal membership in Christian churches endows one with few social benefits. Following Christ thus becomes a matter of personal transformation that is expected, in turn, to lead one to actively work for a transformation of one's surrounding reality. Following Christ, therefore, does not constitute a claim for *Christianity* as affiliation to a certain established church, not to say a certain civilization (*Christendom*). Rather, it should be driven and nurtured by the desire for *Christ-like-ness* in the sense of a quality of life transformed by the power of the Spirit, thus elevated to a level of being authentically human.

Second, incarnational discipleship provides us with a complementary perspective on what it means to be a part of *missio Dei*. Correctly placing much emphasis on God's continuous engagement with creation, *missio Dei* as an inclusive concept potentially implies a danger of neglecting the importance of personal formation of people as agents of mission. Incarnational discipleship constantly reminds us that to be an agent in God's mission means to be a disciple molded into the image of one's Master, Jesus of Nazareth. To put it differently, the proclamation of the gospel does not only entail "making disciples" (see Matt 28:19) but also the mutual formation of a community of Christ's followers and their joint moving—together with other people and the rest of creation—toward kin-dom, our common life in God.

50. World Council of Churches, *Statement on Just Finance*, art. 9.

51. See, for instance, World Council of Churches, *Economy of Life, Justice, and Peace for All*, art. 25–26.

52. Missiologically, the language of *missio Dei* is often used to describe this process. I am going to adopt this hermeneutical lens in the second point below.

Third, incarnational discipleship subverts certain understandings of salvation, including especially those that construe salvation as nothing but an individual reality, and mission as a mere religious project rather than God's story aiming at the transformation of the entire God's creation. As Deenabandhu Manchala puts it, preaching salvation as marvelous life after death to those who are daily sold, enslaved, tortured, raped, deprived of food, and killed is nothing but abomination done in the name of God.[53] Understanding salvation in relation to incarnational discipleship contrasts with such an individualistic and "other-worldly business." Such an approach puts relationality—as well as embodiment—at the center of being Christian. Thus, being Christian actually means being in relation to others—following the example of Christ and empowered by the Spirit. In other words, Christian existence is a journey that Christians walk together with others toward life for the whole creation—life characterized by the values of God's kin-dom.

Finally, incarnational discipleship helps us find a new imagination to see the church not so much as a fellowship of believers but rather a fellowship of partners engaged in God's story and mission with creation.[54] The church as a community of people called forth to pursue a certain purpose (Greek *ekklesia*) is not primarily visible through official structures, traditions, and institutions but in concrete places where the Spirit is in action for the sake of justice, peace, and life. In this way, Christ's followers become a community embodying the promises of the coming reign of God. In this view, the rationale for the existence of the church is found in its sharing and living God's story with creation as enacted through relating to and being with human and nonhuman others in their daily embodied existence, joys, and struggles and striving—together with them—toward transformation and consummation. I suggest referring to this kind of existence as "kenotic presence."

Toward Kenotic Presence

The theological idea of "kenosis"—or self-emptying—refers to the Christological hymn in Philippians 2:1–11. Early church fathers used this concept to express the reality of God's affirmation of humankind and creation in the incarnation of Christ. Inspired by this apostolic account of Jesus's own

53. See Manchala, "Moving," 209–10.

54. See Manchala, "Moving," 211.

mode of being, I take kenotic existence as rooted in a holistic and embodied understanding of Christian faith. It can be characterized by certain features of theological importance. First, if the church is to be present kenotically within creation, it needs to strive for truly being salt and yeast. In the New Testament, Jesus likens his followers to salt (Matt 5:13). As we know, salt is not the only ingredient needed when one is trying to bake bread or, for that matter, prepare any other meal. Jesus's parable of yeast (Matt 13:33) seems to point in a very similar direction: to bake bread, other ingredients are needed in addition to yeast. This means that less is often more. Rather than quantity-driven, then, the mission of the church should seek to be quality-oriented, introducing the values of God's reign, kin-dom, in the world. Christians are to do that by being for and with others, preserving the diversity of creation and seeking to affirm the unity ingrained in creation through the creative intention of God.

To use another gospel image, Jesus, referring to himself as "the light of the world" (John 8:12), also hails—in another gospel—his followers as "the light of the world" (Matt 5:14). Instead of using the symbolism of light and its counterpart, darkness, in a dualistic way to reinforce our concepts of good and evil—and to associate with them the phenomena that we regard as good and evil accordingly—I would suggest, in the light of the discussion in this chapter on mutuality as a balance between diversity and unity, exploring the ways to discover the multidimensional potential of this powerful dyad. This approach could perhaps contribute to our resisting one of the identitary temptations of fostering an apocalyptic view of the world when we identify ourselves with the Good, while often condemning our opponents to be yoked together with the forces of evil. Such an unpresumptuous and hospitable attitude reflects kenotic presence that seeks to authentically and meaningfully relate to the other.

Next, the proposal for kenotic presence of the church in the world, as introduced here, supports a relational anthropology. With reference to 1 Corinthians 6:19–20, one can assert that a Christian does not belong to her or himself but rather to God. In this way, such a person is invited—through one's life—to "glorify God in their (individual and collective) body," the latter referring to the church as the body of Christ.[55] Thus, Paul the apostle can be taken as considering the body—and, by implication, human existence—to be relational and interdependent, rather than an autonomous

55. See Hearon, "1 and 2 Corinthians," 615.

monad.[56] Christian tradition perceives human life as "eccentric existence," that is, humans as bodies striving to transcend their being-in-the-physical-body by relating to other people, their context, creation, and God.[57] As a result, a theological view of human existence is one of living enmeshed in various contextually contingent relationships that make the flourishing of human—and, for that matter—nonhuman life possible. This is what I have been throughout this book referring to as our common life in God.

Another aspect of kenotic presence can helpfully be highlighted by reference to shalom, the biblical concept that we have already introduced in this chapter. In this perspective, human and nonhuman flourishing is a result of shalom. As such, it presupposes relationality since it perceives all dimensions of life as always interwoven and present at every moment. Rather than on utopia, it is concentrated on, as Mary Grey formulates it, modest *eco-topias* in the here and now.[58] These *eco-topias* represent efforts aimed at transcending the absolute minimum for social survival by way of establishing relationships of mutuality, providing welfare for all, securing just employment, self-esteem, and the recognition of the community.[59] Due to their capacity to create trust and relationships, the church (as well as other religious communities), if present with creation truly kenotically, plays a significant role in the process of giving rise to the *eco-topias*, serving as "incubators of civic skills" and social cohesion.[60] Moreover, I would suggest that forming these *eco-topias* calls for a more relational imagination of the space that people inhabit together with the rest of creation. What emerges is, as Andrew Davey says, "a new ethical understanding of both place and individual identity in relational space."[61]

Finally, yet another way to conceive of the kenotic presence of the church while considering the relationality of human existence to be at the heart of one's theological reflection is to speak, together with Tim Gorringe, of *ec-clesia* as a community of those who affirm the giftedness of all life and promote the kin-dom of God—not as a reality of the hereafter but, conversely, as the world being called home by grace from the alienation

56. This point has already been argued in chapter 2 where I dealt with the human body in detail.

57. The idea of eccentric existence comes from Kelsey, *Eccentric Existence.*

58. See Grey, "Shape," 103.

59. See Grey, "Shape," 102.

60. See Pierson, "Faith," 82.

61. Davey, "Better Place," 43. Davey refers to Massey, *World City*, 216.

of sin. The "ec-clesians" are not willing to be manipulated by both plausible structures and determinist views that admit no alternatives, holding on to the conviction that it is Jesus's reign—rather than the logic of "empire"—that is worth betting one's life on.[62] For Christians, this fundamental conviction not only results in an understanding that what it means to be human finds an expression through reflecting on the ways that God relates to God's creation but also in a calling to think and act in an analogous manner. Theologically speaking, such a mode of existence is what I refer to as kenotic presence with human and nonhuman others for the sake of our common life in God.

The motif of kenotic presence is closely connected with our earlier theme of incarnational discipleship. Finding its role model in Jesus as the Master and Lord, it is subversive because it turns upside down all our conventional ideas about "good relations," power, and success. Rosemary Radford Ruether is helpful in this respect when she interprets Jesus as a representative of liberated humankind and the liberating Word of God. Furthermore, he is a herald of new humanity founded on the life style that dismisses any caste privileges, champions the marginalized, and strives for genuine and equal relationships.[63] However, incarnational discipleship that takes kenotic presence seriously is also cruciform because it is decisively defined by the cross of Christ. Jesus as the Master and Lord provides direction and guidance for his disciples who are thereby called to follow him. Christian discipleship is characterized by bearing the sorrows of others to whom Christians are to relate as to their neighbors. Dietrich Bonhoeffer describes this process as follows:

> The disciple-community does not shake off sorrow as though it were no concern of its own, but willingly bears it. And in this way they show how close are the bonds that bind them to the rest of humanity. . . . Sorrow cannot tire them or wear them down, it cannot embitter them or cause them to break down under the strain; far from it, for they bear their sorrow in the strength of him who bears them up, who bore the whole suffering of the world upon the cross.[64]

Bonhoeffer's profound theological grounding of discipleship in God's infinite love does not at all diminish the role that the human is to play in this

62. See Gorringe, "Shape," 81.

63. See Radford Ruether, *Sexism*, 137.

64. Bonhoeffer, *Cost of Discipleship*, 121–22.

process—the role of fear, anxiety, exhaustion, or disgust, but also the courage, strength, and hope that Christ's disciples find in his cross and resurrection. Last but not least, incarnational discipleship in the mode of kenotic presence is also defined by joy because it is a "road of boundless mercy."[65] To be sure, the gospel initiates and nurtures the joy of the disciples/followers of Christ being transformed, thus becoming active agents of God's transformation of the whole creation toward our common life in God.[66] And this is when the theme of comm/unity steps in again as the fundamental element of human embodied existence. Alienated from one another and incapable of relating to fellow human others genuinely and purposefully, the characters in *Borgman* fell short of attaining such comm/unity. We can imagine these characters asking, together with Cain, "Am I my brother's keeper?" (Gen 4:9 NRSV). It is worth noting that—even though meant sarcastically—this actually was the first ethical question that humans ask God. Significantly, God's response is an emphatic "yes." Yes, we are accountable before God for the well-being of the other.[67] To even start this relating to the other for their well-being and flourishing, human imagination needs to be transformed so that people can be "uncurved," freed from the self-encapsulation of their beliefs, images, and behaviors. Such "uncurving" is a creative activity of the Spirit. Daniela Augustine comments,

> This uncurving is the creation-mending work of the Spirit, who convicts "the world concerning sin" (John 16:8), renews and sanctifies (1 Pet 1:2) humanity (including its sociopolitical imagination, its dreams, longings, and desires), and pours the love of God into the human heart (Rom 5:5), enabling it to image once again the divine communal face with and for the other.[68]

Comm/unity is a fragile endeavor, yet—from a Christian perspective—one worth aspiring to. It represents an important manner through which we as God's creatures pursue our common life in God as the vision for a shared, just, and reconciled future in communion with others. In the Scriptures, this vision is symbolized by the image of "feast" that is both a promise of

65. Bonhoeffer, *Cost of Discipleship*, 41.

66. See also Ross, "Brexit," 387–88.

67. See Augustine, *Spirit*, 70. See also De La Torre, *Genesis*, 96.

68. Augustine, *Spirit*, 79. In a similar vein, Walter Brueggemann speaks of the "prophetic imagination" as a way to effectively deconstruct the claims of "domination imagination as a practice that cannot give life because it fails in truth-telling." Brueggemann, *Practice*, 42.

transformation and a means for resilience against sin, injustice, and evil. Feast will be the theme of the next chapter.

6

Feast

When the Feast Is Over

Feast and feasting both presuppose and imply interpersonal encounter, presence, communication, eating and drinking, and enjoyment of cultural inventions, such as music, singing or dancing. Not only being a holistic image that stimulates one's intellectual, imaginative, and sensual faculties, it is also an emphatic image to represent human relationality, including vis-à-vis other human beings, creation, and God. As such, this image acquires a certain liturgical quality as it affirms the dynamic of human-divine action. Moreover, it gives a robust expression to the central idea of this book, namely, that a theological anthropology based on the essential significance of story, body, imagination, and the relational nature of being human enables us to seek and pursue a common life for the whole creation in the force field of God's radical and transformative reign—our common life in God.

In my opening cinematographic reflection in chapter 5, I decided to apply a *via negativa* to make my point on relationality. When discussing feast and feasting as a symbolic climax of my argument in this book, I will likewise turn to this approach. The first film to be considered is *Into the Wild*, written and directed by Sean Penn in 2007. It narrates the story of Christopher McCandless, a young and idealistic university graduate.[1] Intelligent, privileged, and endowed with prospects for a bright future, he

1. For further information on the film, see "Into the Wild," IMDb, accessed December 6, 2021, https://www.imdb.com/title/tt0758758/?ref_=fn_al_tt_1.

decides to leave everything behind to reinvent his identity as Alexander Supertramp, "on course to a noble, albeit misguided, pilgrimage toward a purer life of utter simplicity."[2] This pilgrimage involves a pursuit of close and intimate connection with nature, nevertheless seen through a lens of idealized romanticism. This is beautifully captured in the scene when Supertramp sits alone on a bridge in the middle of the woods, enjoying a break and an apple. In uplifted spirits, he addresses the apple aloud in the following odic way:

> SUPERTRAMP: You're really good. You're like a hundred thousand times better than any apple I've ever had. I'm not Superman, I'm Supertramp . . . you're Super Apple. You're so tasty, you're so . . . organic, you're so natural. You're the apple of my eye![3]

This scene not only expresses the pure pleasure of enjoying food but also suggests that there is a spiritual dimension to human affirmation of being dependent on the fruits yielded thanks to nature's fertility and human labor. From a theological perspective, Norman Wirzba recognizes an essential link between eating, God's grace, and celebration:

> Eating reminds us that we participate in a grace-saturated world, a blessed creation worthy of attention, care, and celebration. . . . Real food, the food that is the source of creaturely health and delight, is precious because it is a fundamental means through which God's nurture and love for the whole of creation is expressed.[4]

The words above imply that food is not a mere means to secure survival. Having enough to eat and drink calls for a response in thanksgiving—truly, eucharistic response. Eating thus becomes a matter of both material and spiritual significance. Such a step presupposes that one recognizes one's embodied existence in an act of imagination. Furthermore, it also requires that one acknowledge relationality as a sine qua non for one's existence: the fact that one has food to eat and can enjoy it is inseparably connected to the fact that one is deeply rooted in a web of multiple relationships—the relationships that highlight human hunger for material, cultural, interpersonal, and spiritual nutrition. Therefore, I would suggest, feast represents a symbol that aptly brings together the intersection of storiedness, corporeality, imagination, and relationality for the sake of transformation.

2. Sison, *Sacred Foodways*, 13.

3. Quoted in Sison, *Sacred Foodways*, 15.

4. Wirzba, *Food*, 2.

For this very reason, it is clear that Supertramp's pursuit is doomed from the outset. On the one hand, he decides to leave civilization precisely to become more aware of his soul—and body. It is the shackles of the late capitalist, achievement-driven, and consumerist society that he sees as an obstacle preventing him from becoming his true self. This endeavor necessarily calls for a new imagination enabling transformation of his entire life. The scene with the apple exquisitely illustrates the point. And yet, on the other hand, Supertramp's efforts completely neglect relationality. He leaves people, including those who love and care for him, to rediscover and reshape his authentic body-self. He seeks to awaken his imagination apart from other human beings. However, this is necessarily failed business. Human beings cannot meaningfully relate to apples as to their equal others. When one turns down an invitation to God's feast of life in an attempt to pursue one's romanticized vision of the "noble" creation in which the "fallen" humankind has no place, one will ultimately starve oneself to death. In *Into the Wild*, this emphasis is dramatically portrayed in the scene that shows Supertramp standing on a small island in the middle of a river, haphazardly shooting up in the air with his shotgun and yelling in apparent despair:

> SUPERTRAMP: Where are the f*cking animals now!? I'm hungry! I'm f*cking hungry! I'm f*cking hungry![5]

As Sison suggests, this scene represents a hermeneutic key to understanding Supertramp's experience. Supertramp's starvation "ultimately lies in his self-imposed exile from vital human relationships."[6] Refusing his invitation to join the others in the feast toward our common life in God, Supertramp—and, we should say, Christopher McCandless—died of hunger: for food—and for human relationships.[7] The tragedy of McCandless's experience can be perhaps better understood through what Wirzba refers to as "eating in exile":

> The truth, of course, is that none of us can stand alone. To try is invariably to flail about and fall. It is also to die by starvation. Each of us is held in "creatureliness" through the multiple food webs that constitute and circulate through every living organism. Eating

5. Quoted in Sison, *Sacred Foodways*, 17.

6. Sison, *Sacred Foodways*, 17.

7. *Into the Wild* is based on a true story as captured in McCandless's journal and a book by Jon Krakauer. See also Sison, *Sacred Foodways*, 18.

> is the daily confirmation that we need others and are vulnerable to them. . . . But when we eat in exile we eat alone and with considerable violence, without deep connection or affection, experiencing food and each other as mere objects and threats or as the means to our power, control, and convenience.[8]

The other film I would like to consider here is *Buried*, a mysterious drama-thriller directed by the Spanish filmmaker Rodrigo Cortés in 2010.[9] It tells the story of a man, an American truck driver in war-stricken Iraq, who wakes up from unconsciousness only to find out that he is trapped in a wooden box—a coffin. Using a cellphone, which is, besides a handful of other little things, the only device that the man is left with, he discovers that he has been kidnapped and buried somewhere underground. If he fails to meet the requirements of his kidnappers, he is left with only a few hours to live. His struggle for deliverance can begin.

Cortés completely redefines our understanding of minimalist cinema. The entire film takes place within the confines of the coffin illuminated by a lighter or a hand torch only. There is no space for either special effects or medium- and wide-angle shot cinematography. Music too serves a rather auxiliary role when it helps co-create a disquieting atmosphere. *Buried* is effectively a one-man show as the kidnapped American, Paul, is the only character that actually appears on screen throughout the film. The remaining cast are stylized as "Phone-a-Friend" characters since the viewer only hears their voices.[10] To turn the central idea into a feature film, the crew has had to employ various elements and strategies, such as an action scene with a snake or a moving call with Paul's senile mother. However, these ultimately result in developing a coherent work of cinema.

One can naturally disagree with the director's views expressed in the film. However, if we accept his hermeneutic lens, *Buried* can be interpreted as a surprisingly stimulating critique of transnational corporations that are not interested in the safety and well-being of their employees but only in their own profit and unblemished image; of governmental institutions that first and foremost strive to keep undesirable situations secret from the public; and war-induced poverty that turns desperate peasants into terrorists.

8. Wirzba, *Food*, 77.

9. An alternative Spanish name of the film is *Enterrado*. For further information on the film, see "Buried," IMDb, accessed December 6, 2021, https://www.imdb.com/title/tt1462758/?ref_=nv_sr_srsg_0.

10. Altogether, one can hear twenty different voices in *Buried*.

In addition, the film also offers implicit yet poignant social criticism when it suggests that an adult, hard-working citizen of the wealthiest country in the world has nothing else to bequeath to his son except for his personal clothes.

Unlike *Into the Wild*, the solitude, lack of resources, and, eventually, death of the main character in *Buried* is not an outcome of his voluntary action. To put it metaphorically, while Paul, unlike Christopher the Supertramp, did not turn down the invitation to the feast of life, the feast is nonetheless certainly over for him. Importantly, it has been over even before Paul gets kidnapped and imprisoned. The reasons are systemic; they do not necessarily have to do anything with his individual will and decision-making. They involve socioeconomic, political, and cultural factors that shape human existence, often preventing them from participating in what I call our common life in God.

The two films are important for my argument in this book as they shed light on the nature of human embodied existence: it is both characterized by a desire to go beyond the given and shaped by contingency, context, and circumstances. While the first aspect can be fathomed in terms of promise that an alternative to the status quo is possible, the latter finds its expression in resilience against malign and destructive phenomena of life. As already outlined in the opening paragraph of this chapter, I would like to turn to the image of feast to interconnect the aspects of human storiedness, corporeality, imagination, relationality, and the quest for transformation. Employing the dynamic of promise and resilience, the image of feast then represents, from a theological-anthropological perspective, a robust way to speak about our common life in God. However, before we engage in discussion on this twofold dynamic—and, later, on comm/unity[11]—the image of feast itself needs to be considered from a biblical and theological point of view.

The Image of Feast: Biblical and Theological Considerations

To capture the dynamics that my argument on our common life in God seeks to express, the image of feast can be usefully turned to as it fittingly represents both the way that God communicates with people and human response to divine action. In biblical tradition, meals in general, and feasts

11. This term has already been briefly introduced in chapter 5.

in particular, serve as a metaphor for God's reign, kin-dom.[12] A polysemantic term, feast importantly emphasizes God's inclusive stance toward various kinds of people.[13] Exegeting the gospel passage of the parable of the Great Dinner in Luke 14:15–24, Robert Goss forcefully asserts that "these meals metaphorically express God's promiscuous invitation of grace, compassion for all, and inversion of hierarchy."[14] To be sure, this "promiscuous invitation of grace" that gives a practical expression to Jesus's code of hospitality is rooted in the insistence to avoid inviting to feasts those who are in the position to return the favor of being invited. To the contrary, there is a clear intention to host those who are unwelcome and expandable, forced to live at the margins of society.[15] Furthermore, as the 2005 Faith and Order study document, *Christian Perspectives on Theological Anthropology*—already discussed earlier in this book—reminds us, Jesus befriended and feasted with various kinds of people who would not otherwise meet and engage with each other, thus effectively showing that "the gift of relatedness overcomes fear of difference to create true community, true koinonia."[16] This not only buttresses my point made in chapter 5 on the central significance of relationality for being human, but also indicates the radical nature of God's hospitality.

To make a point on God's radical hospitality, Daniela Augustine turns to the image of household; God welcomes around God's table all those who welcome the coming reign of God and its logic. To be sure, God "becomes their home."[17] Sallie McFague coins the term "incarnational inclusiveness"

12. The latter term was discussed earlier in chapters 3 and 4.

13. See Goss, "Luke," 532.

14. Goss, "Luke," 533.

15. See Goss, "Luke," 532. See also how John Dominic Crossan elaborates on this point further when he outlines how the historical church has struggled with the radical challenge posed by Jesus's teaching and praxis: "Jesus' kingdom of nobodies and undesirables in the here and now of this world was surely an egalitarian one, and, as such, it rendered sexual and social, political and religious distinctions completely irrelevant and anachronistic. . . . But the radical lack of social differentiation remained as a permanent challenge to all specifications, interpretations, and actualizations of the Kingdom proclaimed by Jesus." Crossan, *Historical Jesus*, 298.

16. Faith and Order Commission, *Christian Perspectives*, art. 89. Hereafter referred to as *CPTA*.

17. Augustine, *Spirit*, 44. To find support for her argument, Augustine draws from hermeneutic insights by Douglas Meeks on the Greek term *oikos* that stands for household but also family, house, or family's property. For Meeks, oikos represents "access to livelihood." See Meeks, *God the Economist*, 33. Based on this understanding, Meeks

to refer to the logic of God's radical hospitality. It involves partaking in the life of all creation, including its flourishing and suffering.[18] Those who are invited to feast with God in God's household, must be ready to offer themselves as nourishment for others.[19] John Dominic Crossan invites us to consider yet another take on divine hospitality that has cosmic dimensions and relevance. He argues that the Sabbath is the true climax of creation as it is within this space-time that all creatures can enjoy the unlimited care of and communion with the God of life.[20]

Furthermore, the Scriptures frequently turn to the images of food and eating to convey God's provision and care for people—and creation—in different ways, including bodily nourishment and spiritual sustenance. One should add that the distinction between the various spheres of God's provision are systematically blurred by biblical authors.[21] One example can be found in the book of Psalms when the existential phenomenon of putting one's faith in God is mediated through the sensorial image of enjoying delicious food: "O taste and see that the LORD is good; happy are those who take refuge in him" (Ps 34:8 NRSV). Moreover, the Gospels contain numerous food metaphors, with Jesus admittedly most significantly identifying himself as the "bread of life" (John 6:35) and sharing bread and wine as his flesh and blood during the final Passover meal with his disciples (John 6:53–55).[22]

For the argument of this chapter, however, it is of ultimate importance to note that social, cultural, and political dimensions are implied in the scriptural image of feast in addition to the material and spiritual sense, as our discussion so far has indicated. David Ford makes this point eloquently when he argues that Jesus was deeply rooted in "the religion, economics, and politics of his time," with his preaching and ministry both being conversant with and having ramifications for these areas of human existence. The standing task for Christians as Jesus's followers, then, is to creatively reenact their Master's deeds and words, including his teaching and practice

---

maintains that home is "where everyone knows your name. Home is where you can always count on being comforted, forgiven, loved, and cared for. Home is where there is always a place for you at the table. And, finally, home is where you can count on sharing what is on the table." Meeks, *God the Economist*, 36.

18. See McFague, *Blessed*, 118–19.

19. See Augustine, *Spirit*, 208.

20. See Crossan, *God and Empire*, 53–54. See also Augustine, *Spirit*, 133.

21. See Sison, *Sacred Foodways*, 4.

22. For further discussion, see Sison, *Sacred Foodways*, 4.

regarding meals and feasting, for today and to "be involved in our situations with compatible perception and sharpness, in ways that testify to the abundant generosity of God, our acceptance of it, and our imitation of it."[23] Together with Ford we can, therefore, say that feast is an image that not only anticipates a time when "saints" are facing God and each other "at home . . . in peace, in the trust and confidence of mutual love," but also offers a chance to experience the reality in a different way, being freed from manifold constraints of daily existence.[24] The WCC affirmation on mission and evangelism, *Together towards Life*, for its part, postulates the image of feast as theologically and missiologically significant because of its ability to constructively intertwine relational, celebratory, and liberational emphases vis-à-vis human existence.[25] As such, it is instrumental for understanding our common life in God.

Drawing from these biblical and theological insights, I would like to suggest that the image of feast can fruitfully be construed in terms of the double dynamic of promise and resilience. This suggestion concurs with the understanding proposed by Stephen Bevans and Roger Schroeder that they refer to as "prophetic dialogue." In their quest for a faithful and relevant Christian theology of mission for the twenty-first century, the two theologians assert that the way that God relates to the world, waiting on people to respond to God's calling, can appropriately be theorized through the notion of prophetic dialogue. The dialogical dimension acknowledges and values human experience, insisting that God reaches out to invite people to be part of the reign of God (kin-dom), symbolized by feasting as notably portrayed in the parable of the Great Dinner in Luke 14:15–24. At the same time, however, the prophetic dimension urges people to come out of their comfort zones, when unambiguously speaking for and firmly standing with "the world's excluded, against human and ecological violence, and on behalf of God's reign of justice and peace." The prophetic dimension furthermore involves proclaiming "unhesitantly, faithfully—and yet respectfully—the name, the vision and the Lordship of Jesus Christ."[26] In God's involvement with the entire creation in which people are invited

23. Ford, *Self and Salvation*, 268–69.

24. See Ford, *Self and Salvation*, 266 and 267.

25. See *TTL*, especially art. 101.

26. Both citations are from Bevans and Schroeder, *Constants*, 4 and 285. For a monographic treatment of the notion of "prophetic dialogue," see Bevans and Schroeder, *Prophetic Dialogue*.

to participate, therefore, a promise of abundant life for all comes together with the accent on resilience vis-à-vis life-suffocating powers (see *TTL*, art. 1).[27] In the following sections of this chapter, the double dynamic of promise and resilience, as embodied by the biblical image of feast, will be explored through the lens of relevant passages from ecumenical documents (*TTL* and *CPTA*) in conversation with some additional scholarly resources and artwork.

Feast as Promise

In this section of the present chapter, I would like to suggest that the image of feast and feasting is central to the promise of redemption for the entire creation as the Scriptures account for it. David Ford interprets this promise in terms of invitation and acceptance, when he states—from a Christian perspective—that "Christian vocation can be summed up as being called to the feast of the Kingdom of God," whereas the "salvation of selves is in responding to that invitation."[28] *TTL*, for its part, seconds this articulation when it conceives of mission as "an invitation to the 'feast in the kingdom of God,'" explicitly referring to Luke 14:15 (art. 101). Moreover, one should add that it is the whole pericope on the parable of the Great Dinner, as rendered by Luke (14:15–24), that is relevant for the topic of our discussion. Inferring from this parable, one can say that it is no other than God who takes the initiative to lead humankind and, to be sure, the entire creation to what *TTL* symbolically calls the "Feast of Life" (see art. 112).[29] This fundamental belief highlights the aspect of togetherness that finds its expression in the scriptural call addressed to Christians to pursue fellowship with the rest of creation. Later in this chapter, I will seek to theorize this conviction through the notion of "comm/unity." To turn to *TTL* once again, Christians as "a redeemed community" are not only to share with others "the waters of life" but also "to look for the Spirit of unity to heal, reconcile, and renew the whole creation" (art. 103). As such, God's promise of feast also implies a

27. Here, *TTL* refers to John 10:10.

28. Ford, *Self and Salvation*, 272.

29. In that very paragraph, the authors of the affirmation make this point in trinitarian terms when they say: "The Triune God invites the whole creation to the Feast of Life, through Jesus Christ who came 'that they may have life, and may have it in all its fullness' (John 10:10, REB), through the Holy Spirit who affirms the vision of the reign of God, 'Behold, I create new heavens and a new earth!' (Is. 65:17, KJV)."

vision and mission for the church to "prepare the banquet and to invite all people to the feast of life" (art. 101).

And yet, David Ford stimulates our theological imagination further still as he contemplates "the ultimate feasting," characterized as "an endless flow of communication" between loving and caring individuals that involves conversation, body language, food, drinks, music, and much more.[30] Such thinking about the "ultimate feasting" leads to appreciate the twofold nature of feast as promise: it is not only something already given and experienced in ordinary, daily encounters among human beings—both religious and otherwise (e.g., church, community, "commonplace" interactions)—but also something that is yet to come in fullness.[31] It is kin-dom, the reality marked by God's reign of liberation, reconciliation, justice, and fulfillment. It is our common life in God that includes the entire creation. The inherent link between the present and the eschatological with regard to feast as promise is also foregrounded by *TTL* when it describes the feast as "a celebration of creation and fruitfulness overflowing from the love of God, the source of life in abundance," considering it in the framework of the Isaian vision of new heavens and a new earth (art. 101 and 112; see also Isa 65:17).

Fundamentally, this prophetic vision is profoundly materialistic. And yet, it is more than a mere material reality. In other words, the prophet insists that, while carried on and nurtured by God's Spirit, this new reality can by no means be spiritualized away. In line with the main thrust on embodied existence, as suggested throughout this book, God's feast of life—inaugurated and implemented by God's liberating action of love, compassion, and reconciliation—therefore, represents a dynamic interplay between the materialistic and the spiritual. Theodor Adorno, in his deliberations on negative dialectics, provides some guidance on how to approach this intricate reality. He writes,

> At its most materialistic, materialism comes to agree with theology. Its great desire would be the resurrection of the flesh, a desire utterly foreign to idealism, the realm of the absolute spirit. The perspective vanishing point of historic materialism would be its selfsublimation, the spirit's liberation from the primacy of the material needs in their state of fulfillment. Only if the physical urge were quenched would the spirit be reconciled and would become

30. See Ford, *Self and Salvation*, 271.

31. Thus the use of the adjective "ultimate."

> that which it only promises while the spell of material conditions will not let it satisfy its material needs.[32]

Further expanding on Adorno's thoughts, Joshua Delpech-Ramey emphasizes the role of liturgy in human liberation fulfillment and of shared life together with the rest of creation as I have outlined it using the discourse of feast as promise.[33] Concurring with this logic, it is first and foremost the Eucharist that becomes crucial for our discussion as it decisively symbolizes the anticipated future as it is celebrated, savored, and lived in very particular ways today. The Eucharist, to use the words of Jean-Luc Marion, "constitutes the first fragment of the new creation" that "anticipates what we will be, will see, will love . . . facing the gift that we cannot yet welcome, so, in the strict sense, that we cannot yet figure."[34] *CPTA* opts for a complementary perspective when it posits the Eucharist as "a foretaste of the heavenly banquet prepared for all humankind," thus giving an eschatological orientation to both Christian theology and anthropology (art. 112). Liturgy in general and the Eucharist in particular are thus theologized in terms of an imminent reality that epitomizes a promise of abundant life for the whole creation.[35] Our discussion, drawing from the insights of David Ford and *TTL*, helps us appreciate the dynamic and intricate nature of feast as promise in more detail: it is at the same time present and anticipated; it is both a given and a task. Moreover, it has to do with transformation in expectation of and cooperation with God who is making all things new (Isa 43:19; Rev 21:5). A stimulating context for this understanding of the Eucharist is provided by Walter Brueggemann, who relates it to the common good. Reading it as "a replay of the manna narrative" from the book of Exodus, the Eucharist represents, for Brueggemann, "a liturgical interpretive offer to reimagine the world differently," as a transformed humankind

32. Adorno, *Negative Dialectics*, 207.

33. See Delpech-Ramey, "Supernatural Capital," 125.

34. Marion, *God*, 174. See also Noble, "Apophatic Aspects," 46.

35. An interesting point is made by Daniela Augustine, who makes distinction between the Eucharist and the agape feast as known from the Scriptures and the history of the early Jesus movement. She writes: "While the Eucharist takes place in heaven, the agape feast takes place on earth. It embodies the ultimate purpose of the Eucharistic pedagogy—it is the life of heaven on earth captured by the household table of the family of God, where all share their resources and freely receive access to life, so that there is not a single one left hungry and needy among them." Augustine, *Spirit*, 150. While I appreciate the distinction, I believe that the two should not be perceived as separated from one another. Thus I suggest considering liturgy in a broad sense, as will be argued below.

starts on a journey "from anxious scarcity through miraculous abundance to a neighborly common good."[36]

Transformation has already been in detail discussed from a Christian perspective in chapter 4. Here, therefore, I will only reiterate the main findings very briefly. First, transformation is embedded in the vision of the inbreaking kin-dom of God. This reality encompasses reconciliation between God, humankind, and the entire creation; liberation from the power and consequences of sin; and hope for the final consummation of God's reign. As a reality that is *already* in effect, but *not yet* accomplished in full, it epitomizes both a promise of what will be and a call to participate in the historical struggle for justice and peace.

Second, transformation has both personal and structural aspects. This feature of transformation focuses on the whole of humankind and creation, that, by virtue of God's accepting grace and emancipating action, seeks to be purified, perfected, and healed from the detrimental power of sin. Furthermore, third, transformation is profoundly linked with both the immanent and transcendent dimensions of human existence. Our participation in what I refer to as our common life in God is not only restricted to the hereafter but encompasses our embodied existence in the here and now.

Fourth, transformation, in a Christian understanding, is distinctively praxis-oriented. Featuring very prominently especially in various liberation theologies, the hermeneutic lens of praxis sensitizes us to the fact that although the factuality of human embodied existence involves much positive and desirable, it should at the same time be approached critically vis-à-vis all the malign phenomena which are to be questioned, critiqued, and called to transformation.

Fifth, it is a Christian belief that transformation is nourished and sustained by transformative spirituality. As *TTL* has it, the latter represents energy for life in its fullness, calling people to actively resist all life-denying structures, while providing dynamism and orientation for their lives (see art. 29). Theologically, transformative spirituality is the driving force behind human involvement in God's transformative work with creation. Transformation—giving a focus to our exploration of the image of feast—thus directly leads us to another aspect of our theme, namely, feast as resilience.

36. Brueggemann, *Journey*, 32.

Feast as Resilience

According to the *Merriam-Webster Dictionary*, resilience refers to "the ability to become strong, healthy, or successful again after something bad happens."[37] This definition implies that contingencies of life do not have an ultimate say but can be actively addressed and confronted. When discussing this notion in chapters 2 and 5, I suggested that resilience is theologically significant as it makes us aware of the fact that overcoming injustice and other consequences of sin does not represent an end to one's striving for human and creational flourishing. As such, resilience insists that our embodied existence is enabled by the grace of God who relates to humankind and the whole creation, while reminding us of our calling to relate to others in solidarity and respect. In this chapter, I would like to add that our understanding of resilience can be enriched when viewed through the lens of feast, since the latter is closely connected with the idea of transformation, as we have just seen.

One example of such resilient transformation—or transforming resilience—vis-à-vis the reality of everyday life is the care of the poor and hungry that the image of feast implies. David Ford again points out that in the preaching and ministry of Jesus of Nazareth it is the "poor, sick and needy [who] are at the centre of the feast as the honoured guests."[38] The scriptural testimony unambiguously indicates that Jesus challenges the conventional rules of hospitality when he refuses to invite those who can return the favor of the invitation. Instead, he reaches out to those who are undesirable in different ways, including the poor, physically afflicted, or socially stigmatized.[39] Moreover, the poor and the needy are regarded as God's honored guests at God's feast and to reject them means "to exclude oneself from their host's presence."[40] We can, therefore, legitimately infer that one excludes oneself—and is not excluded by God—as a consequence of one's own unwillingness to be open to and emulate God's generosity.

TTL enriches our discussion with an additional aspect when it makes a case for "mission from the margins," a concept based on the active agency

37. *Merriam-Webster.com*, s.v. "resilience."

38. Ford, *Self and Salvation*, 270.

39. See Goss, "Luke," 532. For a scriptural reference see, for example, Luke 14:7–14. It is the passage that immediately precedes the parable of the Great Dinner that I referred to earlier in this chapter.

40. Ford, *Self and Salvation*, 270.

of marginalized individuals and groups.[41] This concept elaborates on the gospel account of Jesus of Nazareth and his relating to all those who are in various ways marginalized in society. Such affirmatively subversive action seeks to expose and transform the structures and powers that suffocate life. In a theological perspective, this conviction is buttressed by the teaching about God's preferential option for the marginalized as, for instance, the parable of the Great Dinner introduces it in a narrative way. Mission from the margins subverts our common understandings of what it means to be in the center vis-à-vis the margins, *TTL* postulates, when it insists that even the privileged ones have much to learn from people living in marginalized situations (see art. 38). The particular gifts that the marginalized can offer include active hope, collective resistance, and perseverance in the face of various hardships (see *TTL*, art. 39). The aim of such mission—and, to be sure, every form of Christian mission—then is to transform power structures so that they sustain, rather than deny, life and to uphold the dignity and worth of every human being and creation.

TTL explores the issue of resilience even further, even though it employs the language of resistance instead (see art. 43–45).[42] Framed in the missiological discourse of *missio Dei*, it asserts that those involved in God's continuous work of liberation, reconciliation, and restoration are, by implication, also engaged in resisting the systems and structures of patriarchalism, racism, casteism, xenophobia, and other life-denying ideologies. The strength to resist is engendered by the active hope that a change is possible. After all, so the conviction goes, it is God's will that the entire creation will be restored and achieve its ultimate purpose. Those who take part in God's mission of resilience in the face of pernicious contingencies of life are invited to follow the way of Jesus, marked by "mutuality, reciprocity, and interdependence" (*TTL*, art. 45). This approach finds its unambiguous expression not only in Jesus's preaching and teaching but also—and even more significantly—in his practice of sharing meals with various kinds of people.

To be sure, socializing and celebrating together at feasts is "the most radical of all implications of the teaching and practice of Jesus" because feasting unmasks injustice for what it is—a parasite living on God's story with creation; an obstacle on the way to our common life in God. Even such

41. For an in-depth treatment of the concept of mission from the margins, see *TTL*, art. 36–54.

42. As I have already noted in chapter 5, I prefer resilience to resistance since the former implies the awareness that overcoming various instances of injustice and evil does not represent an end to human quest for flourishing and common life.

a seemingly negligible factor as one's behavior and action at the personal level is of political importance since "feeding the hungry is not a matter of the well-fed offering handouts and getting on with their private feasting: the vision is of everyone around the same table, face to face."[43] This structural, and therefore, truly, political dimension is further constructively developed by *TTL*. The affirmation expands on feast as an image of liberation and reconciliation of the entire creation (see *TTL*, art. 101). If such liberation and reconciliation are to be genuine, they must necessarily become vehicles for resisting the status quo characterized by oppression, inequity, and injustice. And they must inevitably go beyond the level of individual and even group efforts to improve conditions for life within the "playing field" defined by the currently dominant political and economic system. Instead, they should strive to critically yet constructively address the political with its structures of shared life. Feast, as scriptural renderings introduce it, represents a model that enables individuals and communities to confront "structures and cultures of oppression and dehumanization that are in contradiction to the values of God's reign" (*TTL*, art. 106).

There is yet another facet of resilience that I would like to discuss here, namely, the dynamic of what I would refer to as "dreaming" and "struggling." To get a better apprehension of what I have in mind, it is useful to consider how Arthur Bradley and Paul Fletcher interpret Christian life. Together with Heidegger, they suggest it is identified by "ontological messianism." For them, human existence, from a Christian perspective, can be described in terms of the "messianic now":

> Just as *Dasein*'s being-towards-death is not simply an awareness that life will end at some point in the future, but rather the knowledge which individualizes our being as authentic in the present, so Christians do not await a future event that will arrive "one fine day" because that expectation structures their life today, now. In this sense, the "messianic now" becomes the uncanny basis of a phenomenological description of human existence itself.[44]

Such an understanding of resilience ushers a radical praxis of the here and now, aimed at rupturing the social, political, cultural, and religious givens.[45]

43. This and the previous citations in this paragraph are from Ford, *Self and Salvation*, 269.

44. Bradley and Fletcher, "Introduction," 184.

45. See also Beare, "It Gets Better," 354. This understanding is also indebted to Walter Benjamin's notion of "weak messianic power." See Benjamin, "On the Concept," 389–400.

This dynamic between "dreaming" and "struggling" is artistically portrayed in the 2019 South Korean acclaimed and award-winning film *Parasite*.[46] The plot follows the story of the Kim family, which includes the father, the mother, and their two young adult children, struggling to secure their living in the capitalist society of contemporary South Korea. The family dwells in the tragicomically cramped premises of a basement apartment, pursuing low-paying temporary jobs. In the midst of their struggle, dreaming represents the reference point and certainty of their daily existence. This is symbolically portrayed not only by the Kim family members being almost permanently glued to the displays of their smartphones—in spite of the omnipresent no signal issues—but also, and primarily, by a scholar's rock which they are given by a family friend and which is in Korean culture believed to bring wealth and prosperity to whoever possesses it.[47] At the same time, however, all family members also actively strive to resist their ill fortune and make a better future for themselves. The son and the daughter of the family are particularly creative in this regard. As their struggle proves to be successful, their dream comes true. Significantly for the purpose of this chapter, the Kim family throws a feast for themselves in the house of their rich employers to celebrate their achievements. Nevertheless, their "realized eschatology" is short-lived and heads toward a tragic ending. The final scene is therefore reminiscent of the beginning of the film's narrative arc with the son single-mindedly pursuing the aim of resisting the recurring hardships through diligent work and dreaming about liberation for his entrapped father, thus reuniting the family.

However, it should be clearly stated that dreaming can be a risky endeavor. One does not need to go further than different kinds of supremacist visions of future to make one's case. The point is not that these "alt-visions" would not be fostered by a certain hope, nor that they would be disinterested in resisting the status quo. The problem lies in their exclusivism.

Though I appreciate that Benjamin accentuates the significance of the here and now, I perceive a potential danger in his apparent overemphasis on the realization of eschatology in history. Examples include former and current communist regimes around the world.

46. The Korean name of the film is *Gisaengchung*. Directed by Bong Joon-ho, *Parasite* was the first non-English-language film ever to win an Academy Award for Best Picture. For further information on the film, see "Parasite," IMDb, accessed December 27, 2021, https://www.imdb.com/title/tt6751668/?ref_=nv_sr_srsg_0.

47. For some background information on the scholar's rock (Korean *suseok*), see *Wikipedia*, s.v. "Suseok."

What all of them have in common is the exclusivist stance of their propagators vis-à-vis different groups of people who do not belong to the story they hold as viable and desirable. In other words, their "dream" becomes a "nightmare" for others.

Inclusive images, such as feast, have a potential to challenge these destructive and life-denying visions. In Jesus's imagination and practice, dinners and feasting stand for God's inclusiveness embodied in the reality of God's reign.[48] This is what I have throughout this book referred to as kin-dom, or, our common life in God. For *TTL*, inclusiveness represents an essential feature of God's reign (see especially art. 46–50). The ecumenical affirmation makes a point that the church demonstrates its commitment to the values of God's reign to the extent that it practices radical hospitality (see *TTL*, art. 47). However, instead of standing in solidarity with the poor, alas, the church is in reality frequently "much more concerned with being in the centres of power, eating with the rich, and lobbying for money to maintain ecclesial bureaucracy" (*TTL*, art. 48). To accept invitation to God's Great Dinner means being committed to resist these temptations and to actively dream and struggle for transformation. It means searching for one's place in God's story of acceptance, inclusion, and reconciliation. It means striving for an imagination to relate one's embodied existence to the personality and needs of the other. It means seeking and pursuing a common life for the entire creation in the force field of God's radical and transformative reign. It means enjoying the feast.

Comm/unity: Journeying Together toward God's Kin-dom

Drawing from our discussion so far, it is the thesis of this chapter that feast stands for an image that fittingly epitomizes the corporeal, imaginative, relational, and transformative nature of being human—in spite of human brokenness as a result of sin. Now I would like to take the argument in this final chapter further. The aspects of feast that I have discussed so far constitute the building blocks of what I have in chapter 5 termed as "comm/unity." The latter term refers to a meshwork of multiple relationships by dignified individuals that appreciate the interdependence and essential unity of humankind based on their createdness in the image of God as well as human interconnection with the rest of creation. The aim is to pursue

48. See Goss, "Luke," 532.

kin-dom, common life in the force field of God's love, mercy, and acceptance, thus attaining the genuine vocation of being human. In this way, the notion of comm/unity helps to shed light, from a Christian perspective, on human embodied existence as a pursuit of our common life in God. In the following section of this chapter, I will seek to elucidate some aspects of comm/unity that are of theological and missiological relevance.

At the most fundamental, yet very powerful, level, comm/unity is pursued in ordinary situations of interpersonal interaction. It is pursued wherever people look after each other, relating to their fellow humans in deeds of solidarity and bearing one another's burdens (see Gal 6:2). In this regard, special consideration should be given to those who lose a chance to enjoy the benefits provided by the current sociopolitical order, those who do not belong or fit in the system due to their otherness and nonconformity, whether real or imagined.[49] The church has a significant role to play in this process as it can invite people to metanoia, that is, the reorienting of the general mindset in society in order to make us all more sensitive to the needs of the marginalized and poor.[50] Nevertheless, this is not a mere didactic function. More importantly, Christians are called—through their pursuit of comm/unity—to embody what they believe and preach, thus contributing their share to the transformation of the world. Thereby they demonstrate their commitment not to resign themselves to the brokenness of humankind and creation as a result of sin. As I argued in chapter 2 with respect to human embodied existence, brokenness is not to be helplessly undertaken as fate but approached as something which—although a part of the earthly reality—is to be struggled against and eventually overcome. At the same time, such attitude bears a witness to the belief in the deep unity of humankind, and even creation, that is sustained—rather than diminished—by diversity.

Such an understanding indicates that comm/unity is a profoundly missiological concept because it contextualizes relational anthropology in the framework of the everyday. To foreground the missiological aspect, two points can be distinguished here. First, to be sustainable and fruitful, comm/unity must be nourished by prayer. Even though much can be said with regard to prayer, I would like to reiterate the idea of prayer as world-mending and world-making that has already been discussed in chapter 2. Prayer and world-mending/making represent two aspects of the same

49. See Schreiter, "Locating," 348.

50. See Máté-Tóth, "Wounded Words," 369.

dynamic when human beings come before God's face in anticipation and readiness to action.[51] Prayer thus becomes a way to pursue a divine-human partnership for the sake of transformation of the world. In prayer, people open themselves to God-talk, willing to be inspired and changed. They are aware that it is through God only that their ontological brokenness can be restored and comm/unity formed. At the same time, however, prayer is a locus for action since one who prays cannot really be passive and resigned. Prayer represents a creative act as one becomes part of what one prays for: justice, peace, reconciliation, and transformation. It is through prayer that a new, redeemed reality emerges. As such, prayer can be seen as a dimension of *missio Dei*, God's story and mission with creation.

The second point to be made with regard to comm/unity as a missiological concept is the acknowledgment of lamenting with others, standing in solidarity with those who suffer, and offering hope to the desperate as a form of mission. *CPTA* identifies lament as an ancient response to human suffering and to the challenges related to human embodied existence. While being a sort of mourning, it also is much more. Both an individual and communal act, lament brings together past events with present orientations and future anticipations. Being deeply aware of the reality of brokenness, lament "instinctively creates a link between healing and mourning, a link which makes new, just relationships possible in the future" (*CPTA*, art. 72). It does turn a blind eye to anything that is human, including various longings and attitudes; it provides space for both desires for vengeance and quests for forgiveness and healing (see *CPTA*, art. 73). Lament, therefore, epitomizes suffering as something intensely real and hope as something not to be taken for granted, yet viable. Lamenting belongs to the missional dimension of comm/unity as a pursuit of relational anthropology because it sensitize us to the idea that being human implies not only brokenness but also—importantly for the thesis of this book—corporeality, imagination, and relationality.

The theological and missiological significance of what lament stands for is ingeniously elaborated by Judith Gruber in her deliberation on the cross and resurrection through the lens of "ghost story."[52] The cross represents both an exhibition of Roman imperial power and a specter of death

51. For further discussion on this point, see Augustine, *Spirit*, 54.

52. I drew upon Gruber's insights on the relevance of the notion of "ghost stories" in my discussion on human brokenness and vulnerability in chapter 2. See Gruber, "Salvation," 382.

that unmasks the "Pax Romana" for what it is—a project built on violence. Similarly, while the wounds on Jesus's crucified body testify to a spectacle of imperial power, they also provide the hope that empire and the story of its legitimacy and might can be undermined. When rendered through the lens of haunting and lamenting, the cross and resurrection "breaks with a triumphant narrative from death to life, but does open our eyes to life that emerges from the midst of suffering that remains."[53] A ghost-story reading of the gospel thus immunizes against any triumphalism and a lack of care for the other, holding on to a hope for life that cannot be taken for granted. And such hope finds a practical expression in comm/unity amid brokenness.

In addition to the everyday and missiological aspects, what I would call a cosmic aspect also needs to be examined to acquire a more complete view of comm/unity. A point of departure for this inquiry can be found in a widely ecumenical awareness of relationality not only among humankind but within the entire creation. When collaborating with God on pursuing such comm/unity, one of the implied duties for Christians is to cultivate and spread this awareness. It is through this awareness of and a willingness to actively participate in comm/unity that Christians—together with other human beings—are invited to partner with God in writing chapters in God's story with the whole creation. Human beings are capable of doing this because they are first drawn by the Spirit into a relationship with God. Furthermore, it is through the Spirit that all humankind, alongside the rest of creation, is invited to make its dwelling in God, its "habitat in the intersectionality of the Trinity."[54] The Scriptures employ the image of Pentecost community as an example par excellence of the Spirit's communal and eschatological presence. It is here that biblical inaugurated eschatology meets radical egalitarianism.[55] This is what I have throughout this book referred to as our common life in God.

However, it is not only that humankind and the rest of creation find their home in God.[56] We can also view this process from the opposite, yet complementary, perspective, namely, as creation being the material embodiment of divine communal life; to be sure, it is an essential feature of our embodied existence. Still, one needs to emphasize that this process is

53. See Gruber, "Salvation," 386. To build her argument, Gruber draws upon Liew, "Gospel," 129–71.

54. Augustine, *Spirit*, 51. See also *CPTA*, art. 82.

55. See Augustine, *Spirit*, 59. See also Zizioulas, 131.

56. See Isa 11:1–9. See also Augustine, *Spirit*, 107.

conditioned upon a transfigured humankind, a true comm/unity, should it have a potential to become a viable home for divine presence. Such transfiguration takes place wherever people are respected and related to in their diversity, the image of God is honored in all human beings, and the temptation is resisted to sacrifice the other for the sake of idols, such as power, money, ideology, sex, nation, etc.[57] For Christians, the Christ event makes tangible and effective the reality of forgiveness that can be perceived, together with Daniela Augustine, as "a return to the other as homecoming in a recovered Eden."[58]

While relating to the other is essential in this respect, one would do well to go beyond the idea that a return to the "lost paradise" represents a desirable goal. Working toward comm/unity is much more than a mere "recovery" as it allows for an element of the innovative and unique to enter into the world. Transformation implies a dynamic of continuity and discontinuity; the unprecedented comes to constructively join that which has been here before to give rise to a new reality. One can thus conceive of a shared, just, and reconciled future with the other, God's kin-dom, in terms of a multiplicity of creation in harmony. Through the power of the Spirit, creation becomes the communal body of God.[59] In this interpretation, our common life in God, a leading image used throughout this book, is the result of a dynamic process. It can appropriately be understood as the exaltation of the diversity of embodied humanity. As such, it is a communal event: the consummation or finalization of God's creation (see *CPTA*, art. 115).[60] However, human beings are to respect, care, and bear responsibility for all living creatures and the rest of creation: "God created us to be in loving relationship not only with one another, but also with the entire creation" (*CPTA*, art. 90). Therefore, the fundamental relationality of humankind has both its anthropic and non-anthropic dimensions. I would propose that comm/unity as a concept that enables understanding Christian existence and mission as relational anthropology involves human beings relating to their human and nonhuman others.

57. See Augustine, *Spirit*, 93. See also Sacks, *To Heal*, 28.

58. Augustine, *Spirit*, 172.

59. See Augustine, *Spirit*, 173 and 228.

60. Needless to say, this consummation or finalization is to be understood as inseparable from the material reality of creation. *CPTA* puts it that heaven is not to be conceived as "a dream or distraction from endeavour on earth, but as the assurance of the final vindication of God's children and the knowledge that in the Lord their labour is not in vain" (art. 113). This emphasis concurs with the thesis of chapter 2.

Finally, there is a liturgical aspect that helps explicate the theological and missiological significance of comm/unity. I appreciate liturgy in a broad sense, going beyond and not necessarily connected to the action taking place in houses of worship. An interesting dynamic of God acting on behalf of creation and creation responding to God's call with thanksgiving, liturgy is indivisible from the cosmic aspect discussed above. Comm/unity, embracing both human beings and all the other creatures of God, is thus a liturgical entity. Liturgy, particularly in relation to salvation and transformation, is elucidated by David Ford's deliberations on what he refers to as the worshipping self. As already discussed in chapter 5, Ford turns to the image of the face and the dynamics of facing the other to establish a point of departure for theologizing. In addition, this image represents a symbol of the self. Moreover, it is the symbol of God's face that provides a clue to the selfhood of "the worshipping self, before the face of Christ and other people, in an economy of superabundance."[61] Jesus Christ and his face are of ultimate relevance in this respect. Elaborating on his notion of the worshipping self, Ford interprets Jesus of Nazareth, the Christ, as "a person who in facing God and other people embodies the other-oriented concept of self."[62] Worship, or liturgy, is thence introduced as relational, communal action: through the power and grace of the Spirit, human beings relate to God and their fellow humans, experiencing a reciprocal type of relationship with them. Furthermore, as both the Scriptures and *CPTA* unequivocally emphasize, the entire creation is invited to join in this liturgical comm/unity.[63] No less significantly for Christian existence and mission, liturgy is also intimately connected with the experiences of daily life, including longing, communication, suffering, mourning, caring, and—as has the argument of this chapter underlined—feasting.

Another useful view on the liturgical aspect is offered by Daniela Augustine. She asserts that humans are liturgical beings when she expounds on the notion of *homo adorans*.[64] Starkly juxtaposed with the concept of *homo sapiens*—and, especially, *homo faber*—this notion highlights the intercessory engagement that people commit to for the sake of each other and the rest of creation. Embracing embodied existence with all its features and

61. Ford, *Self and Salvation*, 9.

62. Ford, *Self and Salvation*, 166.

63. See, for instance, Pss 98 and 100. See also *CPTA*, art. 114–15 and 117.

64. See Augustine, *Spirit*, 52 and 137. On *homo adorans*, see also Schmemann, *For the Life*, 15.

standing in solidarity with the fellow other, both human and nonhuman, intercession is a way to counter brokenness and journey together toward God's kin-dom in hope. Human beings are much more than mere producers and consumers; they are beings for and with others—pursuing comm/unity to attain our common life in God. As *homo adorans*, a worshipping creature (or Ford's worshipping self), each individual human being is created in the image of God to exercise a priestly function, standing at the center of creation and helping it fulfil its destiny. To put it in other words, people are called to "the continual eucharistic discernment of the world as a sacrament toward cultivating a cosmic community of shared life and flourishing with the other—with God as well as with the anthropic and nonanthropic neighbor."[65] As such, Augustine relates the existence and calling of humankind to the life of God as she conceives of human beings as agents of the "world's transfiguration into the likeness of God's communal life."[66]

We have already examined the crucial importance of the Eucharist in relation to feasting earlier. At this place I will, therefore, conclude my discussion by referring to *TTL* that turns to the poetic image of feast to account for what I have referred to as the liturgical aspect of comm/unity. The feast of life—a trope introduced by *TTL*—is eucharistic in the sense that it evocatively appeals to the comm/unity of all God's creatures to respond in thanksgiving to what their Creator, Liberator, and Reconciler has done and continues to do.[67] Celebrating God's radically loving and transformative reign—or, kin-dom—as the foundation and fountain of superabundant life for all, it epitomizes our common life in God, "the liberation and reconciliation of the whole creation which is the goal of mission" (*TTL*, art. 101).[68]

Feasting Together: Our Common Life in God

Engaging in dialogue with *TTL*, *CPTA*, and a variety of theological (and other) voices, this chapter has examined the scriptural image of feast to give

65. Augustine, *Spirit*, 136.

66. Augustine, *Spirit*, 48.

67. To help illuminate what interrelatedness might mean, Robert Schreiter theologizes the Eucharist as the symbol of a prototypical community. See Schreiter, "Locating," 348.

68. Similarly, Daniela Augustine turns to J. B. Metz's understanding of sacraments as an anticipatory memory to argue that the source and purpose of the eucharistic life of the church is to be found in "union with God and neighbor in a wholesome, ontologically renewed creation." Augustine, *Spirit*, 180. See also Metz, *Faith*, 117–18.

an emphatic expression and pinnacle to the overall thesis of the present book; that is, a case for a theological anthropology based on the fundamental importance of the body, imagination, and the relational nature of being human in order to enable pursuing a common life for the entire creation in the force field of kin-dom—God's radical and transformative reign of inclusion, love, justice, and reconciliation. Drawing on the dynamic of promise and resilience, the relevance of feast as an image then lies in its power to relate to various dimensions of life, interlinking the human with the nonhuman, the physical with the spiritual, the personal with the communal, and the past with the presence and the future. This is the reality that I have referred to as comm/unity. In addition, feast as a symbol addresses three specific aspects that also are of theological and anthropological relevance. First, feast is closely connected with human experiences, both positive and negative, celebrating and lamenting. It offers space for sharing stories and seeking transformation. As such, second, feast has an eschatological thrust and direction. It both "dreams of" and "struggles toward" the relationships and realities that are not yet part of our current created order. Therefore, third, it nurtures and sustains a certain type of utopianism, following the praxis of Jesus Christ to subvert the relations and structures in service of powers that be. The combination of these three aspects fosters hope—a hope that transformation is possible, that the entire creation can have a common superabundant life in God.

From a Christian perspective, however, I believe that stopping here would be both irresponsible and dangerous. Not every kind of transformation is desirable. The image of feast, I suggest, helps address this challenge. While giving assurance about the transformation of all reality in the coming reign of justice, reconciliation, and peace, the image of feast, with its accentuation of inclusiveness and equality, also empowers us to resist all life-denying forces. Called to journey together with the rest of creation toward God's kin-dom, Christians are thus enabled to discern and actively live their vocation, entering into fellowship with various guests, both human and nonhuman, and their common Host at the Great Dinner. Given the scriptural emphasis on togetherness, this vocation necessarily includes building the structures of shared life, in close collaboration with the rest of humankind and in deep solidarity with the entire creation, so that "God may be all in all" (1 Cor 15:28 NRSV).

Bibliography

Adorno, Theodor. *Negative Dialectics*. Translated by E. B. Ashton. New York: Continuum, 1973.

Althaus-Reid, Marcella. *Indecent Theology: Theological Perversions in Sex, Gender and Politics*. London: Routledge, 2000.

Alves, Rubem A. *El enigma de la religion*. Montevideo, Uruguay: Tierra Nueva, 1979.

———. *The Poet, the Warrior, the Prophet*. London: SCM, 1990.

Arendt, Hannah. *The Human Condition*. Chicago: University of Chicago Press, 1958.

Auerbach, Erich. *Mimesis: The Representation of Reality in Western Literature*. Princeton, NJ: Princeton University Press, 1953.

Augustine. *The City of God*. Translated by Marcus Dods. New York: Modern Library, 1999.

Augustine, Daniela C. *Pentecost, Hospitality, and Transfiguration: Toward a Spirit-Inspired Vision of Social Transformation*. Cleveland, TN: CPT, 2012.

———. *The Spirit and the Common Good: Shared Flourishing in the Image of God*. Grand Rapids: Eerdmans, 2019.

Avis, Paul. "Apologetics and the Rebirth of the Imagination." Editorial, *Ecclesiology* 9 (2013) 303–10.

———. *God and the Creative Imagination: Metaphor, Symbol and Myth in Religion and Theology*. London: Routledge, 1999.

Balabán, Milan. "Člověk jako hlína, prach a popel." In *Kvete-li vinný kmen*, 242–44. Prague: Kalich, 2002.

———. "Člověk jako sadař světa a pastýř mimolidského tvorstva." In *Hebrejské člověkosloví*, 58–64. Prague: Herrmann & synové, 1996.

———. "Člověk je muž a žena." In *Hebrejské člověkosloví*, 42–52. Prague: Herrmann & synové, 1996.

———. "Člověk - královský správce všeho mimolidského tvorstva." In *Hebrejské člověkosloví*, 53–57. Prague: Herrmann & synové, 1996.

———. "Člověk - syn Boží v mimolidském světě." In *Hebrejské člověkosloví*, 65–69. Prague: Herrmann & synové, 1996.

———. "Hřích jako scestnost a netrpělivost." In *Hebrejské člověkosloví*, 87–98. Prague: Herrmann & synové, 1996.

———. "Nový model vztahu člověk - kosmos?" In *Hebrejské člověkosloví*, 122–26. Prague: Herrmann & synové, 1996.

———. "Obraz člověka v hebrejském pojetí." In *Kvete-li vinný kmen*, 423–32. Prague: Kalich, 2002.

———. "Odposvátnění veškerenstva?" In *Hebrejské člověkosloví*, 115–22. Prague: Herrmann & synové, 1996.

———. "Radost člověka a pomíjivost života." In *Kvete-li vinný kmen*, 231–42. Prague: Kalich, 2002.

———. "Tvořící Pravda nás předchází." In *Hebrejské člověkosloví*, 104–6. Prague: Herrmann & synové, 1996.

———. "Vina a trest." In *Kvete-li vinný kmen*, 97–99. Prague: Kalich, 2002.

———. "Vrženost?" In *Hebrejské člověkosloví*, 112–15. Prague: Herrmann & synové, 1996.

Bargár, Pavol. "'Imagine!': Culture, Theology, and the Power of Imagination." *Communio Viatorum* 63 (2021) 164–77.

———. *Narrative, Myth, Transformation: Reflecting Theologically on Contemporary Culture*. Jihlava, Czech Republic: Mlýn, 2016.

———. "Relating to Others: The Coronavirus, the Imagined Body, and Enfleshment." *Communio Viatorum* 62 (2020) 46–66.

———. "Toward Comm/unity amidst Brokenness: Christian Mission as (a Pursuit of) Relational Anthropology." *International Review of Mission* 110 (2021) 231–45.

Bavinck, Herman. *Reformed Dogmatics*. Vol. 2, *God and Creation*. Edited by John Bolt. Translated by John Vriend. Grand Rapids: Baker Academic, 2004.

Beare, Zachary. "It Gets Better . . . All in Good Time: Messianic Rhetoric and a Political Theology of Social Control." *Journal for Cultural Research* 19 (2015) 352–64.

Benhabib, Seyla. *Situating the Self*. New York: Routledge, 1992.

Benjamin, Walter. "On the Concept of History." In *Walter Benjamin: Selected Writings*, edited by Howard Eiland and Michael W. Jennings, 389–400. Cambridge, MA: Harvard University Press, 2006.

Bevans, Stephen B., SVD. "Contextual Methods in Theology." In *Essays in Contextual Theology*, 1–29. Boston: Brill, 2018.

———. "Contextual Theology as Practical Theology." In *Essays in Contextual Theology*, 30–46. Boston: Brill, 2018.

———. *Models of Contextual Theology*. Maryknoll, NY: Orbis, 1992.

Bevans, Stephen B., and Roger P. Schroeder. *Constants in Context: A Theology of Mission for Today*. Maryknoll, NY: Orbis, 2004.

———. *Prophetic Dialogue: Reflections on Christian Mission Today*. Maryknoll, NY: Orbis, 2011.

Binsbergen, Wim van. "*Ubuntu* and the Globalisation of Southern African Thought and Society." *Quest* 15 (2001) 53–89.

Bong, Sharon A. "Ecclesiology: Becoming the Queer, Postcolonial, (Eco-)feminist Body of Christ in Asia." *Concilium* 5 (2019) 70–80.

Bonhoeffer, Dietrich. *The Cost of Discipleship*. 2nd ed. New York: Macmillan, 1959.

Bosch, David J. *Transforming Mission: Paradigm Shifts in Theology of Mission*. Maryknoll, NY: Orbis, 1991.

Bourdieu, Pierre. *Outline of a Theory of Practice*. Cambridge: Cambridge University Press, 1977.

Boyle, Gregory. *Barking to the Choir: The Power of Radical Kinship*. New York: Simon and Schuster, 2017.

Bradley, Arthur, and Paul Fletcher. "Introduction: On a Newly Arisen Messianic Tone in Philosophy." *Journal for Cultural Research* 13 (2009) 183–89.

Bretherton, Luke. *Christ and the Common Life: Political Theology and the Case for Democracy*. Grand Rapids: Eerdmans, 2019.

Brueggemann, Walter. *Journey to the Common Good*. Louisville: Westminster John Knox, 2010.

———. *The Practice of Prophetic Imagination*. Minneapolis: Fortress, 2012.

Burke, Kenneth. *Language as Symbolic Action: Essays on Life, Literature and Method*. Berkeley: University of California Press, 1966.

Cathey, Robert Andrew. *God in Postliberal Perspective: Between Realism and Non-Realism*. Burlington, VT: Ashgate, 2009.

Cavanaugh, William T. *Theopolitical Imagination: Discovering the Liturgy as a Political Act in an Age of Global Consumerism*. London: T. & T. Clark, 2002.

Chau, Carolyn. "The Church: Mission-Led Ecclesiology for Today." In *Christian Mission, Contextual Theology, Prophetic Dialogue: Essays in Honor of Stephen B. Bevans, SVD*, edited by Dale T. Irvin and Peter C. Phan, 229–45. Maryknoll, NY: Orbis, 2018.

Clawson, Julie. "Imagination, Hope, and Reconciliation in Ricoeur and Moltmann." *Anglican Theological Review* 95 (2013) 293–309.

Congdon, David W. "'A Beautiful Anarchy': Religion, Fascism, and Violence in the Theopolitical Imagination of Guillermo del Toro." *Cultural Encounters* 6 (2010) 43–67.

Cook, Roger F. "Angels, Fiction, and History of Berlin: Wings of Desire." In *The Cinema of Wim Wenders: Image, Narrative, and the Postmodern Condition*, edited by Roger F. Cook and Gerd Gemünden, 163–90. Detroit: Wayne State University Press, 1997.

Costas, Orlando. *The Integrity of Mission: The Inner Life and Outreach of the Church*. New York: Harper & Row, 1979.

Coupe, Laurence. *Myth*. London: Routledge, 1997.

Crites, Stephen. "The Narrative Quality of Experience." In *Why Narrative? Readings in Narrative Theology*, edited by Stanley Hauerwas and L. Gregory Jones, 65–88. Eugene, OR: Wipf & Stock, 1995.

Crossan, John Dominic. *God and Empire: Jesus Against Rome, Then and Now*. New York: HarperOne, 2007.

———. *The Historical Jesus: The Life of a Jewish Mediterranean Peasant*. New York: HarperCollins, 1991.

Crouch, Andy. *Culture Making: Recovering Our Creative Calling*. Downers Grove: InterVarsity, 2008.

Davaney, Sheila Greeve, and Delwin Brown. "Postliberalism." In *The Blackwell Encyclopedia of Modern Christian Thought*, edited by Alister E. McGrath, 455. Oxford: Blackwell, 1993.

Davey, Andrew P. "Better Place: Performing the Urbanisms of Hope." *International Journal of Public Theology* 2 (2008) 27–46.

De Chickera, Duleep Kamil. "Just Peace: Beyond Rhetoric." *Ecumenical Review* 65 (2013) 181–98.

De Gruchy, John W. *Reconciliation: Restoring Justice*. Minneapolis: Fortress, 2002.

DeHart, Paul J. *The Trial of the Witnesses: The Rise and Decline of Postliberal Theology*. Malden, MA: Blackwell, 2006.

De La Torre, Miguel A. *Genesis*. Louisville: Westminster John Knox, 2011.

Delpech-Ramey, Joshua. "Supernatural Capital: A Note on the Žižek-Milbank Debate." *Political Theology* 11 (2010) 121–25.

Derrida, Jacques. "Living On: Border Lines." In *Deconstruction and Criticism*, edited by Harold Bloom, 62–142. New York: Seabury, 1979.

———. "The Villanova Roundtable: A Conversation with Jacques Derrida." In *Deconstruction in a Nutshell: A Conversation with Jacques Derrida*, edited by John Caputo, 3–28. New York: Fordham University Press, 1996.

Downey, Martha Elias. "A Perspective on Narrative Theology: Its Purpose, Particularity and Centrality." *Theoforum* 43 (2012) 291–307.

Eglinton, James. *Trinity and Organism: Towards a New Reading of Herman Bavinck's Organic Motif*. London: T. & T. Clark, 2012.

Eisland, Nancy L. *The Disabled God: Toward a Liberatory Theology of Disability*. Nashville: Abingdon, 1994.

Eliade, Mircea. *The Myth of the Eternal Return: Cosmos and History*. Translated by Willard R. Trask. Princeton, NJ: Princeton University Press, 2018.

Evans, Jeanne. *Paul Ricoeur's Hermeneutics of the Imagination*. New York: Peter Lang, 1995.

Ewell, Samuel E., III. *Faith Seeking Conviviality: Reflections on Ivan Illich, Christian Mission, and the Promise of Life Together*. Eugene, OR: Cascade, 2020.

Faith and Order Commission. *Christian Perspectives on Theological Anthropology: A Faith and Order Study Document*. Faith and Order paper no. 199. Geneva: World Council of Churches, 2005.

Fiddes, Paul S. "Concept, Image and Story in Systematic Theology." *International Journal of Systematic Theology* 11 (2009) 3–23.

Fiske, John. *Understanding Popular Culture*. London: Unwin Hyman, 1989.

Flood, Gavin. "Religious Practice and the Nature of the Human." In *Interreligious Comparisons in Religious Studies and Theology: Comparison Revisited*, edited by Perry Schmidt-Leukel and Andreas Nehring, 130–41. London: Bloomsbury, 2016.

Ford, David F. *Self and Salvation: Being Transformed*. Cambridge: Cambridge University Press, 1999.

———. "System, Story, Performance: A Proposal about the Role of Narrative in Christian Systematic Theology." In *Why Narrative? Readings in Narrative Theology*, edited by Stanley Hauerwas and L. Gregory Jones, 191–215. Eugene, OR: Wipf & Stock, 1995.

Frei, Hans W. *The Eclipse of Biblical Narrative: A Study in Eighteenth and Nineteenth Century Hermeneutics*. New Haven, CT: Yale University Press, 1974.

———. *Theology and Narrative: Selected Essays*. Edited by George Hunsinger and William C. Placher. New York: Oxford University Press, 1993.

Fuentes, Agustín. *Race, Monogamy, and Other Lies They Told You: Busting Myths about Human Nature*. Berkeley: University of California Press, 2012.

Gendlin, Eugene T. "How Philosophy Cannot Appeal to Experience, and How It Can." In *Language Beyond Postmodernism: Saying and Thinking in Gendlin's Philosophy*, edited by David Michael Levin, 3–41. Evanston, IL: Northwestern University Press, 1997.

Genette, Gérard. *Narrative Discourse*. Oxford: Basil Blackwell, 1980.

Godzieba, Anthony. "'Stay with Us . . .' (Lk. 24.29)—'Come, Lord Jesus' (Rev. 22.20): Incarnation, Eschatology, and Theology's Sweet Predicament." *Theological Studies* 67 (2006) 783–95.

Gorringe, T. J. *Furthering Humanity: A Theology of Culture*. Aldershot: Ashgate, 2004.

———. "The Shape of the Human Home: Cities, Global Capital, and *Ec-clesia*." *Political Theology* 2 (2000) 80–94.

Goss, Robert E. "John." In *The Queer Bible Commentary*, edited by Deryn Guest et al., 548–65. London: SCM, 2006.

Graf, Alexander. *The Cinema of Wim Wenders: The Celluloid Highway*. London: Wallflower, 2002.

Graham, Elaine. "Words Made Flesh: Women, Embodiment and Practical Theology." *Feminist Theology* 7 (1999) 109–21.

Greenberg, Irving. "Religion as a Force for Reconciliation and Peace: A Jewish Analysis." In *Beyond Violence: Religious Sources of Social Transformation in Judaism, Christianity, and Islam*, edited by James L. Heft, SM, 88–112. New York: Fordham University Press, 2004.

Grenz, Stanley J. "Ecclesiology." In *The Cambridge Companion to Postmodern Theology*, edited by Kevin J. Vanhoozer, 252–68. Cambridge: Cambridge University Press, 2003.

Grey, Mary. "The Shape of the Human Home: A Response to Professor T. Gorringe." *Political Theology* 2 (2000) 95–103.

Grimes, Ronald. "Of Words the Speaker, of Deeds the Doer." *Journal of Religion* 66 (1986) 1–17.

Gruber, Judith. "Salvation in a Wounded World: Towards a Spectral Theology of Mission." *Mission Studies* 37 (2020) 374–96.

Harrison, Beverly W. *Making the Connections: Essays in Feminist Social Ethics*. Edited by Carol S. Robb. Boston: Beacon, 1985.

Hauerwas, Stanley, and William H. Willimon. *Resident Aliens*. Nashville: Abingdon, 1989.

Haughton, Rosemary. *Beginning Life in Christ*. Westminster, MD: Newman, 1969.

Hearon, Holly E. "1 and 2 Corinthians." In *The Queer Bible Commentary*, edited by Deryn Guest et al., 606–23. London: SCM, 2006.

Henriksen, Jan-Olav. *Religious Pluralism and Pragmatist Theology: Openness and Resistance*. Leiden: Brill Rodopi, 2019.

Hopkins, Jerry, and Danny Sugerman. *No One Here Gets Out Alive*. London: Plexus, 1980.

Hošek, Pavel. *Kouzlo vyprávění: Proměňující moc příběhu a „křest fantazie" v pojetí C. S. Lewise*. Prague: Návrat domů, 2013.

Hošek, Pavel, and Pavol Bargár. "Lidé žijící v příbězích." In *Kdo je člověk? Teologická antropologie ekumenicky*, edited by Ivana Noble and Zdenko Širka, 71–88. Prague: Karolinum, 2021.

Irenaeus of Lyons. *Against the Heresies*. Grand Rapids: Christian Classics Ethereal Library. https://ccel.org/ccel/irenaeus/against_heresies_v/anf01.ix.vii.vii.html.

Isasi-Diaz, Ada Maria. "Solidarity: Love of Neighbor in the 1980s." In *Lift Every Voice: Constructing Christian Theologies from the Underside*, edited by Susan Brooks Thistlethwaite and Mary Potter Engel, 31–40, 303–5. San Francisco: Harper, 1990.

Ivancic, Mary Karita, SND. "Imagining Faith: The Biblical Imagination in Theory and Practice." *Theological Education* 41 (2006) 127–39.

Jennings, Willie James. *Acts*. Nashville: Abingdon, 2017.

Jenson, Robert W. *Systematic Theology*. Vol. 2, *The Works of God*. New York: Oxford University Press, 1999.

Johnson, Luke Timothy. *Faith's Freedom: A Classic Spirituality for Contemporary Christians*. Philadelphia: Augsburg Fortress, 1990.

Joustra, Jessica. "An Embodied *Imago Dei*: How Herman Bavinck's Understanding of the Image of God Can Help Inform Conversations on Race." *Journal of Reformed Theology* 11 (2017) 9–23.

Kearney, Richard. *On Paul Ricoeur: The Owl of Minerva*. Burlington, VT: Ashgate, 2004.

———. *On Stories*. London: Routledge, 2002.

———. *Poetics of Imagining: From Husserl to Lyotard*. London: HarperCollins, 1991.

Keenan, Oliver James, OP. "The Politics of Sacred Vulnerability." *Medieval Mystical Theology* 28 (2019) 80–96.

Kelsey, David H. *Eccentric Existence: A Theological Anthropology*. 2 vols. Louisville: Westminster John Knox, 2009.

Kirk, J. Andrew. *Being Human: An Historical Inquiry into Who We Are*. Eugene, OR: Wipf & Stock, 2019.

Klaasen, John. "Open-Ended Narrative and Moral Formation." *Acta Theologica* 32 (2012) 103–17.

Kristeva, Julia. *Crisis of the European Subject*. New York: Other, 2000.

Kritzinger, J. N. J. (Klippies), and Willem Saayman. *David J. Bosch: Prophetic Integrity, Cruciform Praxis*. Pietermaritzburg, South Africa: Cluster, 2011.

Labrecque, Cory Andrew. "The Glorified Body: Corporealities in the Catholic Tradition." *Religions* 8 (2017). http://doi:10.3390/rel8090166.

———. "Morphological Freedom and the Rebellion against Human Bodiliness: Notes from the Roman Catholic Tradition." In *Religion and Transhumanism: The Unknown Future of Human Enhancement*, edited by Calvin Mercer and Tracy J. Trothen. Santa Barbara, CA: Praeger, 2015.

Lash, Nicholas. "Ideology, Metaphor, and Analogy." In *Why Narrative? Readings in Narrative Theology*, edited by Stanley Hauerwas and L. Gregory Jones, 113–37. Eugene, OR: Wipf & Stock, 1995.

Lausanne Movement. *The Cape Town Commitment: A Confession of Faith and a Call to Action* (2011). https://lausanne.org/content/ctcommitment.

Lebacqz, Karen. *Justice in an Unjust World: Foundations for a Christian Approach to Justice*. Minneapolis: Augsburg, 1987.

Lederach, John Paul. *The Moral Imagination: The Art and Soul of Building Peace*. New York: Oxford University Press, 2005.

Leidinger, Miriam. "Vulner-*ability*: A Systematic Theological Approach to an Ambivalent Term." *Mission Studies* 37 (2020) 397–415.

Levinas, Emmanuel. *Totality and Infinity: An Essay on Exteriority*. Dordrecht: Kluwer, 1991.

Lewis, C. S. *An Experiment in Criticism*. Cambridge: Cambridge University Press, 2008.

Lewis Hall, Elizabeth. "What Are Bodies For? An Integrative Examination of Embodiment." *Christian Scholar's Review* 39 (2010) 159–75.

Lewis Hall, Elizabeth, and Erik Thoennes. "At Home in Our Bodies: Implications of the Incarnation for Embodiment." *Christian Scholar's Review* 36 (2006) 29–46.

Liew, Tat-siong Benny. "The Gospel of Bare Life: Reading Death, Dream and Desire through John's Jesus." In *Psychoanalytic Mediations between Marxist and Postcolonial Readings of the Bible*, edited by Tat-siong B. Liew and Erin Runions, 129–71. Atlanta: SBL, 2016.

Lindbeck, George A. *The Nature of Doctrine: Religion and Theology in a Postliberal Age*. Philadelphia: Westminster, 1984.

Loughlin, Gerard. "The End of Sex." Introduction to *Queer Theology: Rethinking the Western Body*, edited by Gerard Loughlin, 1–34. Oxford: Blackwell, 2007.

———. *Telling God's Story: Bible, Church and Narrative Theology*. Cambridge: Cambridge University Press, 1996.

Lucie-Smith, Alexander. *Narrative Theology and Moral Theology: The Infinite Horizon*. Aldershot, UK: Ashgate, 2007.

Lynch, Gordon. *Understanding Theology and Popular Culture*. Malden, MA: Blackwell, 2005.

Lynch, William F., SJ. *Christ and Prometheus: A New Image of the Secular*. Notre Dame, IN: University of Notre Dame Press, 1970.

MacIntyre, Alasdair. *After Virtue: A Study in Moral Theory*. 2nd ed. London: Duckworth, 1985.

Manchala, Deenabandhu. "Moving in the Spirit: Called to Transforming Discipleship: Reflections from the Vantage Points of the Marginalized People." *International Review of Mission* 106 (2017) 201–15.

Marion, Jean-Luc. *God Without Being*. Chicago: University of Chicago Press, 1991.

Marshall, Bruce D. "Absorbing the World: Christianity and the Universe of Truths." In *Theology and Dialogue: Essays in Conversation with George Lindbeck*, edited by Bruce D. Marshall, 69–102. Notre Dame, IN: University of Notre Dame Press, 1990.

———. *Trinity and Truth*. Cambridge: Cambridge University Press, 2000.

Martin, Dale B. *The Corinthian Body*. New Haven, CT: Yale University Press, 1995.

Massey, Doreen. *World City*. Cambridge, UK: Polity, 2007.

Máté-Tóth, András. "Wounded Words in a Wounded World: Opportunities for Mission in Central and Eastern Europe Today." *Mission Studies* 37 (2020) 354–73.

Mbembe, Achille. *Critique of Black Reason*. Translated by Laurent Dubois. Durham, NC: Duke University Press, 2017.

McFague, Sallie. *Blessed Are the Consumers: Climate Change and the Practice of Restraint*. Minneapolis: Fortress, 2013.

———. "Human Dignity and the Integrity of Creation." Epilogue to *Theology That Matters: Ecology, Economy, and God*, edited by Darby Kathleen Ray, 199–212. Minneapolis: Fortress, 2006.

McFarland, Ian A. "The Body of Christ: Rethinking a Classic Ecclesiological Model." *International Journal of Systematic Theology* 7 (2005) 225–45.

———. *Difference and Identity: A Theological Anthropology*. Cleveland: Pilgrim, 2001.

Meeks, M. Douglas. *God the Economist: The Doctrine of God and Political Economy*. Minneapolis: Fortress, 1989.

Meiring, Jacob. "Theology in the Flesh: A Model for Theological Anthropology as Embodied Sensing." *HTS Teologiese Studies/Theological Studies* 71 (2015) art. 2858. https://doi.org/10.4102/hts.v71i3.2858.

———. "*Ubuntu* and the Body: A Perspective from Theological Anthropology as Embodied Sensing." *Verbum et Ecclesia* 36 (2015) art. 1423. https://doi.org/10.4102/ve.v36i2.1423.

Méndez-Montoya, Ángel F., OP. "Eucharistic Imagination: A Queer Body Politics." *Modern Theology* 30 (2014) 326–39.

Merleau-Ponty, Maurice. *Phenomenology of Perception*. Translated by Colin Smith. London: Routledge, 2002.

Metz, Johann Baptist. *Faith in History and Society: Toward a Practical Fundamental Theology*. New York: Seabury, 1980.

Michener, Ronald T. *Postliberal Theology: A Guide for the Perplexed*. London: Bloomsbury T. & T. Clark, 2013.

Mikoski, Gordon S. "On Cultivating a Transgressive Theological Imagination." *Theology Today* 70 (2013) 105–8.

Moloney, Francis J., SDB. *The Gospel of John*. Sacra Pagina 4. Collegeville, MN: Liturgical, 1998.

Moltmann, Jürgen. *The Coming of God: Christian Eschatology*. Translated by Margaret Kohl. Minneapolis: Fortress, 1996.

———. *Creating a Just Future: The Politics of Peace and the Ethics of Creation in a Threatened World*. London: SCM, 1989.

———. *The Living God and the Fullness of Life*. Translated by Margaret Kohl. Geneva: World Council of Churches, 2016.

———. *On Human Being: Christian Anthropology in the Conflicts of the Present*. 2nd ed. Minneapolis: Fortress, 2009.

Murphy, Francesca Aran. *God Is Not a Story: Realism Revisited*. New York: Oxford University Press, 2007.

Nelson, James B. *Body Theology*. Louisville: Westminster John Knox, 1992.

Neyrey, Jerome H. *Paul, in Other Words*. Louisville: Westminster John Knox, 1990.

Niebuhr, H. Richard. *Christ and Culture*. San Francisco: Harper, 2001.

———. "The Story of Our Life." In *The Meaning of Revelation*, 43–81. New York: Macmillan, 1941.

Niebuhr, Reinhold. *The Nature and Destiny of Man*. Vol. 1, *Human Nature*. London: Nisbet, 1941.

Nietzsche, Friedrich. *The Gay Science: With a Prelude in Rhymes and an Appendix of Songs*. Translated by Walter Kaufmann. New York: Vintage, 1974.

Noble, Ivana. "Apophatic Aspects of Theological Conversation." In *Essays in Ecumenical Theology I: Aims, Methods, Themes, and Contexts*, 36–52. Boston: Brill, 2019.

Panotto, Nicolás. "Otherness, Paradox, and Utopia: Theological Imagination and the Deconstruction of Power." *Ecumenical Review* 69 (2017) 45–59.

Pecknold, C. C. *Transforming Postliberal Theology: George Lindbeck, Pragmatism and Scripture*. London: T. & T. Clark, 2005.

Phillips, Timothy R. "Postliberal Theology." In *Evangelical Dictionary of Theology*, edited by Walter A. Elwell, 938. Grand Rapids: Baker, 2001.

Pierson, John. "Faith and Politics in the Public Square: Citizen Organizing in Urban Neighbourhoods," *Political Theology* 3 (2001) 80–87.

Pope Francis. *Laudato Si'*. Encyclical. May 24, 2015. https://www.vatican.va/content/francesco/en/encyclicals/documents/papa-francesco_20150524_enciclica-laudato-si.html.

Pope John Paul II. *Man and Woman He Created Them: A Theology of the Body*. Translated by Michael Waldstein. Boston: Pauline, 2006.

Radford Ruether, Rosemary. *Sexism and God-Talk: Toward a Feminist Theology*. Boston: Beacon, 1983.

Ricoeur, Paul. *Lectures on Ideology and Utopia*. Edited by G. H. Taylor. New York: Columbia University Press, 1986.

———. *Time and Narrative*. Vol. 1. Translated by Kathleen McLaughlin and David Pellauer. Chicago: University of Chicago Press, 1990.

Robinson, John A. T. *The Body: A Study in Pauline Theology*. London: SCM, 1957.

Ross, Kenneth R. "Brexit, Trump, and Christ's Call to Discipleship." *International Review of Mission* 106 (2017) 369–88.

Sacks, Jonathan. *The Politics of Hope*. London: Vintage, 2000.

———. *To Heal a Fractured World: The Ethics of Responsibility*. New York: Shocken, 2007.

Schmemann, Alexander. *For the Life of the World*. Crestwood, NJ: St. Vladimir's Seminary Press, 1983.

Schneiders, Sandra M. "Biblical Spirituality." *Interpretation: A Journal for Bible and Theology* 70 (2016) 417–30.

Schreiter, Robert. "Locating European Mission in a Wounded World in Deep Transformation." *Mission Studies* 37 (2020) 333–53.

Schroer, Silvia, and Thomas Staubli. "Bodily and Embodied: Being Human in the Tradition of the Hebrew Bible." *Interpretation: A Journal of Bible and Theology* 67 (2013) 5–19.

Sedmak, Clemens. *The Capacity to Be Displaced: Resilience, Mission, and Inner Strength*. Leiden: Brill, 2017.

Segundo, Juan Luis. *Evolution and Guilt*. Dublin: Gill & Macmillan, 1980.

———. *Grace and the Human Condition*. Dublin: Gill & Macmillan, 1980.

———. *The Liberation of Theology*. Maryknoll, NY: Orbis, 1976.

Shakespeare, Steven. Review of *Telling God's Story*, by Gerard Loughlin. *Modern Believing* 38 (1997) 60–62.

Sison, Antonio D. *The Sacred Foodways of Film: Theological Servings in 11 Food Films*. Eugene, OR: Pickwick, 2016.

———. *World Cinema, Theology, and the Human: Humanity in Deep Focus*. New York: Routledge, 2012.

Song, Choan-Seng. *The Believing Heart: An Invitation to Story Theology*. Minneapolis: Fortress, 1999.

Spivak, Gayatri C. *A Critique of Postcolonial Reason: Toward a History of Vanishing Present*. 4th ed. Cambridge, MA: Harvard University Press, 1999.

Sremac, Srdjan, and Ruard R. Ganzevoort. "Trauma and Lived Religion: Embodiment and Emplotment." In *Trauma and Lived Religion: Transcending the Ordinary*, edited by Ruard R. Ganzevoort and Srdjan Sremac, 1–11. New York: Palgrave Macmillan, 2018.

Tanner, Kathryn. *Theories of Culture: A New Agenda for Theology*. Minneapolis: Fortress, 1997.

Taylor, Charles. *Modern Social Imaginaries*. Durham, NC: Duke University Press, 2004.

———. *Sources of the Self: The Making of Modern Identity*. Cambridge, MA: Harvard University Press, 1989.

Tizon, Al. "Preaching for Shalom: Life and Peace." *Asian Journal of Pentecostal Studies* 19 (2016) 17–29.

Tolkien, J. R. R. "On Fairy Stories." In *The Tolkien Reader*, 33–90. Princeton, NJ: Princeton University Press, 1968.

———. *The Two Towers: Being the Second Part of The Lord of the Rings*. London: HarperCollins, 2008.

Tutu, Desmond. *The Rainbow People of God*. New York: Doubleday, 1994.

Vattimo, Gianni. *The Transparent Society*. Translated by David Webb. Cambridge, UK: Polity, 1992.

Vollmer, Ulrike. "Blessed Are Those Who Are Seen? Incarnation as Cinema's Destiny." *Religion and the Arts* 10 (2006) 524–38.

Volpe, Medi Ann. Review of *The Trial of the Witnesses*, by Paul J. DeHart. *Modern Theology* 24 (2008) 525–28.

Wallace, Mark I. *The Second Naiveté: Barth, Ricoeur and the New Yale Theology*. Macon, GA: Mercer University Press, 1990.

Ward, Graham. *Christ and Culture*. Oxford: Blackwell, 2003.

———. *Cultural Transformation and Religious Practice.* Cambridge: Cambridge University Press, 2005.

Wenders, Wim. *Logik der Bilder: Essays und Gespräche.* Frankfurt: Verlag der Autoren, 1988.

Whitehead, James, and Evelyn Whitehead. *Method in Ministry: Theological Reflection and Christian Ministry.* Rev. ed. Kansas City: Sheed and Ward, 1995.

Wilder, Amos Niven. *Theopoetic: Theology and the Religious Imagination.* Philadelphia: Fortress, 1976.

Wild-Wood, Emma. "Ecumenism and Independency in World Christianity." Introduction to *Ecumenism and Independency in World Christianity: Historical Studies in Honour of Brian Stanley*, edited by Alexander Chow and Emma Wild-Wood, 1–19. Leiden: Brill, 2020.

Williams, Rowan. "The Literal Sense of Scripture." *Modern Theology* 7 (1991) 121–34.

Wirzba, Norman. *Food and Faith: A Theology of Eating.* New York: Cambridge University Press, 2011.

World Council of Churches. *Economy of Life: An Invitation to Theological Reflection and Action.* Last modified November 28, 2014. https://www.oikoumene.org/en/resources/documents/wcc-programmes/public-witness-addressing-power-affirming-peace/poverty-wealth-and-ecology/economy-of-life-an-invitation-to-theological-reflection-and-action.

———. *Economy of Life, Justice, and Peace for All: A Call to Action.* Last modified July 20, 2012. https://www.oikoumene.org/en/resources/documents/wcc-programmes/public-witness-addressing-power-affirming-peace/poverty-wealth-and-ecology/neoliberal-paradigm/agape-call-for-action-2012/economy-of-life-justice-and-peace-for-all.

———. *Statement on Just Finance and the Economy of Life.* Last modified September 2, 2009. https://www.oikoumene.org/en/resources/documents/central-committee/2009/report-on-public-issues/statement-on-just-finance-and-the-economy-of-life.

———. *Theological Perspectives on* Diakonia *in the 21st Century.* In *Ecumenical Visions for the 21st Century: A Reader for Theological Education*, edited by Mélisande Lorke and Dietrich Werner, 401–6. Geneva: WCC Publications, 2013.

———. *Together towards Life: Mission and Evangelism in Changing Landscapes—with a Practical Guide.* Edited by Jooseop Keum. Geneva: WCC Publications, 2013.

Wyschogrod, Edith. *Saints and Postmodernism: Revisioning Moral Philosophy.* Chicago: University of Chicago Press, 1990.

Yoder, John H. "How H. Richard Niebuhr Reasoned." In *Authentic Transformation: A New Vision of Christ and Culture*, edited by Glen H. Stassen et al., 31–89. Nashville: Abingdon, 1996.

Young, Frances Margaret. "What Does It Mean to Be a Creature? Reflections from the Early Christian Theologians." *Medieval Mystical Theology* 28 (2019) 130–42.

Ziegler, Luther. "The Many Faces of the Worshipping Self: David Ford's Anglican Vision of Christian Transformation." *Anglican Theological Review* 89 (2007) 267–85.

Zizioulas, John D. *Being as Communion: Studies in Personhood and the Church.* Crestwood, NJ: St. Vladimir's Seminary Press, 1995.

———. *Communion and Otherness.* New York: T. & T. Clark, 2006.

Filmography

Apocalypse Now. Directed by Francis Ford Coppola. 1979. Lionsgate, 2010, DVD.
Blancanieves. Directed by Pablo Berger. 2012. Sony, 2016, DVD.
Borgman. Directed by Alex van Warmerdam. 2013. Drafthouse, 2014, DVD.
Boyhood. Directed by Richard Linklater. 2014. Paramount, 2015, DVD.
Buried. Directed by Rodrigo Cortés. 2010. Lionsgate, 2011, DVD.
Calvary. Directed by John Michael McDonagh. 2014. Universal, 2014, DVD.
The Endless. Directed by Justin Benson and Aaron Moorhead. 2017. Arrow, 2018, DVD.
Faraway, So Close! Directed by Wim Wenders. 1993. Sony, 2000, DVD.
First Reformed. Directed by Paul Schrader. 2017. Universal, 2018, DVD.
Her. Directed by Spike Jonze. 2013. Warner Brothers, 2014, DVD.
Into the Wild. Directed by Sean Penn. 2007. Paramount, 2008, DVD.
Parasite. Directed by Bong Joon-ho. 2019. Curzon Artificial Eye, 2020, DVD.
Resolution. Directed by Justin Benson and Aaron Moorhead. 2012. Crystal Lake, 2013, DVD.
Wings of Desire. Directed by Wim Wenders. 1987. Axiom, 2008, DVD.

Index

Milton Keynes UK
Ingram Content Group UK Ltd.
UKHW020135260224
438413UK00005B/162